'An O
Campaign'

The Ross and Cromarty By-Election of 1936

Rob McInroy

TIPPERMUIR
· BOOKS LIMITED ·

The right of Rob McInroy to be identified as the author of the Work
has been asserted in accordance with the Copyright, Designs & Patents Act 1988.
This first edition published and copyright 2025 by Tippermuir Books Ltd, Perth, Scotland.
mail@tippermuirbooks.co.uk – tippermuirbooks.co.uk.

ISBN 978-1-913836-49-8 (paperback).
A CIP catalogue record for this book is available from the British Library.

Project coordination and editorial by Paul S Philippou.
Cover design by Matthew Mackie.
Editorial support: Olivia Wood, Steve Zajda.
Co-founders and publishers of Tippermuir Books:
Rob Hands, Matthew Mackie and Paul S Philippou.
Cover Design: Kate Osmond.
Text design, layout, and artwork by Bernard Chandler [graffik].
Text set in Joanna MT Std Regular 11/14pt; Joanna MT Std Bold/Italic titling.

Printed and bound by CPI Group (UK) Ltd, Croydon, CR0 4YY.
This book has been printed in the UK to reduce transportation miles
and their impact on the environment. It has been printed to comply with
the Forest Stewardship Council (FSC) Chain of Custody requirements
and paper sourcing from responsibly managed sources.

When former Prime Minister Ramsay MacDonald and his son Malcolm lost their seats in the 1935 General Election, Prime Minister Stanley Baldwin wanted both men returned to Parliament quickly.

The seemingly safe seat of Ross and Cromarty became vacant in January 1936. Malcolm MacDonald was selected to be the National Government candidate. What should have been a formality became a bitter and extraordinary by-election.

Enraged by this apparent attempt to foist a former Labour MP on them, the local Liberal and Unionist Associations decided to field independent candidates. The Unionists' choice of candidate – Randolph Churchill, son of Winston Churchill – proved explosive.

So began a memorable, abusive and 'odious' campaign contested by the sons of two British Prime Ministers, men who loathed one another and made no attempt to conceal the fact. Remarkably, no fewer than six children of previous, current or future Prime Ministers would be involved in the campaign, a record that is unlikely to be beaten.

The campaign, occurring during the worst winter for 50 years, encompassed the death of King George V, the hospitalisation of a candidate, car crashes aplenty, rampaging deer and candidates coming perilously close to being run out of town by enraged locals.

The 1936 Ross and Cromarty by-election is an entertaining slice of history that resonates with current British Parliamentary politics.

✡ ✡ ✡

Praise for Rob McInroy

About **Burials and Other Stories**

'A dark and very well-crafted mini thriller.'

Rachel Seiffert, author of Booker Prize shortlisted novel **The Dark Room**

About **Moot**

'Trust me when I say read this book.'

Jim C Mackintosh, poet and **'Scots Writer o the Year' 2024**

'As evocative as it is thrilling.'

Nick Quantrill, author of the ***Joe Geraghty*** novels

About **Barossa Street**

'A powerful and resonant novel that explores the prejudices and injustices of the time and their impact on policing. Dark, thrilling and sinister, it will keep you guessing until you reach the last page.'

C L Taylor, *Sunday Times* bestselling author of ***The Accident*** and **The Lie**

'Part murder mystery, part gritty crime, part immersive historical fiction – 100% excellent.'

Dan Malakin, author of ***The Wreckage of Us*** and **The Box**

About **Cuddies Strip**

'Very much a contemporary novel. It deals with misogyny, it deals with institutional corruption, it deals with the problem of policing. I highly recommend it.'

Val McDermid, bestselling Scottish crime writer

'I read this wonderful novel with a tear in my eye. I could hardly bear to read the ending but it was beautiful.'

Cathi Unsworth, author of ***That Old Black Magic*** and ***Weirdo***

✲ ✲ ✲

Acknowledgements

Malcolm MacDonald's collected papers are held in the Archives of Durham University in the Palace Green Library. I am very grateful to the staff there for their kindness and professionalism.

Thanks to the archivists at Cambridge University for help in tracking down some recalcitrant newspaper articles.

Thanks to Boyd Mackenzie for help with identifying photographs and for memories of his family's involvement in the by-election.

Thanks to Neil and John Ferguson for their assistance in tracking down several photographs.

I am very grateful to Dr Margaret MacLean Ferguson for permission to use photographs taken by her husband, the late Dr Charles Ferguson.

✡ ✡ ✡

For my father, Bob McInroy,
an autodidact who would have enjoyed this

About the Author

Rob McInroy is primarily a novelist. He was born in Crieff, Perthshire, and his fiction is mostly set in his home county, particularly Crieff, the Knock Hill and the River Earn. He is the author of the acclaimed Bob and Annie Kelty series of historical crime fiction which follows the central characters from the 1930s to the 2010s.

In 2018, he was a winner of the Bradford Literature Festival Northern Noir Crime Novel competition with an early draft of *Cuddies Strip* and this first novel was subsequently longlisted for the Crime Writers' Association John Creasey First Blood Dagger Award.

He has an MA in Creative Writing and a PhD in American Literature, both from the University of Hull. He currently lives in Yorkshire.

* * *

Also by Rob McInroy

Fiction

Cuddies Strip (2020)
Barossa Street (2022)
Moot (2024)
Burials and Other Stories (2024)
Barvick Falls (2025)

Non-Fiction

'Cormac McCarthy and the Cities of God, Man and the Plain'
(Unpublished PhD thesis, University of Hull, 2013)
One Final Hurdle: A Fans' History of St Johnstone FC (2014)

* * *

Notes

Randolph Churchill's father and son are both called Winston Spencer Churchill. This is rather awkward when writing about them, particularly when quoting from Winston Junior's biography of his father, which often also refers to his grandfather. In this book, Churchill Senior is referred to as Winston Churchill and Churchill Junior as Winston S Churchill. That Winston's father was also called Randolph is an added complication, at least alleviated by the fact he was *Lord* Randolph Churchill.

At the time of the Ross and Cromarty by-election, the Universities of London, Queen's (Belfast), Wales, Oxford and Cambridge each had their representation in Parliament. There were two additional university constituencies, the Combined English Universities and the Combined Scottish Universities.

✡ ✡ ✡

Introduction

Days of Fuss and Tub-Thumping

Prime Minister Stanley Baldwin called a general election in November 1935, the second to be contested by a coalition of parties representing the National Government established by Ramsay MacDonald in 1931. George Lansbury had stepped down as leader of the Labour opposition earlier that month over the party's policy on Abyssinia and, sensing disorder, Baldwin considered this a propitious time to go to the country.

The 1931 election – won in a landslide by the National Government – had been fought on domestic issues, primarily the financial emergency that had erupted in August of that year due to a banking crisis in central Europe which depleted gold reserves held in Britain, and a projected British budget deficit of £120 million.[1] The 1935 election, however, ostensibly had international affairs to the fore. Italy's invasion of Abyssinia, in the face of entreaties from the League of Nations not to do so, was creating a full-scale crisis with the viability of the League as a peacekeeping force. The future governance of India was hugely contentious: despite 'diehard' opposition to Indian self-determination, led by Winston Churchill, the Governance of India Act was ratified in August 1935, granting a large degree of autonomy to Indian provinces. The growing authoritarianism and militarism of Japan was causing concern, as was the emergence of the Nazi regime in Germany.

The election manifesto published in the names of the three party leaders, Baldwin, MacDonald (National Labour) and Sir John Simon (National Liberal), laid out their general aims and policy on key aspects of home and foreign affairs. They were, in order:

The League of Nations
Peace and Defence
Limitation of Armaments
Imperial Policy
Overseas Trade
Agriculture
Fisheries
Employment

Unemployment Assistance
Special Areas and the Coal Mining Industry
Social Reform
Scotland.[2]

It is worth noting that the manifesto talked of 'Limitation of Armaments' and not 'Rearmament'. This would become a crucial factor in the years that followed, and would be central to the way Baldwin's government came to be judged by historians. Baldwin wanted rearmament to be an election issue but seemed reluctant to discuss the matter. As a result, he could later claim a mandate without having debated it during the campaign.

The election resulted in another huge victory for the National Government, albeit on a lesser scale than 1931. In particular, National Labour, the small grouping of former Labour MPs who followed MacDonald in 1931 when he established the National Government, was badly defeated by the resurgent opposition Labour Party, losing five of their thirteen seats. The National Liberals, too, lost more than half of their seats, marking the moment when they ceased to be a major political force in the country.

Among the National Labour losers were MacDonald and his son Malcolm. Baldwin was now faced with a difficult situation, his supposed National Government being largely Conservative, with only 33 National Liberals and eight National Labour. Moreover, Malcolm MacDonald, although no longer a member of the House of Commons, was still in the Cabinet as Secretary of State for the Dominions. Winston Churchill – a constant thorn in Baldwin's side – noted in a letter to his wife, Clementine:

> Here are these two MacDonalds whom we are told must be elected, in order that the Labour element should be represented in a National Government, otherwise it cannot be called 'National'.[3]

Baldwin might not admit this publicly, but Churchill's analysis was correct: he needed both MacDonalds back in Parliament as quickly as possible. Plans were laid. Baldwin asked Ramsay to stay on as Lord President and fight a by-election to enable his return to Parliament.

MacDonald agreed, with the proviso that 'suitable provision shd be made for [James Henry] Thomas and agreement re Malcolm'. Thomas was currently Dominions Secretary and unpopular with foreign officials, and Baldwin accepted the conditions. The next day he swapped Thomas and Malcolm in their respective roles as Dominions and Colonial Secretaries, making Malcolm Dominions Secretary.[4]

Next, Ramsay MacDonald was lined up for a vacant seat in the Scottish Universities constituency, which left Malcolm MacDonald still to be accommodated. The solution appeared quickly.

Sir Ian Macpherson, veteran Member for the Ross and Cromarty constituency in the Scottish Highlands, tendered his resignation on doctors' orders, creating a vacancy in a constituency conveniently just to the west of the MacDonalds' family home in Lossiemouth. A by-election would be required, and Malcolm MacDonald would stand as the National Government candidate, easing his return to Parliament and Cabinet.

What could be simpler?

And yet the Ross and Cromarty by-election of 1936 would prove to be one of the most astonishing in British electoral history. As the *Edinburgh Evening Telegraph* suggested:

> Many of the quiet-going electors in the North must be marvelling at the Press-made excitement over the by-election, but we live in days of fuss and tub-thumping.

The counties of Ross and Cromarty were, the *Telegraph* continued, 'so much in the news today that they seem likely to stage a political comedy with several rival candidates'.[5]

As it turned out, the *Telegraph* didn't know the half of it. The 1936 Ross and Cromarty by-election, an 'odious campaign' fought over the 'politics of the dunghill' by a 'freak' and a 'nondescript', would electrify the country for six long weeks.

* * *

Monday, 16 December 1935

The Highlands, Ill-health and Hoare-Laval

Change Ahead

A small paragraph in a newspaper full of seemingly more interesting news laid the foundations for the 1936 Ross and Cromarty by-election. The *Inverness Courier*'s leader dealt with the Hoare-Laval Pact, through which the 'Governments of Great Britain and France have made a bold bid for peace with dishonour'.[6] This affair would unravel quickly and result in the resignation of British Foreign Secretary Sir Samuel Hoare. Closer to home, the paper reported at length on an 'eloquent speech' by Mr C I Fraser on the present-day problems of the Highlands, including the condition of the roads, tourism, the lack of understanding of the Highlander by the Lowlander and a 'New Deal' for the Highlands.[7] Several column inches were expended on the death of Sir Hector Munro of Foulis, Lord-Lieutenant of Ross and Cromarty,[8] and on the appointments of a new Chief Constable, Burgh Assessor and Burgh Prosecutor.[9] But it was the event described next which would set everything in motion.

Sir Ian Macpherson
photo: Walter Stoneman

Sir Ian Macpherson, it said, was suffering from ill-health. Macpherson was the long-standing National Liberal Member of Parliament for Ross and Cromarty, having been elected, unopposed, for the fourth time at the general election the previous month. The following May would mark his 25th anniversary as a Member of Parliament. Now, though, he advised a meeting of the Ross and Cromarty Liberal Association that he may have to undergo a period of enforced rest.[10] *The Scotsman*'s 'Special Correspondent' recorded that Macpherson had been advised his health required 'a long holiday in a sunny climate' and was considering invitations to visit the West Indies and South Africa, where he had business interests. He was still to decide whether this would be through a leave of absence or a formal resignation.[11]

If it were the latter, there would be a by-election.

Given what was about to transpire, it is hard not to imagine that, in the days before and after Sir Ian's revelation, secret and excitable conversations were being held behind closed doors in Westminster, Edinburgh and Dingwall.

The game was afoot.

Tuesday, 24 December 1935

A Resignation, Some Kite-Flying and MacDonalds Enter Stage Left

Eight days later, the resignation of Sir Ian Macpherson was confirmed in the press. While the fact of the resignation was widely reported, it is a curiosity that the farther the distance away from Ross and Cromarty, the firmer the speculation was about the likely identity of Sir Ian's replacement. The *Inverness Courier* reported that Sir Ian would resign immediately, after taking the advice of two specialists, who concurred with his GP's original diagnosis and recommendation of a rest cure.[12] However, it made no mention of who might replace him in its news report nor leader column on the loss of the 'Member for the Highlands'. In an unwitting foreshadowing of events, it finished by declaring it did not envy the Ross and Cromarty Liberal Association in trying to find a suitable successor'.[13] Down the coast, the *Aberdeen Press and Journal* also made no mention of successors,[14] while farther south the *Dundee Courier* did suggest that Malcolm MacDonald had been 'considered tentatively' but gave no further information.[15]

Malcolm MacDonald
photo: Creative Commons

The *Scotsman* named Thomas Bridgehill Wilson Ramsay and Sir John Wallace 'possible' candidates but also reported the 'interesting suggestion' that the local Association may invite Malcolm MacDonald to stand. He had the advantage, the paper said, of being a near neighbour of the constituency through his home in

Lossiemouth. Moreover, Highland constituencies had a 'well-known partiality for the services of distinguished statesmen, especially when they happen to be Scots'. MacDonald could lay claim to both these criteria. However, it stressed the decision would rest with the Liberals of Ross and Cromarty.[16] The wording of this is intriguing: MacDonald's possible candidature was an 'interesting suggestion' but the article ended with the firm assertion that the decision must be made locally. This sounds suspiciously like kite-flying, somebody in high places floating a possibility to see what the public reaction might be.

It certainly seems that, in official circles, the idea was being downplayed. The London correspondent for the *Daily Record*, who prided himself on his good connections, wrote that 'so far as I can learn, such a contingency [MacDonald standing] is so remote that it can be safely dismissed'. There may be an element of wishful thinking here: the correspondent went on to suggest that Sir Ian might remain in post until May 1936 at the behest of his local supporters, completely contradicting what he had written in the previous paragraph when he said that Sir Ian had told him personally of his desire to resign 'as soon as possible'.[17]

However, it was in the English press, which may have been less aware of or less interested in the sensitivities around such conjecture, that Malcolm MacDonald's prospective candidature was most talked up. The downmarket *News Chronicle* suggested that 'three or four names of probable candidates' had been considered, but named only one – MacDonald – and the article's sub-heading was explicit: 'MacDonald Jnr May Step In'.[18] MacDonald's name was mentioned in a series of English regional papers, including the *Hartlepool Northern Daily Mail*, *Gloucestershire Echo*, *Liverpool Echo*, *Staffordshire Sentinel*, *Derby Daily Telegraph*, *Shields Daily News*, *Leicester Mercury*, *Nottingham Journal*, *Belfast Telegraph*, *Birmingham Daily Gazette* and the *Sunderland Daily Echo*. The *Yorkshire Evening Post* was clear:

> If events move as their friends expect, Mr Ramsay MacDonald will be adopted as Parliamentary candidate for the Scottish Universities vacancy, and Mr Malcolm MacDonald for Ross and Cromarty, the seat resigned by Sir Ian Macpherson.[19]

It may be, of course, that the English papers were later editions which could have been updated with news that wasn't available to the Scottish press. That said, the *Birmingham Daily Gazette* dated its story as Monday, 23rd, the day before.[20] The national (and right-wing) *Daily Mail*, too, reported Ross and Cromarty was a 'probable seat' for Malcolm MacDonald in an item also written on the 23rd.[21] *The Belfast Telegraph*, reporting that MacDonald was being considered as the National candidate, was quick to point out a potential problem: '[Ross and Cromarty] is, of course, a Liberal National seat and Mr MacDonald is National Labour'.[22]

The Nottingham Journal featured the story prominently, no doubt because MacDonald had until a few weeks before been the MP for Bassetlaw in Nottinghamshire. It concluded that it was 'probable' that MacDonald would stand but, like the *Belfast Telegraph*, suggested there were difficulties to overcome. There was a chance the constituency would not support him if he were to stand as a National Labour candidate and it was by no means certain the Liberal Association would allow the seat to be transferred to him 'without a fight'. If a Liberal candidate stood in the by-election, it concluded, the result 'could not be counted upon as a foregone conclusion'.[23]

Thus, it appears that while the Scottish papers were scarcely covering the matter, the English and Northern Irish press were already considering the ramifications. Traditionally, Scottish matters were not discussed in much detail in the English press, but this was to set the tone for the coming weeks.

* * *

Wednesday, 25 December 1935

First Intimations of Difficulty

Although many newspapers did not print editions on 25 December, Christmas Day was not a public holiday in the 1930s and journalists and correspondents worked normally. News broke that the local Liberal Association was preparing to speak to Malcolm MacDonald, and Dr George Middleton, chairman of the Association, was pressed for a statement. He could not comment, he said, until the Association had held a meeting on Saturday. He did confirm to the *Press and Journal* that MacDonald's name, along with two others, had been brought to the Association's notice. He would not offer any opinion on MacDonald's chances of success but said: 'One thing is certain, and that is that the man whom our association adopts will be a supporter of the National Government'.[24] That was as good as an admission that MacDonald was their man. MacDonald, of course, was Labour National, not Liberal National, and this formulation of a 'National Government' candidate, which was not official parlance, was an attempt at obfuscation.

If that was the case, then there could still be obstacles. The paper's London correspondent, while – like *The Scotsman* the day before – stressing that the final decision on a candidate would rest with the local association, considered there to be one factor of the greatest importance in considering MacDonald's prospects: the Liberal National leadership, it suggested, was determined to maintain the Liberals' representation and strength in Parliament. HQ would 'not lightly agree to the seat being given over to another party, even though in this instance it be a National Government Minister'. In government, though, there was support for MacDonald. 'There is a strong feeling in Government circles that a Cabinet Minister, especially in this case the Dominions Secretary, should not be without a seat in Parliament longer than can be avoided', the correspondent wrote. He named the same two alternative candidates identified by *The Scotsman* the day before. In addition, he recorded that Wilson Ramsay – like Sir Ian Macpherson a native Gaelic speaker, which was considered advantageous – was thought unlikely to wish to stand against MacDonald.[25]

Whatever disputes in London, there was every prospect that greater confrontation could arise back in Dingwall, the county town of Ross-shire. Sir William Martineau, chairman of the local Unionist Association, told the *Press and Journal* his association was aware of the situation. (Until 1965 the Conservatives were known in Scotland as the Unionist Party, while the Labour Party were referred to as the Socialists. Since most of the newspaper reports quoted in this book use that nomenclature, that practice has been adopted throughout the book.)

Although there was an expectation that the Liberals and Unionists, as partners in the National Government, would work together, tensions were inevitable. Ewan Cameron records that Ross and Cromarty was a constituency with a history of Liberal representation unbroken since 1832, ranging from Whig lairds such as Sir James Matheson and Alexander Matheson to the Crofters' Party MP Roderick Macdonald, elected in 1885, and orthodox radical Liberals such as John Galloway Weir.[26] Indeed, in twelve general elections, a Liberal was returned unopposed, and the last time a Unionist candidate stood was in a by-election in 1911. The Unionists felt, all the same, that perhaps this time they should have a greater say in the choice of candidate.

'We are not going to be sat on', Martineau warned, saying that a meeting would be called to discuss the matter. 'I suppose we will have to leave it principally to headquarters to choose a candidate', he continued, somewhat oddly as it was certainly the convention that local associations were responsible for choosing their candidates. Was this an attempt to distance himself from any decision? He considered it would please many constituents if the candidate were a Unionist but, he added, 'We will naturally support the National Government'.[27]

Whether or not MacDonald was to be the candidate, there would certainly be a Socialist opponent. Arthur Woodburn, the Scottish Secretary of the Labour Party, reported that they would fight the by-election and declared their chance of winning excellent, largely because of wholesale dissatisfaction with the government's Italo-Abyssinian policy.[28]

Hoare-Laval Pact

Behind Woodburn's assertion was the revelation of the Hoare-Laval Pact the week before, which had developed into a full-blown crisis for the government. They had fought the general election the previous month on support for the League of Nations. Sir Samuel Hoare, British Foreign Secretary, had addressed the League of Nations in September 1935 and called for collective resistance to acts of unprovoked aggression and for all nations to share the risks and responsibilities that come with war. This was greeted enthusiastically around the world as a fine piece of statesmanship, but within a month Italy mounted a full-scale invasion of Abyssinia. Britain imposed sanctions which proved insufficient but gave the impression of the country – and the League – standing firm against aggressors. It was at this point that Stanley Baldwin chose to call a general election and Abyssinia became an election issue, not least because Labour's official position on rearmament and foreign policy was distinctly dovish. George Lansbury, a pacifist, resigned as Labour leader over the issue. Officially, the government remained of the opinion that Italy's aggression should be repelled, which chimed with the public mood. However, in December 1935, news broke of secret plans by Hoare and his French counterpart, Pierre Laval, to partition Abyssinia and hand over half of its lands to Italy. In both Britain and France, there was popular outrage at the proposals.

On the evening of 18 December, Hoare resigned. After a blistering debate in Parliament the next day, the government lost an opposition motion that the peace proposals be immediately repudiated, by 397 votes to 165, an astonishing reverse for a government with such a huge majority. Hoare spoke, stating that his obsessions since becoming Foreign Secretary were the avoidance of a new European conflagration and the prevention of an isolated war with Italy. His conscience was clear, he said. In fairness to Hoare, he was unwell at the time and many parliamentarians had questioned the appropriateness of allowing him to conduct such vital diplomacy in that condition.

Clement Attlee, the new leader of the Labour Party, was vituperative. If the Cabinet agreed to the Paris proposals – which they had – then he could not understand how the Foreign Secretary was the only person to resign. 'The Government did more than try to find a basis for discussion, it sided with the aggressors', he said. 'It betrayed the League and the people of this country who voted for the Prime Minister.'[29] There were two issues at stake, Attlee said, the honour of the country and the honour of the Prime Minister. If the Prime Minister had won the election on one policy and immediately afterwards was prepared to carry out another, that had 'an extremely ugly look'. What he had done was worse than doing nothing at all: 'If you turn and run away from the aggressor, you kill the League, and you do worse than that, or as bad as that: you kill all faith in the word of honour of this country'.

Baldwin, replying, said that when Cabinet first debated the proposals they did not like them. 'We thought they went too far', he said. They wanted to modify them, but there was insufficient time and he explained that Cabinet decided, reluctantly, to put forward the proposals. 'You may say it was an act of weakness on my part', he said. 'It certainly was, and an error of judgement.' The decision was the collective responsibility of Cabinet, but responsibility was principally his, he concluded.[30] This was a humiliation for Baldwin and his government.

Sir Ian Macpherson, in one of his final statements in Parliament, declared that voting for the Socialist motion implied a vote of censure on the government and the conduct of the Prime Minister. His words carried little weight and the vote was carried. The proposals were now dead; Sir Samuel Hoare had resigned and Pierre Laval would follow.[31]

It was in this context that the Socialists felt confident that a by-election would be conducted in an atmosphere of disapprobation of the government. It is no wonder, then, that Arthur Woodburn felt confident. Unfortunately for him, this was only one of the issues on which the ensuing campaign would be fought.

✡ ✡ ✡

Thursday, 26 December 1935

Rumours, Scones and Growing Tensions

Rumours circulating in London about the health of the King were denied by Buckingham Palace. 'The King is in excellent health', we were told.[32] As will be seen, official statements are not always what they seem.

First Contact

In the afternoon, a deputation, comprising Dr Middleton, chairman of the Ross and Cromarty Liberal Association, Alexander (Sandy) Macrae, secretary, Dr Johnstone and one other member of the Association, who would no doubt be livid to learn his name has not been recorded for posterity, visited the home of Ramsay and Malcolm MacDonald at the Hillocks, Lossiemouth, for what would come to be known as the Lossiemouth Tea Party. Malcolm MacDonald's sister, Sheila, made the scones and later confessed: 'If I had known what an important party it was going to turn out, I should have been too excited to eat any tea'. 'The truth is', Sheila MacDonald explained, 'that neither side was committed to anything after that tea party'.[33]

It may have been an important meeting,
but it was not a wholly productive one.

That may have been slightly economical with the truth. Alexander Macrae recorded later that the delegation suggested that either Malcolm or Ramsay should be proposed as candidate to the Liberal Association. On hearing this, Ramsay said, 'Take the laddie'.[34]

The idea of Liberals and former Labour politicians coming to some form of agreement is not far-fetched. Ramsay MacDonald, particularly after the Great War, was clear that Labour, rather than the Liberals, should take the lead in promulgating radical democratic reform. He was, nonetheless, quite prepared to work with the Liberals.[35] Unlike in England, however, where MacDonald established a Liberal-Labour pact with Herbert Gladstone, there was no formal alliance in Scotland.[36] Nonetheless, he recognised that an element of the Liberal Party shared Labour's desire for radical reform. For that reason, and also because many trade unionists desired it, he was open to the establishment of a loose alliance with the Liberals.[37] This was highly unlikely to happen, however: Sir Archibald Sinclair, leader of the independent Liberals in Parliament, was avowedly opposed to going 'cap in hand' to Labour or any other party. Any alliance, he suggested, would cause the party to 'commit suicide'.[38] This approach to the MacDonalds by the local Liberal Association, then, was going to have ramifications one way or the other.

Later that day, Malcolm MacDonald repeated Sheila's suggestion that nothing concrete had been agreed. 'We may hear something on Saturday', he told a reporter. That was when the Liberal Association was next due to meet and they would have the opportunity to debate their options. Although other names had been suggested, the *Dundee Courier* believed it was 'practically certain that MacDonald would receive most support' while it was anticipated that the Unionist Association would join forces, as they had during the previous three elections.[39]

That belief, though, may have underestimated the strength of feeling among the Unionists. They were also due to meet in Dingwall on Saturday and there was talk that they could nominate their own candidate. Many influential Unionists were expressing the view that on this occasion the Liberals should be supporting them, without necessarily articulating why. Several prospective candidates had been mooted, including

Sir William Martineau, chairman of the Unionist Association, vice-chairman Sir Robert Brooke and Major John Stirling.[40]

The MacDonalds
photo: *Aberdeen Press and Journal*

While tensions emerged in Dingwall, the same could be said in London. The *Daily Herald* was the first paper to explicitly state that the proposal to nominate MacDonald had come from Downing Street, and it reported that the suggestion had angered the Simonites – the Liberal National members of the government, named after their leader Sir John Simon. Their preference was again suggested to be either Sir John Wallace or Wilson Ramsay.[41] The *Edinburgh Evening News* reported that the speed with which the local association was moving had 'embarrassed' the Liberal National Party Executive, for whom Leslie Hore-Belisha had been actively working on plans for several days.[42] The background to this was that, in the general election, the National Liberals won only 33 seats. Giving up one of those to MacDonald, then, would be hugely undesirable.

And the national leadership was about to receive even worse news. *The News Chronicle* reported that Dr Middleton had phoned Sir Ian Macpherson on Christmas Day to advise him that MacDonald was going to be approached and to canvass his opinion on who his successor should be. Sir Ian let it be known that he would warmly support MacDonald's candidature. This placed the national leaders in a quandary. They would know they held little sway with the Ross and Cromarty Association which, the *News Chronicle* added somewhat tartly, had acted 'independently of financial or other assistance from party headquarters for thirty years'.[43]

It was acknowledged, then, that the Ross and Cromarty Liberals were fiercely independent. *The Scotsman*'s London correspondent made clear that the selection of either MacDonald or a Simonite would be made by the local association 'without regard to outside influence or pressure'. They were financially independent and threats of an independent Liberal candidate standing against them were unlikely to alarm them, given the independents had no organisation in the constituency.[44]

This independence at the local level was not unusual. In 1885, radical Liberals established the National Liberal Federation of Scotland. The Federation was created to advance a wide-ranging programme of reform of the House of Lords and disestablishment of the Church of Scotland, and was independent of party political hierarchy. All of this was anathema to the more conservative elements of the party.[45] The result was, according to I G C Hutchison, that the Scottish Liberal Federation 'had only a very tenuous relationship with some constituency parties', with local autonomy the norm and no apparent need for them to liaise with the centre. Ross and Cromarty was not the only association to effectively declare independence: Hutchison points to Montrose Burghs, which never consulted the SLF 'about anything' and had had 'no official connection with the federation for years'. The East Fife, East Perthshire and Greenock parties all refused to stand candidates in by-elections in the 1930s. East Perthshire disaffiliated, and Greenock threatened to do so.[46]

What we were seeing, although it would take time for that to become obvious, was the gradual diminution of the Liberals as a major political force in Scotland and Britain. Hutchison characterised its approach in the late twenties and early thirties as 'rather antiquated', presenting a 'slightly backward-looking, small-town or rural vision of Scotland'. Its traditional campaigning issues of free trade, temperance and the 'land question' seemed less relevant in the modern world. Protectionism was in vogue, the fear of the impact of cheap imports trumping any notions of free trade, while the gradual break-up of the great Scottish estates was lessening demands for sweeping land legislation. Overall, the party seemed to Hutchison to be 'timid and marginal'.[47]

Whatever, the fact that Malcolm MacDonald had previously been a Labour politician was leaving the Liberals in Ross and Cromarty in a difficult position.

Who was in charge? And what did they want?

✲ ✲ ✲

Friday, 27 December 1935

Ramsay MacDonald, the Universities, 'No Surrender'

Ramsay MacDonald
photo: Creative Commons

The first of the MacDonalds to receive a nomination for one of the pending by-elections was Ramsay; the joint representatives of the Unionist Associations of the Universities of St Andrews, Glasgow, Aberdeen and Edinburgh unanimously invited him to accept their nomination as the National Government candidate in the by-election for the Combined Scottish Universities constituency caused by the death of A Noel Skelton. He would face a three-cornered fight with Professor Andrew Dewar Gibb for the SNP and David Cleghorn Thomson for the Socialists.[48] The request to stand was made by telephone to MacDonald's home in Lossiemouth, where MacDonald was in bed. His daughter, Ishbel, took the call and relayed the offer to her father, who authorised her to accept the nomination.[49]

The decision to adopt him was not as clear-cut as this sounds, however. Sheila MacDonald noted in her diary:

> Ever such a lot of wrangling and indecision before fixed that JRM [Ramsay MacDonald] should be nominated. If it weren't for Malcolm, I think JRM would have given up.[50]

This seems to confirm that the move to return the MacDonalds to Parliament was predicated on both gaining seats, not only Ramsay.

There was an irony in MacDonald accepting the nomination for the Scottish Universities seat, since he had voted for Universities' representation at parliament to be abolished some years earlier, in February 1931, when he said, not unreasonably: 'If there is any special institution requiring representation in the House of Commons it is certainly not the universities.

They pervade the whole atmosphere of the House and cannot help being represented there'.[51] The seats were eventually abolished as part of the Representation of the People Act in 1948, with the first general election to exclude them occurring in 1950.

This attempt to manoeuvre Ramsay MacDonald back into parliament was sure to be controversial. MacDonald was an austere and distant man, someone who inspired devotion among his friends and distrust, even hatred, among his enemies.[52] The circumstances behind his formation of the National Government in 1931 remained opaque and resented in Labour circles. The decision to form the National Government, headed by MacDonald and supported by the three principal parties, was made by MacDonald, Stanley Baldwin and then Liberal leader, Sir Herbert Samuel, in conference with King George V on 24 August 1931. Once that decision was agreed, MacDonald returned to his Cabinet and told them. At no point before that had Cabinet discussed the possibility of coalition government, and there was therefore consternation.[53]

Ramsay MacDonald
photo: Edinburgh Evening News

Although many believed MacDonald had gone against his party, there is no evidence that his decision to enter into a coalition was long premeditated. On the night of 23 August, he confided to his daughter Ishbel that he intended to resign and lead the party into opposition. His subsequent decision to obey King George V's request to form the National Government was, according to Kenneth Morgan, born of his progressive tendencies. It was a 'supreme gesture' and the 'supreme tragedy of his career'. Malcolm MacDonald declared that for his father it was a 'matter of duty, 'and damn the consequences'.[54]

It may be, then, that MacDonald hadn't made up his mind until the audience with the King, but the fact he hadn't even discussed the matter with his Cabinet is telling.[55] In the end, only fourteen Labour MPs followed MacDonald into the National Government, the remainder, including most of the Cabinet, formed the official opposition. The fifteen were expelled from the party and a major rift emerged in Labour ranks which it took a decade or more to repair. When the National Government called a general election in October 1931, Labour was trounced pretty much everywhere except their mining heartlands and, according to Juliet Gardiner, 'it seemed to many that Labour would never again come to power democratically'.[56] And Ramsay MacDonald was at the centre of all this acrimony. In the 1935 general election, he was soundly beaten by Labour's Manny Shinwell,[57] and, it seemed, he was being ushered back into Parliament in a somewhat contentious manner. Old wounds would undoubtedly be reopened by his return.

If Liberal National HQ in London was exercised by the course of events, so too were the Scottish Liberal Federation in Edinburgh. Speaking to the press, Ranald Findlay, their general secretary, said he found it difficult to believe there was any truth in the statement that the Ross and Cromarty Liberal Association would seriously accept a National Labour or Unionist candidate:

> Such a surrender would arouse great indignation among Liberals in all parts of the constituency, and would make it necessary to put an independent Liberal candidate in the field. In such an event there would be no difficulty in selecting a strong candidate familiar with the problems of the Highlands.[58]

These were words he would come to regret.

* * *

Saturday, 28 December 1935

Implosion, Randolph Churchill and the Marlborough Vendetta

The Associations Meet

This was the day when the Ross and Cromarty Liberal Association believed matters would be resolved. It turned out to be the day everything imploded.

The Association's Emergency Committee met as planned during the afternoon and spent an hour listening to the report of the four representatives who had interviewed Malcolm MacDonald, following which they agreed unanimously to invite MacDonald to their Executive Committee meeting on Tuesday. His nomination was regarded as a formality: the Executive Committee could make the official request to MacDonald to stand and nobody doubted they would do so. Job done, it seemed. *The Scotsman* did note, however, that rank-and-file Liberals were divided, with some feeling that they were being coerced into a position over which they had no control.[59] It is ironic, of course, that National Liberal HQ felt the same.

The *Sunday Post*'s report was more sensational, though possibly with some basis in truth. The Liberal grouping in Ross and Cromarty was 'seething with dissensions', it said, with political rivalry 'at fever heat'.[60] Amid this growing discontent, an anti-MacDonald faction began a campaign against him. The MP for the neighbouring constituency of Sutherland, Sir Archibald Sinclair – a respected and principled politician – was leader of the independent Liberals in Parliament, and it was being suggested locally that his influence in the Highlands could be sufficient to ensure an independent Liberal candidate would stand if MacDonald were nominated. *Reynolds's Illustrated News* suggested that reports from the constituency made it 'abundantly clear that Mr MacDonald could not hope to win in a straight fight with an independent Liberal'.[61] *Reynolds's*, it should be noted, had links to the Co-operative Party, a centre-left group affiliated to the Labour Party, so one should be in no doubt as to the anti-MacDonald agenda being pursued here. The paper's political correspondent, not a man to hide his political sentiments, reported that: 'It is curious, but true, that when [Ramsay and Malcolm MacDonald] lost their seats neither of them thought fit to resign from the Cabinet'. If they had, he continued, Baldwin would not have accepted Ramsay's resignation 'but would have been glad to get the son off his hands'.[62] Whatever one thinks of MacDonalds Senior and Junior, they had a rare capacity to make enemies.

Further names of potential candidates to stand as an independent Liberal emerged. Sir Murdoch McKenzie Wood, who lost in Banff at the general election, and Sir Robert Hamilton, who lost in Orkney and

Shetland, were two. Thomas Trotter KC, author of standard legal works, was another.[63] Trotter was formerly Sheriff-substitute of Caithness, Orkney and Shetland.[64] The *Dundee Courier*, in its daily *London Letter*, speculated that Sir Herbert Samuel, Isaac Foot and Sir Robert Hamilton could be asked to stand.[65] Samuel, former Home Secretary and Liberal leader in the 1931 and 1935 general elections, was forced to issue a statement emphatically denying the rumour.[66] It was, he said, 'rather disgraceful that my name should be put forward without any foundation'.[67]

Meanwhile, if relations were growing fraught in the Liberal Association they were positively febrile over in the Unionist Association. The *Daily Record* reported that Unionist officials were keenly resentful over having been ignored by the Liberal Association in their apparent choice of candidate. They had not been consulted by the local association or Liberal HQ but were expected to support the Liberal choice during the by-election.[68] They were, one official told *The Scotsman*, 'disposed to support a Liberal National candidate' but they would have nothing to do with a Socialist. The potential nomination of Malcolm MacDonald, then, was hugely unpopular. A group of Easter Ross farmers had come together to agree a series of motions to be raised at the Executive Committee of the Unionist Association on Tuesday. These were:

1. That the meeting reject Mr Baldwin's recommendation that Unionists should support Mr Malcolm MacDonald.
2. That the Association have nothing to do with Mr MacDonald's candidature.
3. Recommend that all Unionists, if there is no Unionist candidate, should vote for any other candidate who opposes Mr MacDonald.[69]

They hadn't really thought through item three. If there were to be opposition to MacDonald, it would most likely come from another Socialist, and motion three would require them to vote for a real Socialist to keep out a National Labour candidate. The farmers were irate, however, to the extent that they now did something which would blow the whole election apart.

They sent a cablegram to Randolph Churchill requesting that he stand as an Independent Unionist.

Enter Randolph Churchill

Randolph Churchill was the only son of Winston Churchill, who would become Prime Minister in 1940 but was, at this time, out of Cabinet and favour, and causing copious mischief from the back benches. Randolph Churchill was only 24 but was already a journalist of some renown and seemed to be as great a provocateur as his father. He shared with him many of the same preoccupations, notably the future of India, the need for rearmament, the weakness of the National Government and the unsuitability of Stanley Baldwin for the role of Prime Minister. When the cablegram reached him, Churchill was on holiday, cruising between Madeira and Tangier in the company of his father, Lord Rothermere and David Lloyd George, which meant he was not in a position to reply immediately.[70] If he were to agree, however, it would create a sensation. The highly partisan correspondent who wrote the *Daily Record*'s *London Letter* was salivating:

Randolph Churchill
photo: Creative Commons

> A scrap between Mr Malcolm MacDonald and Mr Randolph Churchill for the Ross and Cromarty stakes would be the most spectacular political contest Britain has had for some time.

Both, he went on, were 'bonny fechters', although neither had much experience of campaigning in Scotland.[71]

Perhaps not, but in recent times Randolph Churchill had become quite the by-election warrior. In 1935, both Winston and Randolph Churchill were greatly exercised by the Government of India Bill, which would give Dominion status to India. This was hugely contentious and it is a remarkable fact that discussion of the Bill took up 84 per cent of legislative time in Parliament in 1934–5.[72] Winston Churchill had resigned from the government over the issue in 1931.[73] He believed that India was not ready for self-government and that giving the country Dominion status too early would lead to the collapse of central administration and give rise to bloodshed on a colossal level.[74] Future events did somewhat vindicate his position, although it is hard to avoid the racist stereotyping behind his words.

In mid-January 1935, Randolph Churchill visited Liverpool to report on the Wavertree by-election, along with some friends from the India Defence League. James Platt was the official National Government candidate and during an election hustings Churchill and his friends gave him a testing time over the issue of India.

Later that night, Churchill resolved to fight the election himself, standing as an Independent Conservative. His father was unhappy, and wrote to his wife Clementine:

> This is a most rash and unconsidered plunge...In all probability all that he will do is to take enough votes from the Conservatives to let the Socialist in.

That would do no end of harm, he concluded. All the same, he supported his son in public, deeming India to be a worthy cause. Later, he became more sanguine, reflecting that, should Randolph beat the National Government candidate but lose to the Socialist, this would be 'a nasty jar for Ramsay [MacDonald] and [Stanley] Baldwin'. He went on:

> You will see that I am much more easy in mind about it than I was at first sight. Randolph, of course, is in the seventh heaven. This is exactly the kind of thing he revels in and for which his gifts are particularly suited.

At this point, Randolph was assisted by Lady Houston, a woman described by Winston S Churchill, in his biography of his father, as Randolph's 'political fairy godmother'.[75] She had written to Randolph about a series of articles he published in the *Sunday Express* expressing regret that he was 'showing the cloven hoof – or shall I say the fatal flaw of the Churchills' character'. The reason was that he had been lauding Liberalism in some of his pieces. She told him: 'never have a word to say in praise of your opponent'. Churchill responded, 'distressed' at her suggestion and offering assurances she was mistaken. 'Sometimes I have felt that you and I are the only two real Conservatives left in this defeatist world', he wrote. 'We must not start detecting the cloven hoof in each other.'[76] His reply must have satisfied Lady Houston because she gave him a cheque for £1,000 to cover his election expenses.[77]

The by-election was a bizarre affair, described by the *Liverpool Echo* as 'a mad-hatter contest from beginning to end'.[78] Randolph Churchill came third behind James Platt but, as Winston had predicted, split the vote and Platt lost to the Labour candidate, Joseph Cleary. The fallout did indeed cause Randolph a great deal of harm. Sir Samuel Hoare, at the time Secretary of State for India, and later that year briefly (see 25 December on the Hoare-Laval Pact) Foreign Secretary, wrote to Lord Willingdon, Viceroy and Governor-General of India: 'That little brute Randolph has done a lot of mischief'. It is likely that this affected the rest of Randolph's Churchill's career.

If that didn't, then the Norwood by-election in London certainly did. Less than a week after the Wavertree count, Randolph Churchill announced his intention to put forward a candidate, Richard Findlay (previously a member of the British Union of Fascists), to challenge the National Government's India policy. Again, Churchill was bankrolled by Lady Houston. Winston was furious, telling his wife, 'He is quite beyond reason and even parley and I am leaving him alone'. Randolph's candidate went on to lose his deposit, causing Winston to reflect that the experience: 'should teach him prudence, and to work with others'. History shows that it did neither.

And yet, for Winston, there were positives. The Churchills saw themselves as outsiders, trouble-makers beholden to no one. That they had damaged the reputation of the National Government they purported – almost – to support seemed not to bother them. Indeed, *The Times* interpreted the affair as a concerted effort by them to damage the government:

> India...played no real part in the [Wavertree] election. It is significant that MR RANDOPLH CHURCHILL [their upper case], especially during the latter stages of his campaign, widened the front of his assault to attack the whole policy and system of National Government.

The National Government, then, and MacDonald and Baldwin in particular, were the real subjects of the Churchills' ire. Winston Churchill wrote to his wife: 'The Baldwin-MacDonald regime has hit this country very hard indeed, and may well be the end of its glories'.[79] Elsewhere, he said of Baldwin: 'He has no achievements to his record. He is an unknown man'.[80] Randolph Churchill was even more scathing: on a tour of America, he was quoted in the *News Chronicle*:

> Of course I have the greatest admiration for Mr Stanley Baldwin. He shares all the qualities of a suet pudding, is steady, solid, substantial, but as a leader – NO SIR![81]

Randolph had time for one further election foray, standing as the official Conservative candidate in the general election in Toxteth. He lost again but did reasonably well in a campaign characterised by outbreaks of violence. His sister Diana's hat was snatched from her head. A stone was thrown at his car, knocking off Winston's hat. Chairs were hurled in hustings meetings.[82] It would prove a sound training ground for Ross and Cromarty.

MacDonalds v Churchills

The *Dundee Courier* had a more sober analysis of events in Ross and Cromarty and the Scottish Universities, where Ramsay MacDonald's nomination was also receiving heavy criticism. The paper was concerned that in both by-elections National Government candidates were being opposed, although it doubted this opposition would be 'carried to the point of endangering the result'. The imperative should be to keep out a 'revolutionary Socialist Government' and a guiding ideal was to keep the National Government national. The national character of the government had been 'unquestionably weakened by the exclusion of the two MacDonalds from Parliament', it said, calling for all involved to consider the needs of government ahead of those of party.[83]

Their call was aimed, alas, at the deafest of deaf ears.

By a remarkable twist of timing, the day that Randolph Churchill's name was first mentioned in relation to Ross and Cromarty he wrote a column in the *Sunday Dispatch* which focused ostensibly on the ongoing Italo-Abyssinian crisis but which, by the end, had turned into a diatribe against the two MacDonalds. As we will discover, this was something of a default position for Churchill, causing the *Daily Express* to write of him, somewhat approvingly: 'Mr Randolph Churchill sees so red at the mention of a MacDonald that some people think he must be a Campbell in disguise.'[84]

Ramsay MacDonald, Churchill wrote, had 'always talked about retiring from politics', but whenever an opportunity arose which could make that happen he 'never seems anxious to do so'. Of his nomination for the Scottish Universities seat, Churchill wrote, one supposes without firm evidence: '[h]is defeat may be another New Year surprise'. Turning to Malcolm MacDonald, the man with whom he was now fated to be conjoined for the next six weeks, the campaign would be 'one of the fiercest by-elections of recent times', with the 'Socialist clansmen' gathering to encompass his defeat. At this point, he seems to have no inkling that he might somehow join the fight. The defeat of both MacDonalds, he continued, would give the government a 'ticklish problem' by reducing 'almost to nil' any chance that they might gain a return to Westminster during the current Parliament. He suggested that 'many politicians' (which could at least be verifiably counted at two – himself and his father) thought that this could herald the return of party government. He conjectured:

> Mr Baldwin might then relinquish the leadership to Mr Neville Chamberlain, who would invite the Simonite Liberals and the small band of National Labourites to choose between the Conservative party and the different shades of opposition.[85]

While he accepted that such a step was inconceivable 'at this moment', it is impossible to ignore the desire that imbues Churchill's words. Again, we can see the political agendas of the Churchills in tandem. A change of leadership and the return of an exclusively Conservative government would, of course, open the way for Winston Churchill to return to frontline politics. Not only that, but should either MacDonald fail in their attempts to return to Parliament, that would be an elated outcome for Churchill senior and junior. Clive Sangers lists how often the MacDonalds and the Churchills had clashed politically over the years: over Churchill's strikebreaking activity in 1911, their respective views on the First World

War, India, the National Government and Palestine. Chamberlain's Munich Agreement and Malcolm MacDonald's negotiation of the Irish Agreement with Eamonn de Valera, both in 1938, would further strain relations.[86]

And now, in his cabin on his luxury yacht in the Mediterranean, Randolph had received the strangest cablegram from a group of Highland farmers, inviting him into battle.

What would Churchill, a serial candidate against the National Government, do next? The answer seemed inevitable: as Christopher Harvie noted:

> Like a jam jar to a wasp, [the candidatures of the two MacDonalds] attracted Randolph Churchill, standing in for his father as chief nuisance to the Baldwin Government.[87]

✡ ✡ ✡

Monday, 30 December 1935

Will He? Won't He?

On a day when the mood and trajectory of the by-election shifted decisively, it is instructive to view how different parts of the press conveyed the news. There was a growing understanding that the political battles in the Scottish Universities and Ross and Cromarty were much larger than the by-elections which were their catalysts; high politics was being played out in full view of the watching public.

The Daily Herald, a daily newspaper of the labour movement, excoriated the MacDonalds. Ramsay had been fixed up by his friends, the Conservatives, and Malcolm hoped to be fixed up by *his* friends, the Liberals. 'The father will be formally nominated by a Conservative Association, the son – such is his hope – by a Liberal Association', they protested. 'Of men who so behave while yet they pose as "Labour" and claim still to be Socialists, the people of this country are fully capable of forming their own opinion'.[88]

This level of vituperation – five years after the crisis which had caused Ramsay MacDonald to establish the National Government – showed the rancour still affecting the Labour movement. Labour had performed disastrously in the 1931 general election, which Simon Heffer put down to the electorate feeling they had 'behaved irrationally about the crisis'.[89] They did much better in the 1935 election, picking up over a hundred additional seats to end with 154, but they were still not trusted as a party of government. Until such enmities could be overcome, it seemed unlikely this would change.

The Scotsman now reflected that it was 'doubtful' that MacDonald would be adopted.[90] This represents a significant – even improbable – shift from previous reports. Remember, only two days before their correspondent said there was 'little or no doubt' he would become the candidate.[91] How could the situation have changed so radically, so quickly? It seems fairly clear that intense lobbying was going on in the constituency, with vested interests proclaiming as fact what was only opinion or conjecture. Dingwall was embroiled in a fast-shifting and multi-headed intrigue, with Liberals (of various flavours), Unionists and Socialists all claiming the one way to truth. The word from the National Liberal camp was that, if MacDonald was not adopted, there was a high likelihood of a Liberal National candidate being chosen instead. Such a candidate could be acceptable to Unionists and independent Liberals in a way that MacDonald, a Socialist, would never be.

If MacDonald was nominated, however, *The Scotsman* felt that opponents would surely come forward. For the Liberals, the most likely candidate from an ever-changing roster of previous election losers was now Basil Murray, son of Professor Gilbert Murray of Oxford University, who had twice lost in Argyll. In addition to Randolph Churchill, two possibly more palatable names were suggested for the Unionists – Roderick Martineau, son of the Association chairman, Sir William Martineau, and Angus Vickers, son of Douglas Vickers, a former MP.[92] *The term 'nepo-babies' may be new, but their existence assuredly isn't.*

Liberal Traditionalists Flex Their Muscles

The *Daily Record* also presented coverage which appeared to owe much to the views of Liberals on the ground. William Webster, former General Secretary of the Scottish Liberal Federation, visited the constituency to determine the local views on MacDonald. He said it would be dangerous to the prospects of Liberalism if any Liberal Association adopted a

Socialist. However, if MacDonald agreed to stand on a National Liberal ticket they probably would not oppose him.

This was, no doubt, an attempt to put pressure on MacDonald to do just that. If so, it seemed likely to fail, as the view from MacDonald's camp was that he would stand as a National Government candidate, not National Liberal or National Labour. This would set an unusual precedent since nobody else was a member of the National Government without a declared allegiance to one of the three main parties.[93]

Saying the situation had grown 'more obscure and involved', the *Press and Journal* suggested it was older Liberals who were fomenting dissent over MacDonald's candidature. They quoted one:

> We may have had to swallow our Free Trade principles in the light of modern conditions but we are not socialists, and we are not going to have one forced on us even with the excuse that we must support the National Government.[94]

The question of free trade, long a Liberal shibboleth, was still contentious even four years after the National Liberals, at the formation of the National Government, had reluctantly acceded to the government's policy demands on tariffs. The new Cabinet established a Balance of Trade Committee which recommended a general tariff in January 1932. This was too much for the Samuelites in the Cabinet, who threatened to resign. As a result, on advice from Lord Hailsham, the Cabinet relaxed its usual rule of collective responsibility, allowing those whose 'lifelong convictions' supported free trade to be 'free to state that they did not agree in the policy of the Government in this particular matter'.[95]

The idea remained anathema to rank-and-file Liberals, though, to the extent that, during the 1935 election campaign, the Samuelite leadership was forced to produce, as a sop, their manifesto in addition to the official tripartite one. This made no reference to the imposition of tariffs but was of no consequence because tariffs remained official government policy and free trade was consigned to history. This still rankled the old-fashioned, Lloyd Georgian Liberals.[96]

The *Press and Journal* reported that the Socialists were not saying anything officially, but the name of Hector McNeil was being freely discussed in the constituency. If true, he would be a formidable candidate. They reported, too, that Sir William Martineau and Dr G G Middleton, chairmen of the Unionist and Liberal Associations respectively, met in the afternoon. Little progress was made, but Martineau made clear that the Unionist Association was 'not in any way committed' to support the candidature of MacDonald.

Unionists Disunited

Martineau probably now realised that he was facing a greater level of dissent than he had anticipated. The kite-flying exercise undertaken by the Easter Ross farmers had, improbably, succeeded: they had received a cablegram advising them that Randolph Churchill's agent was on his way to the constituency from Liverpool and that Churchill had cut short his holiday and was about to fly home. The resolution, which was going forward to the Executive Committee of the Association calling on them to ignore the recommendations of Central Office, suddenly presented a greater degree of jeopardy.[97] Indeed, the *News Chronicle* (admittedly not the most reliable information source) was certain that Malcolm MacDonald 'would have' Churchill as a rival in the by-election.[98] The *Inverness Courier*, though, was dismissive: 'A touch of humour has been added to the situation' by the cabling to Churchill by the Easter Ross farmers. 'It is not in the least likely that the Association will be so foolish as to adopt Mr Churchill', it stated.[99]

The Easter Ross farmers met in Dingwall to plan their next steps, no doubt as surprised as anyone by the train of events. They outlined their position to the press: they wanted a candidate who 'understood the needs and difficulties of the agricultural industry as they affect the Highlands'.[100] That is a perfectly sensible platform, but to suppose that their ideal candidate might be Randolph Churchill, scion of the Marlborough clan, Eton-educated and Anglophile to his bootstraps, rather than Malcolm MacDonald, a Highlander who had previously represented an agricultural constituency and who was responsible for agreeing agricultural tariffs with the Dominions, was almost breathtaking in its absurdity. *There's none so blind as those who will not see.*

The Scion

At this point, it is worth adding information about Randolph Churchill.

He began his autobiography with the following potted history:

> I was born in London on 28 May 1911 at 33 Ecclestone Square, of poor but honest parents. Born within sound of Bow Bells I was a cockney and, until I was forty, was destined to spend more than half my life in London.[101]

He did, then, have a sense of humour, but he was not an easily likeable man. He was precocious, fiercely intelligent and arrogant, as many school reports made clear. He was 'no willing accepter of drudgery' eager to take 'short-cuts to success'. He constantly interrupted classes with 'queries and quibbles', remarks which were 'largely cheap, pointless and irrelevant'. He was 'handicapped by his obsession for the sound of his own voice'. Calling him 'quarrelsome', his history tutor reflected he enjoyed being in a minority. In fairness, Churchill recognised this in himself, saying of his time at Eton: 'I was lazy and unsuccessful both at work and at games. I did not conform to the general pattern and was an unpopular boy'. And, despite his faults, he could be charming and good company. His headmaster at Sandroyd School said, 'I am heartily sorry to part with a boy so full of the cheerfulness and gaiety of life'. An Eton housemaster alleged that when he could keep his 'wagging tongue' under control he could be 'a most delightful member of society'.[102] His trouble was that he could be, in his son Winston S Churchill's candid description of him, 'boorish, idle and generally objectionable'. Some of the blame for this, he continued, could be placed on Winston Churchill, who had been determined not to be the 'cold, distant, irascible father' that Lord Randolph had been to Winston, and instead spoiled Randolph at every turn.[103]

There is no question that Randolph was a very able thinker. He was not yet eighteen when he first spoke in public, at an election hustings for his father in the general election of 1929, addressing over 2,000 people in Edinburgh for twenty minutes without notes.[104] At the age of nineteen, in 1930, he was invited on a speaking tour of America and in October 1931 he conducted a six-month lecture tour of Britain, during which he was one of the first people to warn about German rearmament – at a point when Hitler wasn't even in power – and criticised the folly of continuing disarmament.[105]

By the time of the Ross and Cromarty by-election he was already a successful journalist. It all seemed to come easily to Randolph Churchill. Writing in the *Daily Despatch* in 1932, he said, 'I wish to make an immense fortune and to be Prime Minister', although he added:

> In twenty years' time, however, when I shall probably have fought four or five unsuccessful elections and have been bankrupted more than once, I do not see why I should then regret my youthful ambition, however laughable this will appear to my more experienced eye.[106]

Even by 1936, the harsh realities of life may have become clearer to him. In an interview with Matthew Halton for the *Toronto Star* during the by-election, he said:

> When I was at Oxford I thought I'd die if I weren't in Parliament by the time I was twenty-one. Now I don't care.

The reason he was fighting, he said, was the tactics of the MacDonalds.[107] What seemed to motivate Churchill – apart from his dislike of the MacDonalds – was the fight, or at least the trouble he could cause through the fight. Returning to the analysis of his former history tutor, Churchill enjoyed, not rubbing people up the wrong way, but the 'result of having rubbed them the wrong way'.[108]

Positions are Taken

The *Edinburgh Evening News* reported on the views of the Scottish National Party, hitherto quiet in the campaign. A statement by John MacCormick, party secretary, attacked both MacDonalds:

The adoption [by the Scottish Universities] of Ramsay MacDonald after long and obscure negotiations...and the manoeuvres now in progress to impose his son...as candidate in Ross and Cromarty arouse wide and justifiable resentment. These two politicians, discarded by their English constituencies, are being foisted upon the Scottish electorate, although wholly lacking in Scottish political antecedents. Scotland is being made, in a peculiarly flagrant fashion, the convenience of caucus politics.[109]

While most of the press were seeking (with varying degrees of success) to show impartiality, the *Inverness Courier* decided that the best course of action was to get its retaliation in first. A stinging leader column focused on the mere suggestion that MacDonald should stand was 'sufficient to let loose a flood of antagonism'. It went on:

> ...we are sorry to see that a few farmers in Ross-shire have been affected by that spirit so far as to cable to Mr Randolph Churchill for permission to submit his name to the Unionist Association as a possible Unionist candidate...though what use Mr Churchill would be to a Highland constituency passes our comprehension.

It suggested there was little likelihood of the Unionist Association countenancing such a proposal (a neat use of an argument from its false authority), and stated that if Malcolm MacDonald stood he would be the 'official candidate of the National Government'. Any Association or individual who declined to support that candidate would, in effect, be declining to support the National Government, and a vote against MacDonald would be a vote against the National Government. This proof by assertion would be played out again and again in the coming weeks. Voting in such a way would be to fall for the 'very transparent efforts to sow discord in the ranks of the Government forces in Ross and Cromarty'.

Any Unionists concerned by MacDonald's candidature, it went on, had plenty of time and opportunity to make their feelings known to the Association, rather than attempting to 'foist a candidate of their own on the constituency before the views of even their own Association had been ascertained'.

It finished with an encomium for MacDonald: he would be a Member able and willing to promote the interests and attend to the needs of Ross and Cromarty.[110]

This leader set the tone for the *Inverness Courier*'s campaign coverage. It refused to fall for the spin that other newspapers were reporting as fact. In its news report, it noted that in certain quarters efforts were being made to create dissension between the Liberals and Unionists by creating the impression that the Unionists were annoyed because they had not been consulted. However, to date MacDonald had only been invited to meet the Executive, meaning no decision had been taken. Moreover, it suggested that Unionist officials were 'not so unaware of the situation' as was being implied.[111]

✡ ✡ ✡

Tuesday, 31 December 1935

The Worst Laid Plans of MacDonalds and Men

The Unionists Meet

The Unionist Association met in Dingwall to consider the proposal for Malcolm MacDonald to stand as National Government candidate at the by-election. There was lingering resentment at the treatment of the Association by the Liberal Association and by Sir Ian Macpherson, the previous Member of Parliament. The source of this resentment could be traced back to the general election in November 1935.

Sir William Martineau spoke at the meeting and declared that, during the election, he was never asked on to any platform or even to take part in any meeting. 'I call that an insult to the Unionist Party', he said. To great applause, he went on:

> After the meeting I was so annoyed that I wrote a strong letter of protest to the Edinburgh Liberal headquarters, to which I received a belated reply thanking the Unionists for their support. Five weeks ago [in the general election] Sir Ian Macpherson was returned with a record majority. And why? Because the Unionists had voted for him. I say that it was the Unionist votes which returned Sir Ian at the top of the poll.[112]

Since Macpherson won with a majority of over 7,500 and the Unionist strength in the county at the time was reckoned to be about 2,500, this was wholly implausible, but it went down well.

Sir William outlined the chain of events in recent days. On 23 December, he received a letter from Sir Ian Macpherson marked 'private and confidential', stating that Sir Ian was to retire. However, he only heard the news that Malcolm MacDonald was likely to be nominated as the National Government candidate through the newspapers. On Saturday, 28 December, he received a letter from Dr Middleton of the Liberal Association, also marked 'private and confidential'. He met Dr Middleton in Dingwall and told him that the only way to secure Unionist support was to come to the Unionist Association 'on equal terms, as equal members and equal partners in the National Government'. Everything needed to be above board, he stressed.

Sir William Martineau
photo: Creative Commons

On Monday, 30 December, he received a phone call from Conservative Central Office to say that the Co-ordination Committee of Whips of the parties in the National Government had met and recommended the Unionists in Ross and Cromarty should support MacDonald. A series of phone calls ensued with Captain David Margesson, the Conservatives' Chief Whip, and Colonel Blair, secretary to the General Whip in Scotland. The official line that Conservative Central Office wanted the Unionists to support MacDonald was reiterated, to which Martineau declared he could offer no such assurance until he had consulted his members. At this point, Margesson appeared to raise the stakes by asserting that, in addition to the Co-ordination Committee approving MacDonald's nomination, this was also the express wish of the Prime Minister.

It is clear that there was considerable discord in the Unionists' meeting, with a perception they were being steamrollered by Central Office. At the conclusion of Martineau's speech, a vote was held and the Association voted unanimously against support being accorded to MacDonald. An official statement was sent to Central Office:

> It was decided unanimously that the Unionist Association was unanimously (*sic*) opposed to Mr Malcolm MacDonald as a candidate. An emergency committee has been appointed, consisting of the executive committee and certain others, to consider the selection of a Unionist candidate who might be acceptable to the Liberal Association. The Unionist Association desires, if possible, to work in harmony with the Liberal Association.[113]

As it happened, Dr Middleton, Alexander Macrae and Malcolm MacDonald were in the hotel where the Unionists' meeting was taking place. Martineau and T H Burns, the Unionists' secretary, met with Middleton and Macrae, but not MacDonald, and advised them of the outcome. The Liberals received the news 'sadly'. Martineau told them it was 'surely time the Liberals supported a Unionist candidate' and asked the Liberals to work with them to find a candidate who could command the support of both parties.

The Unionists' special committee was composed of the Executive Committee along with the Reverend John Sellar of Ferintosh; James Scott, Fearn; W H Gill, Brucefield; Provost Donald Ross, Tain; and Major Alexander Stirling, Strathgarve. Although the statement talked of consideration of an appropriate candidate, it seemed that the Unionist choice had already been narrowed down to a single name, Randolph Churchill.

The carefully contrived plot to return Malcolm MacDonald to Parliament was beginning to unravel.

* * *

Wednesday, 1 January 1936

A Gong, Much Anxiety, Threats of Excommunication and Resolve Maintained

The day began with news that Sir Ian Macpherson had been granted a peerage in the New Year's Honours.[114] One may speculate whether this was in recognition of his 25 years as a Member of Parliament, or for his decision to stand down and create a convenient vacancy.

Malcolm MacDonald told a reporter in Lossiemouth that he had not yet decided whether to stand. He stressed, however, that he would not be standing as a Liberal candidate. 'If I stand I will stand as a National Government candidate and nothing else', he said, adding that he would make up his mind in a few days.[115]

This, at least, seemed to placate those Liberals who had been unhappy with the way MacDonald was being foisted on them. His pledge to stand as a National Government candidate assuaged some of their concerns, but soundings continued to be taken among likely independent Liberal candidates.

MacDonald's statement did nothing to appease the growing disgruntlement among Unionists, however. They believed he had already had ample time to make a decision and suspected this delay was a ruse by Conservative Central Office to put pressure on the local branch to accept his nomination. The *Daily Mirror* ran a report suggesting that Central Office were 'wholeheartedly backing MacDonald' but Stanley Baldwin and his lieutenants were suffering 'much anxiety'. If the local association continued to reject his candidature, the *Mirror* continued, they ran a 'big risk of being excommunicated by party leaders'.[116]

Nonetheless, a meeting of Unionist officials, comprising Sir William Martineau, J Brown, W H Gill, Dr Ross, Captain MacGillivray and J Sutherland maintained their resolve to reject MacDonald's candidature.

Unionists
photo: Aberdeen Press and Journal

With this whiff of rebellion in the air, Randolph Churchill's agent, Tom McDonald, was busy preparing the ground for Churchill's adoption if, as now seemed likely, the Unionists would field their own candidate. The *Press and Journal* reported he was in constant touch with Unionist officials and with the group of Easter Ross farmers who made the initial contact with Churchill via cablegram.[117] Other names were being put forward, too, including Viscount Tarbat.[118]

Meanwhile, the Labour Party confirmed they would contest the seat and convened a meeting on the evening of Friday, 3 January to select the 'strongest possible candidate', with Arthur Woodburn, general secretary of the Scottish branch travelling to Dingwall to take charge.[119]

✡ ✡ ✡

Thursday, 2 January 1936

An 'Astonishing Day', Secret Meetings, Opposition and Possible Names

Another day of intrigue led the *Press and Journal* to state, 'Yesterday's political moves astonished the Highland counties'.[120] A two-hour conference took place in Dingwall between representatives of the Liberal and Unionist Associations, under conditions of great secrecy. Malcolm MacDonald travelled from Lossiemouth to attend the meeting. The other attendees were Sir William Martineau, Sir Robert Brooke, Captain Shaw-Mackenzie, W H Gill for the Unionist Association; and Dr Middleton, D A M Ross and Alexander Macrae for the Liberal Association.

Afterwards, MacDonald declined to speak to the press but, the *Press and Journal* reported:

> [h]is general cheerfulness...seemed to suggest that he was more than pleased with the result of the two hours' conclave.[121]

Sir William Martineau also remained reticent, saying only that the discussions were informal and no decision had been reached. The *Daily Mirror*, though, reported that the Unionists were 'now disposed to accept MacDonald'.[122] There remained considerable resistance in Unionist circles to MacDonald's candidature. The *Press and Journal* reported that a faction, although strongly opposed, might support him for fear of splitting the National Government vote and ushering in a Socialist victory.

Some, however, remained resolute in their opposition. The *Press and Journal* quoted an unnamed but 'prominent' official as saying he did not believe the members of the Association would allow Headquarters to dictate to the local branch. Although, he said, the Liberal Association stated they had no intention of slighting the Unionists that 'would not cut any ice'. 'We are simply not going to support a Socialist', he concluded.[123]

James Scott, a prominent farmer, did go on record, calling MacDonald's candidature 'irregular'. He explained:

> I believe that Ross-shire will go out solidly to fight Mr Malcolm MacDonald in every way possible. There is a danger that if Mr MacDonald is put forward this interference by headquarters will drive Ross-shire solidly to the support of a genuine Socialist candidate. The meeting of the Liberals and the Unionists makes the Unionists more determined than ever to have a candidate of their own.[124]

News of the informal talks was condemned by supporters of Randolph Churchill. The events of the day, however, appeared to boost his hopes of acceptance as an independent Unionist candidate. The *Press and Journal* reported that Churchill was now expected to be in Dingwall in time for the Unionist meeting on Saturday.

Even so, the matter of his candidature was still uncertain. Ross Unionists revealed to the *Press and Journal* that Churchill had cabled them advising that, as the issue affected the Party in general, he felt compelled to consult Lord Stonehaven, the chairman of the Party, on Conservative Central Office's view. He had not yet received a reply but, since we already know from discussions between Sir William Martineau, Captain Margesson and Colonel Blair that Central Office was strongly disposed to support MacDonald, the response can probably be guessed. A further complicating factor was that Central Office would not ordinarily deal with Scottish constituencies, leaving that to the Scottish Unionist Association. The result, then, could be a non-committal reply only serving to further confuse the issue.

Anger at the imposition of a candidate remained strong in Liberal circles, too. Ranald Findlay insisted that independent Liberals were 'quite determined' to fight the vacancy.[125] Findlay was planning to visit the constituency at the weekend to consult with the local association. Basil Murray, who had been mooted as a possible candidate was reported by the *Press and Journal* as willing to stand.

The *Press and Journal* also confirmed rumours that the favoured candidate for the Socialists was Hector McNeil, who had narrowly lost to

Walter Elliot, the Minister for Agriculture, in the Kelvingrove constituency in Glasgow in the November general election. A rumour that A M Mackay, a 'farmer of independent means' from Dornoch, might be asked to stand for the Socialists was firmly rebuffed by the man himself. 'The rumour that I have been invited to stand is as silly as the statement that I am a farmer of independent means', he said.[126]

The people of Ross and Cromarty found themselves anticipating a weekend the like of which they had never before seen.

* * *

Friday, 3 January 1936

An Opportunity Missed

The day began with an early visit by Malcolm MacDonald – symbolically accompanied by Sir Ian Macpherson, the retiring Member – to the Dominion Offices in London of which, despite having lost his seat in the general election, he was still Cabinet Minister in charge. He later consulted with Captain Margesson and one supposes he was reassured that Central Office's position remained unchanged.

The view Central Office had been keen to promote was that MacDonald should be allowed to stand unopposed by the Unionist Party because Ross and Cromarty was a long-standing Liberal seat and the Liberal Association had selected MacDonald as their nomination. He should, therefore, receive support from all parties in the National Government.

Later, MacDonald left London for Inverness on a sleeper train. When it was pointed out that the number of his sleeper was thirteen, he laughed and said he wasn't superstitious.[127] Perhaps if asked the same question six weeks later, he might have propounded a different view.

Another 'unexpected' meeting of leading Unionists took place in Dingwall during the day.[128] Although, again, no official report of the outcome of this meeting was recorded, there was a sense that support was slowly shifting towards MacDonald, leaving the Easter Ross farmers isolated. The *Daily Telegraph*, for example, suggested that MacDonald would probably gain the majority of Unionist votes in Saturday's meeting.[129]

Possible corroboration of the *Telegraph*'s view comes in a draft letter in

Malcolm MacDonald's papers (Durham University). In the letter, which is undated and addressed only to 'P.M.', MacDonald apologised for the events transpiring in Ross and Cromarty. He ended by saying, 'Afraid these dissensions [among the Unionists] make fight very risky one. Hope we may be able pull it off for you (*sic*)'. This suggests the letter is to the Prime Minister, Stanley Baldwin, apprising him of the current situation. From the context, it appears to have been written on Saturday, 4 January. This is supported by the fact that, unlike most of the letters from MacDonald during the campaign, which were written on paper headed 'National Hotel, Dingwall', this paper was not headed. MacDonald, of course, was in London at this point and not Dingwall. In the letter he referred to the Unionist meeting and noted, 'In Association meeting yesterday was actually ~~majo~~ [*sic*] on vote majority of one in favour of getting me in. Why not acted upon I know not'.[130]

Had the Association acted on that vote, the whole campaign would have been transformed and Malcolm MacDonald's success in the by-election would have been assured. But they didn't, and instead, the rebels continued to assert a false authority. The *Daily Telegraph* quoted prominent Churchill supporter, W H Gill:

> You may take it for granted that most of the people who opposed Mr MacDonald on Tuesday will again oppose him tomorrow. We have seen no reason to alter our view since the last meeting. The issue involved is one of principle, and we cannot have outside people foisted on us. I would go as far as to say that two-thirds of the meeting will be against Mr MacDonald.[131]

Gill was busy elsewhere, too, telling the *Dundee Courier*, 'It is quite wrong to say that Mr Churchill is a farmers' candidate, for he has the support of a large number of Unionists of all kinds'.[132] Gill was, of course, a farmer.

This accusation that Churchill was the preference of only a small cabal of farmers seemed to be telling. Tom McDonald, Randolph Churchill's agent, referred to it too, when explaining that the reason for Churchill's vacillation was that he was waiting for an official invitation from the wider Unionist Association:

> There is no question at all of him standing unless adopted as the official

> Unionist candidate. If he is adopted, he will certainly stand. But he will await the decision of tomorrow's meeting. There is no question of Mr Churchill being recommended only by farmers. He is supported by many others in the constituency as well as the farmers.[133]

This vagueness from Churchill was unusual – he was not a man given to doubt – and suggests tensions between him and senior officers in the Unionist party. According to *The Scotsman*, a reporter was informed by Conservative Central Office that Churchill would not contest the by-election. But at 11.15 pm, Churchill sent a wireless message to the Press Association: 'Am astonished Central Office should issue unfounded and unauthorised statement of my intentions'. He went on: 'I have taken no decision'.[134]

It wasn't until 11 January, when Churchill spoke to a Unionist Association meeting, that the full reason for this impasse was revealed. Churchill, he told his audience, had telegrammed Central Office on 1 January, explaining that he had been invited by the Unionist Association to stand and asking whether the long-standing, and recently reaffirmed, rule that Central Office would support any candidate chosen by local Unionist associations, was still valid. Lord Stonehaven, chairman of the party, responded:

> Understand Ross and Cromarty Liberals and Unionists in consultation on question of candidate. Position not analogous with Basingstoke.

'Basingstoke' references Churchill's comment about the rule being 'recently reaffirmed'. During the general election campaign in Basingstoke, Lord Stonehaven wrote to the candidate, Patrick Donner, who had been selected by the local Association, confirming he would receive support from Central Office. This, for Churchill, gave a precedent for Central Office certifying choices made by local associations. He was, not unreasonably, irritated by Lord Stonehaven's evasive reply. Stonehaven had 'deliberately avoided giving me any advice on this point', Churchill later told his audience.[135]

Any question of Churchill's nomination could prove to be moot anyhow because there were suggestions in the constituency that there was a strong and growing feeling in favour of a local Unionist candidate such as Sir Robert Brooke. This desire for a local name was driven by concern with potential 'official wire-pulling' and carpetbagging. The *Edinburgh Evening News* concluded:

> 'Dictatorship' from official sources in Edinburgh and London is also resented by many voters who in the district appear to take their politics very much more earnestly than do voters in other regions. The feeling against 'outside candidates' is particularly strong among some of the women voters.

That said, the paper did concede that MacDonald was practically a local himself.[136]

Anticipating the decisive Unionist meeting the next day, *The Scotsman* expressed little confidence about what would transpire. There was a feeling, it suggested, that the case for Churchill had been 'pressed somewhat too strongly by a group of individuals' and this might not meet favour with the wider membership. While there was no evidence that the joint meeting of the Liberal and Unionist Associations had done anything to assuage the concerns of the Unionists, *The Scotsman* concluded that it was possible that in Saturday's meeting, 'the whole situation be will be considered *de novo*'. Being right back where they started must have been dispiriting for the participants.

Meanwhile, the secretary of the Scottish National Party told the *Edinburgh Evening News* that they had received no information from their northern branch on the likelihood of the party standing. It was reported that Sir Alexander MacEwen, chairman of the SNP, had been asked to stand. Sir Alexander had stood for Parliament twice before, without success, which seems almost to be a prerequisite among people of all parties being touted as potential candidates in this by-election.[137]

Hector McNeil

Hector McNeil (another previous election loser, albeit a very close one) became the first candidate to be officially adopted when the Ross and Cromarty Socialists unanimously announced him as their candidate. McNeil, aged 25, was regarded as a rising star of the socialist movement.

Hector McNeil
photo: Aberdeen Press and Journal

Although there had been a wellspring of opinion that a local candidate should be adopted, the adoption meeting of around 70 members was described by *The Scotsman* as 'most enthusiastic'.[138] Among the speakers in his favour were Hugh Fraser, the rejected Socialist candidate for Inverness--shire and Malcolm Macmillan, Socialist MP for the Western Isles, who appears to have had a robust oratorical style. In a letter to Malcolm MacDonald at the end of the campaign, a local woman, Annie Cameron of Hilton, Fearn, wrote that Macmillan was 'one of your worst enemies' who 'showed a very poor standard of a highland man when his policy was a hymn of hate'.[139]

McNeil did have Highland connections, his father's family originated from Barraand his mother's from Islay.[140] Ewan Cameron quotes Arthur Woodburn reflecting later on the by-election and saying that McNeil 'was well-known, a highlander and [he] had a pleasant manner and appearance and was an able speaker'.[141] He proved to be an unusually high-quality candidate, one of a new breed of Labour candidates. As Cameron explained: 'the Labour intake [of candidates] after the [Great] war was characterized by older figures who had "served their time" in the trades union movement or local government'.[142] McNeil was someone entirely different.

Unrest in the Liberal ranks was beginning to settle, with only the (mostly older) traditionalists still objecting to MacDonald. However, another new name for an independent candidate arose during the day, that of Dr Lachlan Grant.[143] Grant was a 65-year-old doctor from Ballachulish. He was co-founder of the Highland Development League and an early proponent of a 'New Deal' for the Highlands.[144] Names such as Dr Grant's would emerge regularly throughout the campaign, often without any contact with the individuals themselves, and were suggestive of a chaos at the heart of the independent Liberal hierarchy. As it happens, Dr Lachlan Grant, had his candidature come to pass, could have made an enormous impact on the by-election.

Any chaos in the Liberal ranks, however, was nothing compared to the chaos that was going to descend on the by-election campaign the next day.

* * *

Saturday, 4 January 1936

Vilification, a Pile-on, Ringers, a Second Rejection and a Candidate

The Scotsman detected a 'process of disintegration' in both the Liberal and Unionist parties in Ross and Cromarty.[145] By the end of the day, that process would have advanced significantly.

The Unionist and Liberal Associations met in adjoining rooms of the National Hotel in Dingwall to agree their approaches. Malcolm MacDonald arrived at 11 am and waited patiently while the debates about his candidacy raged. The lengthy Unionist meeting was a feisty affair, a battle between toeing the party line and maintaining an independent spirit. While the leadership of the local association had largely swung round to supporting Central Office's position, dissenters remained, and they seemed suspiciously large in number. The rebels quickly criticised senior Unionist officials, including Sir William Martineau and Sir Robert Brooke.

Unionists at *War*

Martineau stressed the need to support the National Government. He stated that he had received a letter from the prime minister supporting MacDonald, but at no point was this read out.[146] Presumably, he feared it would be taken as further proof of London's interference.

If MacDonald stood, Martineau explained, he would do so without a prefix – that is, he would stand as the candidate of the National Government, not an individual party of the government – and in that eventuality, he would probably win. If the Unionists refused to support him, the seat would probably be won by the Socialists. MacDonald, he concluded, may not be a popular choice for Unionists, but he was a useful one for the government. 'The prestige of the Government is in your hands,' he said. 'The country is watching this Association and watching our decision.'[147]

Although many could see the political rationale behind this, anger at the way the matter was being handled persisted. Reverend John Sellar described the circumstances of the by-election as 'political jobbery of the meanest description'. W H Gill insisted the difficulties they were encountering had been caused by interference from Central Office.

P D Robertson and Captain Shaw-MacKenzie (who had himself been considered a possible candidate by the Emergency Committee on Tuesday) spoke in favour of observing Central Office's advice. Colonel Blair thought that a refusal to support MacDonald would create an impression throughout the country that Unionists were not supporting the National Government.

At this point, Lord Tarbat intervened, drawing loud applause when he suggested there was considerable doubt whether, even if he were to be adopted by the Unionists, MacDonald would be returned by the electorate. This appeared to create what, in modern parlance, would be described as a pile-on, with dissenters encouraged to weigh in with negative views of their own.

Captain John MacGillivray of Calrossie declared that if MacDonald stood and failed to be returned, this would seem an even greater rebuff for the government than if he had never accepted the nomination. He was convinced, he said, that MacDonald had little chance of winning.

James Scott suggested that the hundred or so people in attendance did not represent the rank-and-file Unionists in the constituency who were 'quite opposed' to MacDonald's candidature. Joseph Budge of Easter Rarachie betrayed some of the tribalist feeling informing people's stances: 'Mr MacDonald is a Socialist and even if he got the support of the Association he would still be a Socialist'.[148] This theme was taken up by another speaker who protested against the 'Red Flag' being 'planted in the county'.[149]

Martineau made an appeal to the farmers who had attended in significant numbers, claiming that if they returned MacDonald they would not only have an experienced member but also a good Minister who was a Highlander and whose interests were Highland. Reminding the meeting that the man himself was next door, he suggested that MacDonald be asked to appear before them but this was not well-received. Thirty-five people voted in favour of inviting him to address them, 38 voted against and a few abstained.[150]

The meeting concluded and, without a formal vote being taken, the decision was made once again to reject the candidature of Malcolm MacDonald. A brief official statement was given:

> No vote was taken. It was decided to report to Mr MacDonald that we are not in favour of his candidature.
> The matter is remitted back to the co-ordinating committee to reconsider the situation, and to put forward other names acceptable to both Liberals and Unionists.[151]

The Executive Committee gave the news to the waiting MacDonald personally after they convened in the lounge of the National Hotel. MacDonald appeared to take the news with equanimity, the *Edinburgh Evening News* suggesting he was 'smiling and looking in no way distressed by the result'.[152] The reason for that would soon become clear.

Although the decision had been made to remit the matter to the Coordinating Committee, Randolph Churchill was still being touted as the most likely Unionist candidate. His agent, Tom McDonald, was an interested bystander during the Unionists' meeting and later met with Sir Robert Brooke.

Liberals United – Sort of

Meanwhile, in their meeting, officials for the local Liberals had by now rallied around MacDonald. Alexander Macrae had gathered the views of sub-agents and prominent liberals throughout the constituency and he issued the following statement:

> With one small exception the whole of the Liberal organisation in the constituency is unanimously in favour of the candidate proposed by the Ross and Cromarty Liberal Association.[153]

This may have overstated the position. Anger at the imposition of a candidate, although lesser in tenor than among the Unionists, remained. Ranald Findlay, speaking in Edinburgh, announced that a strong independent Liberal would take the field within the next 24 hours. He told the *Press and Journal* that Sir Murdoch Wood, Basil Murray and a third name, not yet made public, had been identified as potential candidates.

Findlay may have consistently exaggerated the Liberal opposition to MacDonald but reservations did exist, and not only in Ross and Cromarty. Writing in the *Manchester Guardian*, Frederick Hindle, former MP for Darwen in Lancashire, wrote:

> Does not this episode prove conclusively that the National Liberal members hold their seats by the favour and grace of the Conservatives, and that while the existing members are good boys and toe the line they may continue to receive that favour and grace, yet on their death or retirements no Liberal, even if he support the National Government, need apply to be their successor? What a humiliating position to be in.
>
> ...
>
> While the dominant Conservative party treat their existing Liberal allies in this shabby, mean, way how can they hope to obtain further Liberal recruits?[154]

Although the National Government had only the previous month secured a second huge mandate, tensions were clear and increasing. Ross and Cromarty exposed them, and further by-elections in the coming years would see local animosity resurface in the face of national diktat. For example in the Greenock by-election only nine months later, caused by the death of National Liberal MP Sir Godfrey Collins, the Unionists refused to accept either of the Liberals' proposed candidates and instead insisted on a Unionist standing as a 'National' candidate. The resulting 6.1 per cent drop in the National Liberal vote, allowing the Labour candidate to win with a swing of 7.85 per cent, is directly attributable to the local Unionists' displeasure.[155]

A Decision Made

After days of uncertainty, and in the face of the Unionists' second disavowal of his candidature, four hours later, Malcolm MacDonald announced that he had accepted the Liberals' invitation to stand. He would fight, he said, on the government's record of achievement and its promise of further progress in the next few years.[156] He would, in particular, seek to focus on the problems of agriculture and fishing in relation to the constituency. There would be, he added, no extravagant promises.[157] In his papers (Durham University), a draft copy of his statement exists. In it, he appealed:

> for the support of all Liberal, Unionist and Labour voters in the Ross and Cromarty [sic] who believe that the problems which the our country has to face today is facing are too grave to admit of a return to unrestricted party politics and require the continuance of a strong National Govt.[158]

In his letter to Stanley Baldwin, MacDonald expanded on his reasoning for making his decision. Apologising for the difficulties, he said he had discussed the problem with Captain Margesson and Sir Ian Macpherson the day before. For some reason, no preparatory work had been done with the Unionists, who were now badly divided. He went on, in an ungrammatical style common at the time because of the need for precision in telegrams:

> My information, from various sources, Unionist and otherwise (sources which I think on whole reliable) that the opponents at meeting rep. only minority of Cons. in county. I was urged by considerable a number of Cons. after yesterday's meeting to go ahead. Would have liked if poss. to delay decision until more time allowed see whether meeting could be persuaded recuse previous unanimous decision to oppose me.
>
> But this would meant delay for several days, with possibility of equally inconclusive meeting of Assoc. at end of it. Delay would have
>
> 1. played into hands of Lab. Opp…
> 2. led to dissensions amongst Libs. who already impatient.
> 3. left me less time than ought have for getting round const.[159]

MacDonald also wrote immediately to Sir William Martineau to explain his decision. He had wanted to acquaint Sir William and the Unionists with his decision before it appeared in the press, he said, but 'before I had made my decision you had left for London, so that it was impossible for me to do so'. His sole concern, he wrote, was that this constituency, which had loyally supported the National Government, should not be lost. He went on:

> I came to the conclusion that any further delay in the choice of a candidate would merely play into the hands of the Labour Opposition and [*sic*] our opponents.
>
> As I say, my only concern is that this constituency should continue to be represented in the H of C by a Nat. Govt. Member, and I hope that all of us who have this object in view can co-operate together to achieve it.[160]

The Liberals and the Unionists were now facing an impasse. Sir Robert Brooke tried to play down the seriousness of the situation, saying he did not anticipate a serious split in the Unionist ranks.

> The Executive will follow the recommendation which was made at Saturday's meeting and refer to the Co-ordinating Committee in London, asking for names of more possible candidates. This is a perfectly correct procedure, because the Co-ordinating Committee exists to suit every possible requirement. It is their duty to supply another name, although it is doubtful whether they will do so as Mr MacDonald is now the National Government candidate.[161]

The last sentence is revealing. Presumably, Brooke knew full well that Central Office would not back down. Indeed, matters had progressed so far it would be politically impossible for it to do so. Sir William Martineau was despatched to London to speak to the Chief Whip, but he set off on the long trip from Dingwall to London with little hope of success.

The *Dundee Courier*, reviewing the events of the day, took the view that, in defying the resolution of the Ross and Cromarty Unionists, MacDonald was making a judgement on the electoral importance of that body that was 'almost certainly correct'. 'Unionist county political associations are often pretty queer assortments of die-hard extremists', it said unsympathetically (and perhaps unexpectedly, being a Unionist-supporting newspaper),[162] before continuing even more dismissively, 'and in this shire of sporting estates and shooting lodges this trait has always been pronounced'.[163] One imagines the already irate Unionists, on reading that in their morning paper, would have found their rebelliousness even further emboldened.

If the Socialists, the first party to commence their campaign, imagined the *Courier*'s editorial line here might translate into support for them, they would be disappointed. In a statement insulting crofters and socialists in equal measure, the paper announced:

> There are probably no real Socialists in Ross and Cromarty, but in these days the crofter voters, who are the decisive factor, can be freakish.[164]

The locals of Ross and Cromarty may have been gentle folks not given to modern politicking, but that deference didn't extend to the press, particularly the press 150 miles down the coast.

* * *

Monday, 6 January 1936

A Fatal Miscalculation and a Third Rejection, a Fascist Fairy Godmother and the Bulls of Bashan

Agriculture was to be one of the defining policy issues of the Ross and Cromarty by-election, which mirrored concerns worldwide. On this day, Franklin D Roosevelt's Agricultural Adjustment Act (AAA) – the New Deal for farmers – was declared unconstitutional by the Supreme Court. 'At one blow', wrote the *Daily Telegraph*, 'the Supreme Court today destroyed the agricultural assistance machinery set up under President Roosevelt's New Deal'. They voted by six votes to three that the AAA was an 'invasion of the rights of States'. All AAA field offices were ordered to cease activity immediately. The decision, reported the *Telegraph*, deprived the government of 'all its anticipated revenues from the processing taxes on such diverse products as wheat, rice, maize, tobacco, sugar beet, jute, paper, and cotton'.[165] The issue was fiercely divisive, with many farmers rejoicing and just as many despairing. Several options to alleviate the crisis were under consideration, among them a domestic allotment programme guaranteeing prices to farmers in proportion to their crops. A British version of this idea would feature in the Ross and Cromarty campaign and beyond, becoming a major global political issue until the outbreak of war rendered any question of subsidies and tariffs obsolete.

Back in the county, a letter published in *The Scotsman* suggested growing concern in Liberal, and probably Unionist, circles about the potential damage to working relationships caused by the MacDonald stand-off. Written by Sir John Wallace, a former Liberal MP (and father of opera singer, Ian Wallace) whose name had been suggested several times in the past week as a potential candidate, it sought to offer a balm for the ongoing tensions. The two associations had worked in harmony for many years in the choice of Parliamentary candidates, he wrote, and he expressed the hope that any misunderstanding which had arisen on this occasion would 'disappear', removing the risk of allowing an anti-National Government candidate to be returned by a minority vote. This 'definite disaster' faced the constituency, he warned.

The need for a National Government in the country was at least as great as it had been in 1931, he said, encouraging the moderate voices in both parties to rally around MacDonald, who was, Wallace suggested, highly regarded by the great majority of members of Parliament. 'No man is more retiring, less pushful, and he achieved Cabinet rank through his own unquestioned ability.' He finished with a final encomium aimed at the traditionalists in this most traditional of constituencies:

✡ ✡ ✡

> If Ross and Cromarty return him as their member to the House of Commons he will fully carry on the traditions of his distinguished predecessor, who has so long represented this great Highland constituency.[166]

If this was a planned attempt to rally the locals, it didn't work. The *Press and Journal*'s sub-headline the following morning, reflecting on the day's events, read: 'Confusion worse than ever: More swift moves expected this week'. Feelings remained high in some quarters against the MacDonalds. Oliver Baldwin, son of the Prime Minister and a journalist, lamented the fact that the 'two MacDonalds are still pursuing their undignified way of re-entering Parliament by the back door after having been ejected by those who know them best [in the general election]'. It was no wonder, he concluded, that Parliament was losing the respect of the public 'when defeated Ministers can sink any political principles they ever had in order to hang on to office'.[167]

Local vs National

David Margesson
photo: Creative Commons

The day began with Sir William Martineau in London to meet the Unionist Chief Whip, Captain David Margesson. The meeting was not a success. While Martineau would have tried to explain the difficulty Central Office's imposition of MacDonald had caused the local Unionists, he must have known there was no possibility of them relenting. Indeed, Margesson made it clear to Martineau that no part of the central machinery of the Government parties could be used to promote any other candidate. The offer was MacDonald or nobody. Martineau was left with the stark reality of relaying to his association Central Office's intransigent position.

On receiving this news from Martineau, a special meeting of the Executive and Emergency Committee of the Ross-shire Unionist Association was convened in the National Hotel in Dingwall, attended by fourteen members. Commencing at 6 pm, it would not finish until 9.40 pm, by which time the ongoing threat of a schism in the party seemed to have come to pass.

Sir Robert Brooke, vice-chairman of the Association and chairman of the meeting, made a strong appeal to observe the instructions of Central Office and support MacDonald. This did nothing to quell the discontent. James Scott launched a stinging attack on MacDonald: '[He] belongs to no party', he said. 'The Labour Party would not have him, and his National value is worthless.'

Alongside animosity towards MacDonald, feelings against Central Office ran high. Hector Forbes of Culloden said that the whole country knew that the Ross and Cromarty Unionists had been sold. Reverend Sellar made a plea for cleaner politics, claiming the action of the government was a 'political expediency'. He went on:

> I am ashamed to belong to the largest party in the Government, which is apparently determined to sell the constituency for a consideration. Coalition has done nothing but sell ideals, and the Liberal Party itself has been put completely out of existence because of the formation of a National Government. Major Walter Elliott thought more of his political future than the interest of the farmer, and Mr Malcolm MacDonald is in the same position.[168]
>
> We have an opportunity now of striking a blow against political jobbery. The whole country is looking to us to put a stop to it. Liberty means freedom, and yet we are not allowed to choose a candidate for ourselves.[169]

A vote on whether to endorse the candidature of MacDonald was rejected by eight votes to four with, remarkably, two abstentions: this did not seem a matter where sitting on the fence could be a viable option. It was later reported that all four who voted for MacDonald did so out of loyalty to Central Office and all of them were thought to be against MacDonald's candidature.

The problem had now become a full-blown crisis. The *Daily Mirror* suggested that Stanley Baldwin had made a 'fatal' miscalculation in trying to impose MacDonald on the constituency. The government 'failed to take into account the pride and, some say, obstinacy, of the clansmen of Ross and Cromarty'.[170]

Captain John MacGillivray moved that Sir Robert Brooke should stand as an Independent Conservative. James Scott supported this, saying Sir Robert was the only man who had a chance of winning in Ross-shire. However, Sir Robert declined, saying he would vote for Mr MacDonald. Reverend Sellar expressed great disappointment, pointing out that the Liberals in the county had promised to support him and it seemed a 'calamity' that Sir Robert would not represent Unionist interests.

Not only would he not stand, however, at this point Brooke resigned his chairmanship of the meeting, to be replaced by Reverend Sellar, and he later resigned his position as vice-chairman of the Association as well.

Talk turned to other candidates and only one name seemed viable:

Randolph Churchill. W H Gill thought Churchill was a young man and a sound member of the Party. He had experience and youth on his side, and would make an impression in the House of Commons, as one who could well represent agriculture in Scotland and particularly in Ross-shire. On the other hand, the *Daily Mirror* reported one unnamed Unionist leader saying, 'a local orator would be preferable to a foreign professional'.[171]

Provost Ross of Tain suggested that both Churchill and MacDonald should be invited to give their views on agricultural policy, but this was not well received, perhaps because most of those in attendance would have known that MacDonald would be rather better versed in such matters than city-boy Churchill.

W H Gill moved, and James Scott seconded that Randolph Churchill be put forward as Unionist candidate. There was no counter-motion and the proposal was carried unanimously.

Chamberlain's agent, Tom McDonald, was present in the hotel and he was called before the committee and asked whether it was possible for Churchill to attend a meeting in Dingwall on Saturday. MacDonald said he could not say definitely but, undeterred, the Association sent a cable to Churchill immediately, inviting him to meet with them.

Churchill had, of course, suggested he would only accept an invitation that was unanimous, which was not the case, making it far from certain that he would accept. Nonetheless, the mood of the meeting was such that, even if Churchill did not stand, an Independent Unionist would certainly be put up.

Afterwards, the Association released an angry statement to the press:

> The meeting, while loath to oppose the nominee of the National Government, was influenced by the complete disregard with which the interest of the county had been treated. In an area almost entirely dependent on agriculture, it is reasonable to suppose that the National Government would have ensured that the candidate they recommend would be one who, from his previous activities and experience, could adequately represent the county in Parliament.
>
> The utilisation of a vacant seat in Ross-shire in order to find a home for a Cabinet Minister met with the most severe condemnation by all present.
>
> Further, the Committee felt that, if unity in the National Government

> had been studied, the name of the prospective candidate would have been submitted to the Unionists as well as to the Liberals and that this important section of political opinion would have been given a fair chance to approve or disapprove of the Government's nominee before the appointment by the Liberal party of the National Government's candidate made the position of the Unionist party in Ross-shire exceedingly difficult.[172]

Political Fairy Godmother

At this point, the somewhat controversial figure of Lady Houston, Randolph Churchill's 'political fairy godmother', entered the drama. Lady Houston was a political activist so eccentric she was possibly insane, and she possessed an even greater hatred of the MacDonalds than Randolph Churchill. In his biography of his father, Winston S Churchill described her as a 'patriotic but eccentric millionairess',[173] which is one way to portray a thoroughgoing fascist. On the day Addis Ababa fell to Italy, Houston telegrammed Mussolini: 'TEN THOUSAND TIMES BRAVO BRAVISSIMO'. On another occasion, she telegrammed Adolf Hitler, encouraging him to join with Britain and fight against Russia: 'I want to tell you that you are a wonderful man', she wrote. 'You have done wonders for Germany'.[174]

Her hatred of Ramsay MacDonald stemmed from his pacifist tendencies, which she thought unsuitable in a Prime Minister. From 1929, she waged a campaign against MacDonald's government and she campaigned, too, against the Conservatives' decision to enter the National Government with him.[175] During the East Fife by-election of 1933, she produced a series of vitriolic leaflets including one proclaiming the spiritual home of politicians must be Hades because Satan was the 'Father of all Liars' and 'FREE TRADE – is the biggest LIE that was ever invented'. She later wrote to T E Lawrence that Ramsay MacDonald was 'one of Satan's own disciples'.[176] In the Norwood by-election of 1935, she produced a leaflet entitled 'Thrown to the Wolves', attacking the 'iniquitous sham' of the National Government introduced by MacDonald to destroy conservatism. He was a 'Political Popinjay' who had made the armed forces a laughing stock.[177] She instructed an assistant to hire 50 women at £5 a week to dress in red, white and blue and march around Bournemouth displaying

Lady Houston
photo: Creative Commons

posters which read 'Baldwin is a Liar' and 'Ramsay MacDonald is a Traitor to Great Britain'. To his credit, the assistant refused and resigned.[178] When her yacht, *Liberty*, was berthed in Portsmouth she had an electric sign erected on it saying, 'TO HELL WITH RAMSAY MACDONALD'. When she refused to remove it, the authorities towed her yacht away.[179] Later, she sailed round the British Isles with another electric sign reading, 'DOWN WITH THE TRAITOR [RAMSAY] MACDONALD'.[180] Her participation in the by-election, then, was unlikely to be dignified.

The *Press and Journal* reported that Randolph Churchill's campaign was being sponsored by somebody in London and speculated that it might be Lady Houston, although her secretary denied the suggestion.[181] However, since her representative, James Wentworth Day, would arrive in Dingwall within days this denial could be safely discounted. That she might get involved in Ross and Cromarty was probably no great surprise, particularly given her previous relationship with Randolph Churchill, but if the campaign was already veering into surreal territory, having this deranged woman involved was likely to see it career even further into the realms of the unknown.

Bulls of Bashan

The ever-doughty *Inverness Courier* responded to the Unionists' implosion with a blistering edition the next day, invoking the Biblical 'Bulls of Bashan':

> Bulls many compass me, strong bulls
> of Bashan me surround;

Their mouths they open'd wide on me
Upon me gape did they,
Like to a lion ravening
and roaring for his prey.[182]

This is Psalm 22 from the 1650 *Scottish Psalter*, also known as *the Psalms of David in Metre*,[183] and the *Courier* compared the position of Sir Robert Brooke, surrounded by the Unionist 'bulls of Bashan', to David, asking 'My God, why have you forsaken me?'[184] Once Sir Robert had refused to support them and left the chair, these 'Bulls of Bashan stampeded the Committee into the most foolish of the many foolish actions which have characterised its behaviour ever since the Bulls began to bellow'. Needless to say, the paper continued, the Bulls did not represent the mass of Unionist opinion in the county.

The paper expressed its satisfaction that Malcolm MacDonald had 'defied this body of reactionaries who have brought discredit upon the Unionist Association' because it had 'the utmost contempt for the campaign of bigotry, prejudice, and intolerance to which Mr MacDonald has been and is being, subjected'.

The man at the centre of the storm, Malcolm MacDonald, had left for Ullapool to commence a tour of the western part of the constituency. He expected to return on Thursday night and his itinerary would include no meetings but would, instead, focus on face-to-face contact with electors. One imagines that farmers, in particular, would be the primary focus of his attention. He was accompanied by Dr Middleton and Alexander Macrae of the Liberal Association. Meanwhile, it was reported that MacDonald's sister, Sheila, and his secretary, Marjory Gordon (daughter of Canadian novelist Ralph Connor), were due to arrive in Dingwall on Thursday to assist with the campaign.[185]

Liberals and Socialists Active

Despite the obvious support for MacDonald from the leadership of the Liberals, there were still machinations about standing an alternative candidate. Three names were prominent: Sir Murdoch McKenzie Wood, previously a Liberal MP for Aberdeenshire and Kincardineshire Central and, later, Banffshire; Mr Basil Murray, who had stood for Parliament unsuccessfully on three occasions; and Sir Alexander MacEwan of Inverness.

This latter name is a fascinating one, as MacEwan was traditionally a Liberal, but he was also a founding member of the Scottish National Party. He was originally a member of the Scottish Party, described by Richard Findlay as 'a collection of disgruntled Tories and Liberals who believed that Scotland was not being treated adequately by the current political system'.[186] He stood for the Scottish Party in a by-election in Kilmarnock in 1933 and, although coming last, had polled well. At this point, John MacCormick, the leader of the National Party of Scotland, which had been founded in 1928 but was still to make any significant impact, decided that a merger of the two independence parties would be the best way to promote the nationalist cause. Using the novelist Neil M Gunn to ease negotiations, MacCormick agreed common ground with the Scottish Party. He expelled several NPS's more radical members (including Hugh MacDiarmid). In April 1934, the Scottish National Party was created from the fusion of the NPS and the Scottish Party.[187] As Ewan Cameron explained in his analysis of the politics of the by-election campaign, MacEwan had remained in touch with the independent Liberals' leader Sir Archibald Sinclair and, when it appeared the SNP would not stand in the by-election, the idea that MacEwan could instead stand as a Liberal took shape.[188]

For the Socialists, Hector McNeil was planning to open his campaign on Friday. Malcolm Macmillan MP had agreed to devote his holidays to assist in the campaign, while George Lansbury and Clement Attlee were also planning to offer support.

* * *

Tuesday, 7 January 1936

MacChurchill is Coming, and Hearing What You Want to Hear

Sir William Martineau, still in London, followed the lead of his vice-chairman and resigned as chairman of the local Association, releasing the following statement:

> In view of the Executive Committee's decision last evening [to oppose MacDonald's candidature and to invite Churchill to meet the Association] I herewith tender my resignation as Chairman of Ross and Cromarty Unionist Association, but not as a member. I intend to give my full support to Mr Malcolm MacDonald, the National Government candidate.[189]

The *Dundee Courier* pondered whether a disagreement between supporters of MacDonald and Churchill on Saturday could result in the Unionist Association dividing in two,[190] but Sir Robert Brooke tried to temper such speculation, saying, 'While I intend to support Mr MacDonald, I shall remain a member of the Association, and shall abide by the decision of the majority, whatever that may be'.[191]

This may or may not have been a symptom of complacency but, regardless, the Association was now in an unenviable position, somehow having to broker a meeting with Randolph Churchill on Saturday to determine whether or not to go against Central Office guidelines, while having neither of their senior office bearers in position. The *Press and Journal* reported that they might appoint a proxy to chair the meeting on Saturday and attend to the permanent appointments at a later stage.[192]

The Unionist rebels hoped that the arrival of Randolph Churchill on Saturday would clarify his campaigning position. Churchill had confirmed in a cablegram to Reverend Sellar that it was his 'duty to consult with you' and he would arrive in Dingwall on Friday to make the meeting on Saturday morning.[193] This involved a tortuous journey, as described by his agent Tom McDonald:

> Mr Churchill will take an aeroplane and leave Casablanca tomorrow morning. He will reach Toulouse tomorrow afternoon, getting to Paris in the early hours of Thursday morning and to Croydon at 11.45 am on Thursday. He will head straight for Dingwall, although I do not know whether he will fly on this last lap of his long journey.[194]

Despite his obvious efforts to comply with the Association, his candidacy was not yet secure, leading some Unionists to caution that it would be better if he met with the Unionist Association Emergency Committee on

Prominent Unionists
photo: Aberdeen Press and Journal

the Friday afternoon prior to the wider meeting on the Saturday.[195]

The *Daily Record*, giddy with excitement at the imminent arrival of this *rara avis*, was moved to poetry:

> He is coming! The Northern gloom
> Rolls back for an end of dule,
> There is laughter along Loch Broom,
> There is singing in Ullapool;
> And the jubilant voices swell
> Like a roll of exultant drums,
> All's well with the North! All's Well!
> For Randolph MacChurchill comes![196]

However, already there was a feeling that support was swinging away from Churchill and back towards the Central Office position. The argument of Martineau and Brooke, that 'at whatever personal sacrifice the National Government must be supported in the election' was beginning to gain traction. There was a strong belief that Martineau and Brooke would make powerful addresses to the meeting on Saturday. One unnamed Unionist source told *The Scotsman*:

> In all probability, it will be found on Saturday, when the Unionist Association meets at Dingwall, and when only those who are members of the Association will be entitled to vote, that support for the National Government candidate will have become more consolidated.[197]

Another (or possibly the same) unnamed official told the *Press and Journal*:

> The confusion that has arisen is remarkable. I cannot understand the action of some of the Unionists in opposing Mr MacDonald. He is undoubtedly the best man to put forward, for he has the influence of his father, he has the power of the Prime Minister behind him, and he has the ear of a fair number of the Cabinet, for he is a Minister. He could help us more than anyone else.
>
> My opinion is that the other side will fall in with us on Saturday so that Mr MacDonald may have our undivided support. Think of the remarkable situation that would arise if a Socialist got in. We frequently have to send deputations to London on questions affecting the county. If we sent up one after a Socialist had been elected, they would simply reply that we had turned out the man they had recommended.
>
> I think there is a lot of hidden support for Mr MacDonald. There are many people who favoured him but did not wish to express an opinion openly in case they should offend the other side. They simply remained quiet. But it is the vote on polling day that will count.

As ever with politics, what you hear depends on who you ask. The independent Liberals were beginning their campaigning and, not surprisingly, the sentiments they heard in the towns and villages of Ross-shire opposed MacDonald. Ranald Findlay, touring the constituency, was well satisfied with what he heard. 'Every vote cast for Liberalism is a vote against jobbery', he said.[198] Of the word on the street, he suggested:

> The news from the west [of the constituency] is highly favourable to an independent Liberal. The Gairloch Liberals will have nothing to do with the candidate which the local executive has allowed the powers-that-be to foist upon them. Mr MacDonald has received a severe rebuff in this quarter, where political intrigue makes no appeal.[199]

Of course, the independent Liberals did not even have a candidate yet, and efforts to do so appeared to be mired in difficulty. One of the names talked up the previous day, Sir Murdoch McKenzie Wood, was now being downplayed.[200]

There was, no doubt, an element of political intrigue in Findlay's statement. Talking up the chances of your candidate is a rite that has been observed by political canvassers through the ages. The Socialists, too, were laying on the hyperbole. With little history in the constituency, their local organisation was not extensive. At the general election, they received 3,284 votes (against 10,810 for the National Government), compared with 6,710 votes the last time the constituency was contested, in 1921. They seemed a party in decline. However, pointing out that their candidate on this occasion, Hector McNeil, was much stronger, a Socialist spokesman suggested, 'We should do much better than at the General Election. With the split vote we should win'.[201]

Meanwhile, Malcolm MacDonald's campaign was taking shape. He was still canvassing in the west of the constituency, meeting prominent residents. As with Ranald Findlay, the views he heard on the doorsteps chimed with his own beliefs. His first speech was now planned for Dingwall on Monday, and by now the focus of his campaign was on agriculture and fishery.

MacDonald's first day on the campaign trail was undoubtedly busy. The *Dundee Courier* noted that, after spending the day motoring through Wester Ross, he and his team then spent the evening visiting and canvassing well into the 'wee sma' oors'. Before the sun had risen the next morning, it recorded, he had 'eaten a hasty breakfast' and embarked upon another day of canvassing along the shores of the Atlantic between Lochbroom and Lochmaree.[202]

The romance of electioneering.

✡ ✡ ✡

Wednesday, 8 January 1936

Indecision, a Dandy and a Whipping Boy, and a Salutation

The independent Liberals believed they were closing in on their candidate, with Basil Murray expected to arrive in the constituency on Thursday. He confirmed he had been approached but said he had not as yet made a decision.[203] A (failed) veteran of two elections in the Highlands (plus one in London), he had most recently lost to F A Macquisten (who once put forward a motion in Parliament to criminalise lesbianism)[204] in Argyllshire in the general election.

The Daily Express weighed into the race, declaring that its support, 'with all its resources, will be placed behind the farmers' candidate in this county if they maintain their attitude of fighting the election'.[205] The mystery surrounding the potential involvement of Lady Houston was resolved by the arrival of James Wentworth Day, a journalist who was, in his own words, Lady Houston's 'spokesman, "personal representative", political buccaneer, editor and general whipping boy'.[206] He told the press he had come to shoot wild geese but, when asked if he would take any part in the election, he conceded he might. 'Mr Churchill has for a long time been a friend of mine, and I like him very much', he said. Day's involvement seemed deeper than mere friendship, however. When pressed on whether he would be much more interested in the situation politically if Churchill didn't stand, he agreed he would. If he were to stand, he said, it would be as an Independent Conservative, not a National Government candidate.[207]

James Wentworth Day
photo: Aberdeen Press and Journal

However circumspect Wentworth Day was in his responses to the press, he was indeed in Dingwall on the instructions of Lady Houston. When Churchill's name was first mentioned in relation to the by-election, she called Wentworth Day to her home and instructed him to do whatever he could to oppose both MacDonalds in their respective campaigns. She later informed Randolph she would support him 'tooth and nail' and sent him a telegram: 'It seems to me that this is a vital crowning point in your career. You must win and I will do all I can to help you'. Again, this included financial support: according to Teresa Crompton, Wentworth Day had a 'wad of banknotes that [Lady Houston] had given him to pay Randolph's expenses'.[208]

Wentworth Day wasted no time and launched an attack on both Ramsay and Malcolm MacDonald (and, by extension, the government):

> I feel that Mr Baldwin, by trying to foist [the MacDonalds] on to the country, is letting down the whole loyal body of Conservative support which put him and his government into power. Mr Malcolm MacDonald is just a political nonentity sheltering behind his father's name.[209]

Wentworth Day also suggested he might take on MacDonald senior in the Scottish Universities by-election. 'I have today spoken to a member of a Scottish university and the question of nominees is now being discussed', he said.[210] He went further than that, getting heavily involved in the campaign. He sent a pamphlet, 'What the late Prime Minster [Ramsay MacDonald] Has Done for England' to every graduate of the Scottish universities. In it, he said MacDonald had enforced disarmament and dragged Britain's armed services 'down, down, down to the depths of despair'. The *Northern Whig* reported this backfired somewhat, with some voters who had not previously favoured MacDonald deciding to vote for him.[211]

The *Inverness Courier* felt that rather than damage Malcolm MacDonald's prospects, Wentworth Day's foray would assist him:

> The resentment naturally created by the intervention of an outsider in the political affairs of the constituency...will gain many sympathisers for the Dominions Secretary [MacDonald] among voters of all political beliefs.[212]

The paper also reckoned support for MacDonald was growing but, having already strongly come out in his favour they probably would say that. That said, other papers concurred. As the day progressed, the feeling was that the swing away from Churchill to MacDonald was intensifying. 'Many Unionists now feel that it is their duty to support the Government', a party member said. 'It may be grudgingly, but they are more inclined now to maintain the Unionist strength intact.'[213]

Today was market day in Dingwall and the *Press and Journal* took advantage to canvass farmers from all over the county on their position. They reported a 'remarkable unanimity' of opinion that 'even in a three-cornered contest, the Socialist [Hector McNeil] would have a good chance of winning, while in a straight fight Mr MacDonald would probably be the victor'.[214] The inference of this for the (mostly Unionist) press was that a three-way contest was to be avoided.

In this context, the mooted meeting of Churchill and the Executive Committee was now confirmed for Friday evening. This would provide both parties with a stronger idea of their respective positions before the full meeting on Saturday.

If there was to be a swing of support towards MacDonald, then as he sat down with his sherry that evening, the outgoing MP, Sir Ian Macpherson, would probably have considered he had played no small part in that, with his extraordinary, 840-word letter published that morning in the press. Addressing Mr MacDonald directly, and at times in terms verging on adulation, Macpherson painted MacDonald as the only candidate suitable to follow in his footsteps. Talking of a dinner they attended at the House of Commons, Macpherson said he was struck by:

> the breadth of your statesmanship, your love of the Empire and of the Constitution, your compelling advocacy of social progress, your approachableness and your generous love of the underdog.[215]

Claiming to know the needs of Ross and Cromarty and the Highlands 'as well as any man alive' – illness hadn't affected his self-confidence – Macpherson contended: 'there is no candidate available who is more suited to represent in the National interest a constituency in the Highlands than you are.' It was absurd, he wrote, to regard MacDonald as being foisted on the Highlands. 'I know that you have a profound love for the Highlands, their tradition, their beauty and their history and that you have a very special knowledge of their needs.' (All of that may be true, but it doesn't specifically address the charge that he had been foisted on them.) His role as a Cabinet Minister, occupying one of the most distinguished offices under the Crown, 'which you occupy…by your own merit and with the goodwill and approbation of all who know you', made him ideally suited to representing the county, he proffered. Picking up on a theme which the National Government side thought was a vote-winner (and loser), he went on:

> You have shown that you have…a very special knowledge of the needs of British agriculture to which no other candidate in the field can possibly lay claim.

While ostensibly addressing MacDonald, there is no question that Macpherson's true audience was much wider:

> It has been a terrible wrench for me to leave my old constituency, but it would be a consolation to me to feel that my old friends rallied round you and supported you, imbued as you are with a desire to help and easily accessible as you are to those who have a grievance to remedy.

Buck up and rally round, in other words. Macpherson might have found a more emollient audience, however, if he hadn't, earlier in the letter, appeared to contradict the Unionists in their judgement that they had not been consulted:

> As a matter of courtesy I tried to get into touch with the Unionist chairman here even before I resigned and may I say, quite contrary to what has been stated, I not only thanked him personally for his services, but I wrote personally to over three hundred people – Unionist, Liberal and Labour – who had in any way given me special help.

There is no reason to doubt Macpherson's words, but it does seem unwise to antagonise people who, later in his correspondence, he was seeking to appease. There are times to speak and times to remain quiet. However, those independent Unionists holding out for Churchill fared even less favourably in Macpherson's account: 'This is no time to listen to to the turbulent and unrestrained outpouring of one section of the community,' he declared. He concluded his letter with a final burst of approbation:

> I cannot help feeling that my friends in Ross and Cromarty are making a profound mistake in searching the ends of the earth for a young man to supplant you.

The letter was designed to bring waverers back into the fold. Time would tell its effect.

* * *

Thursday, 9 January 1936

The Lord Strathcarron, the ILP, a Fiery Cross and a Prediction

Until now, the precise date of the by-election remained uncertain. Sir Ian Macpherson had accepted his peerage, but the UK – then as now – was mired in Gormenghastian ritual and there were still other formalities to be overseen with the actual bestowal. One such was the title Macpherson would take and this was now settled, with his decision to become Lord Strathcarron of Banchor.[216] It was hoped that the writ for the by-election could be published quickly, with the poll taking place as early as the first week of February. What disarray the various parties might be in by that point was very much open to question.

Much of the speculation about the potential victor of the by-election rested on the split nature of the government vote. The Unionists' doomsday scenario – and the Labour dream – was that a two- or even three-way split could clear the path for the sole non-government candidate, the Socialist Hector McNeil, to win by default. McNeil's status as the only anti-government candidate was thrown into doubt, however, by the news that Labour, too, might field an independent candidate, with rumours that a potential contender, as yet unidentified but described as having 'Maxtonian Labour' sympathies, was expected to arrive shortly in Dingwall.[217] This, then, was the Independent Labour Party (ILP), a breakaway grouping which disaffiliated from the Labour Party in 1932 and was now led by charismatic 'Clydesider' John Maxton. The ILP dominated the early history of the Labour Party in Scotland, reaching a high point in the 1922 general election, which saw Labour's breakthrough in Scotland, followed by the 1929 general election when 67 of Labour's 68 candidates were ILP members.[218] I G C Hutchison described the ILP as representing an 'ethical vision of socialism which had certain things in common with Liberal radicalism'.[219] In particular, he noted, land reform, temperance, free trade and the right to national self-determination were all shared values. The first three of those would undoubtedly chime with traditionally Liberal voters in Ross and Cromarty and, while the chances of the ILP succeeding outside its geographical stronghold of Clydeside were remote, a candidate standing in Ross and Cromarty would undoubtedly harm Hector McNeil's prospects.

Randolph Churchill was reported to have arrived at Croydon Airport on his way to Ross and Cromarty, dressed, the *Daily Mail* noted approvingly, in a coat with a heavy fur collar – an 'admirable precaution' which would be useful if he were to campaign in the constituency.[220] The *Mail* didn't know the half of it.

Meanwhile, J Wentworth Day suggested that should Churchill not stand, Roderick McLeod, previously on the staff of Lord Milner and formerly chief Unionist political officer of the Eastern Counties of England, was willing to put his name forward as an independent candidate.[221] Officially, Wentworth Day was still denying he was acting under instruction from Lady Houston, but his identification of a potential candidate does not seem the work of an amateur goose hunter, while Lady Houston herself sent a message wishing success to the Independent Unionists and promising all possible support. The needs of farmers and fishermen had been neglected, she said, implying an independent was the requisite remedy. Quite how the local Unionists, enraged as they were by interference from Central Office, received this apparent intervention from a cabal of posh outsiders, is not clear.

Malcolm MacDonald would no doubt have been cheered by the receiving of a letter sent by Sir William Martineau the day before, acknowledging MacDonald's reasons for accepting the Liberal Association candidature. Martineau explained that he had offered his services to Dr Middleton and would assist in any way to secure MacDonald's victory. Referring to MacDonald's planned meeting in Dingwall on Monday, he said, 'I shall be on your platform & will speak if I am asked'.[222]

This may have been a particularly timely fillip for MacDonald. In a letter to Dr William Grant of Easington, County Durham, sent today, he confessed: 'The odds are that I shall be beaten, but it cannot be helped. Anyway, I shall enjoy the lovely country'.[223] Nonetheless, on his return from his three-day tour of the west of the county with Dr Middleton and Alexander Macrae, he proclaimed to the press that he was much cheered. 'Believe it or not', he said, 'we met hundreds of Liberals, and only one was opposed to the National Government. Unionists are also supporting the Government and Labour people are giving their support'.[224] There is an element of false equivalence here, of course: it is quite possible that people supported the National Government but still felt deeply resentful about the imposition of MacDonald as candidate. There is no question, however, the National Government side felt buoyed by their progress.

They declared they had evidence of growing support. In Easter Ross, a house-to-house canvass was proceeding and, according to one official:

> To use a phrase so often employed in connection with Highland affairs, the fiery cross has been sent round on behalf of Mr MacDonald.[225]

Nonetheless, some farmers' opposition could not be ignored. One landowner said:

> What the farmers want is someone who can help them to get a tariff on barley, and a solid price for oats up to, say, 18s or 20s a quarter.[226]

Agriculture would become one of the main election issues in a county that was heavily reliant on farming at a time when the industry was seriously depressed. Between the end of the Great War and the start of the Second World War, arable land in the UK fell by four million acres, while a quarter of a million agricultural workers left the industry, leaving the country heavily dependent on imported foodstuffs. As much as 70 per cent of food was imported. It was estimated that the total cost of food imports in 1932 which could have been produced at home was £17 million. The impact on farming was severe. In response, the National Government introduced a series of quotas and import taxes on a range of agricultural goods from Europe and later, to a lesser extent, from the Empire. These tariffs were used to provide subsidies to farmers and they did provide some relief. There was still much to be done, however. Subsidies largely benefitted the major landowners and rarely trickled down to the tenant farmers and agricultural labourers, who saw no increase in wages. The subsidies, too, were of greater benefit to English farmers than Scottish. For example, subsidies for wheat under the Wheat Act of 1931 guaranteeing a minimum price. Wheat, though, was grown primarily in England, while Scottish staples like potatoes, barley and oats, did not attract subsidies until the 1937 Agriculture Act. The price of barley dropped by 500 per cent in the interwar period, while the wheat subsidy profited English farmers to the tune of about £6 million per year.[227]

A lengthy article declaring the importance of agriculture to Ross-shire was published in the *Press and Journal* during the campaign. Although it was the county's chief industry, for several years the life had 'been almost crushed out of farming'. The National Government had pledged to find a 'cure for the rheumatic condition of the industry' and the paper reported that the 'most seriously affected limbs' – livestock and cereals – were to receive first attention. It recorded that in Scotland in the past year, arable land had reduced by 16,300 acres, resulting in a 20 per cent reduction in barley yields, with regular and casual farm worker numbers reduced by 1,800. The various foreign trade agreements the country had entered into were identified as a major problem but the article noted that most of these ended in 1936. Even the Ottawa Agreement, which was fiercely criticised by the industry, was due to end as soon as August 1937, and in any case, there was a clause within it which permitted revisions by either party. There were opportunities, then, for improvement.[228]

These arguments would be rehearsed and revisited many times over the coming weeks.

After some days of vacillation, Basil Murray decided against standing as an independent Liberal. He had received no invitation, he said, and if he should receive one now he would feel compelled to refuse. 'I do not choose to stand in opposition to a candidate representing Labour with most of whose aims I am in sympathy, and who supported me at the last election,' he declared, although it is unclear why this spark of conscience could not have been struck days earlier to put an end to speculation.[229]

After another frantic day of political activity, there was still no clarity on the way forward. One Unionist, however, made a bold prediction about the by-election outcome:

> Personally, I think that if Churchill comes forward he will not get more than 1,800 to 2,000 votes, with about 6,000 for the Socialist candidate...I should not be surprised if the total poll amounted to 15,000 or 16,000.[230]

We will return to this in due course to find how close or otherwise our political clairvoyant was.

* * *

Friday, 10 January 1936 Part One

A Considered Morning Prelude to a Day of Frantic Activity

The Scotsman ran a leader with a withering take on the events to date. It offered 'an object-lesson to party managers in the tact necessary in dealing with a democratic electorate'. Pointing the blame at party officials south of the border, it declared:

London is curiously incapable of understanding Scottish conditions, and unfortunately Scots who have been long exiled are in general as lacking in understanding as the English community among whom they live and whose colour they have absorbed. This would not be so serious if Englishmen and Anglo-Scots recognised their own limitations in dealing with Scottish affairs; but they seldom do.

The obvious course of action, it thought, would have been to sound opinion in the constituency before declaring a candidate but this was done, if at all, in 'a very partial and incomplete way', with Unionists not consulted despite being partners in government. With greater diligence, it was possible that Malcolm MacDonald would still be the National Government candidate but 'he would have been assured of Unionist as well as Liberal support from the outset'. That his prospects had now been prejudiced was almost entirely the fault of London.[231] The leader then referred to a letter from Sir Robert Brooke which also featured in that day's newspaper.

In his letter, Brooke bemoaned the 'misdirected efforts of some of our party organisers', which had led to Ross-shire Unionists being deeply insulted.[232] While stating that the leadership should have consulted both Liberals and Unionists before putting forward MacDonald's name, he sought harmony rather than further rancour. 'Two wrongs will not make a right', he said, suggesting the party needed to rally round MacDonald. He went on to echo the sentiments of Sir Ian Macpherson in extolling MacDonald's virtues. His role in Cabinet would prove invaluable to the people of Ross and Cromarty. His position as Dominions Secretary would not affect his view on the importance of UK agriculture. 'He has told me emphatically', Brooke wrote, 'that he places the initerests [*sic*] of the United Kingdom first, those of the Dominions second, and the foreigner third and last'.

Turning to the national scene, Brooke used an appeal to vanity:

> In spite of the large Government majority in the House, a defeat in this stronghold of sanity would be a serious setback to our national solidarity.

He then rather deflated the value of those words when he slid into *ad hominem* territory:

> If the Unionist Party on Saturday decide to put a candidate of their own in the field I shall fear that they are placing what they conceive to be their personal interests before those of their country.

If they were not big enough in spirit, he continued, to treat with 'contempt' the 'stupid slight' placed upon them, then they were 'willing to cut off their nose to spite their face for the sake of getting their own back on some fatuous official'. He moved on to an appeal to tradition, firmer ground for his Unionist audience, warning against dissipating their strength through vacillation and internal dissent and cautioning they would 'cease to be a power' in the county if that happened. It was the duty of 'all loyal Unionists' to 'support the majority finding of their local organisations'. However, it is hard not to escape the notion that his earlier words aimed at the putative independents would have greatly darkened their moods.

Sir William Martineau, in a letter to party members, was equally forceful in attacking the 'rebellious proposition' to put Churchill forward as an independent Unionist. 'Patriotic Unionists who are not members of the Association should join at once and come to the meeting [on Saturday when the matter was to be debated]'.[233]

The split in the senior ranks, however, was becoming clearer. W H Gill also invoked strong rhetoric in his statement. The issue had become national, he said, and it was about 'whether agriculture is to survive and to remain as it has been in the past, the mainstay of the nation'. The election would be fought on the ruinous prices for produce, low wages, the decline of fishing and the concomitant decay of fishing villages. This was a perfectly valid contention – and, indeed, agriculture became a key focus of the ensuing campaign – but Gill lost a degree of credibility by switching directly to an appeal to emotion (which concluded with an echo of Robert Burns):

> Honoured names have been dragged in the mire as the result of the political game of arranging a candidature in this county which is opposed by the official Unionist Association... The people of Ross and Cromarty have shown that, in no uncertain voice, that (*sic*) they resent the county's fair name being associated with such proceedings.
>
> They have taught the 'high heid yins' in London and elsewhere that Highland constituencies may not be bought and sold.[234]

These very public interventions did little to calm the fevered nature of the debate. They served only to ensure the meeting on Saturday, already destined to be feisty, would now be incendiary.

The Scotsman, in its leader, recognised this threat. Siding with the National Government, it praised the 'older and more responsible Unionists' like Brooke and Martineau who accepted it was time to 'forget their resentment and rally round' MacDonald. 'There is a distinct danger', the leader claimed that 'the seat will be lost to the Government'. The Unionists had 'made their protest' but was it necessary 'to carry their resentment as far as the polling booths?' It ended with a coded address to Randolph Churchill:

> Mr Churchill is an able young man, who will find his way to the House of Commons in time; but this is not his opportunity. He himself will no doubt realise that.[235]

This press reporting merely served as *hors d'oeuvres* for another day of bickering politics.

✡ ✡ ✡

Friday, 10 January 1936 Part Two

Lochinvar, a Study in Contrasts, Another Vote and the Price of Oats

Lochinvar Arrives

The most striking development of the day was the arrival, finally, of Randolph Churchill. According to the *Daily Mirror*, which was fond of a historical analogy, 'Like another Lochinvar, [he] descended upon us this afternoon and told waiting Dingwall his decision'.[236] His arrival marked the point when the campaign became national news, prompting the *Daily Mail* to suggest it would be 'one of the grandest elections of our time'. The *Mail*'s correspondent, Percy Cater, sent to the constituency for the duration, pondered poetically (if somewhat meaninglessly):

> Who would have thought that you had to risk stepping off the northern edge of Great Britain into ice-floes and sealschools to encounter political consciousness?[237]

Churchill was met at Inverness by Reverend Sellar and they completed the journey to Dingwall by road, where they were met by W H Gill, Captain M T Tindal of Kinnairdie and Hector Forbes. His arrival was described by the *Press and Journal* as 'unobtrusive', as he slipped into the National Hotel largely unrecognised. His dozen suitcases and golf clubs must surely have raised some comment, however. When questioned by the *Press and Journal*, he said airily, 'I am not one of those people who travel light'. He went on: 'And as I do not carry it myself it does not matter to me whether I have one bag or more'.[238] Even his son, Winston S Churchill, in his balanced biography of his father, accused Randolph Churchill of 'unbridled arrogance' and, on one occasion 'boorish, idle and generally objectionable behaviour.[239]

It would be fascinating to see how this *boulevardier* would be received in ultra-traditional Dingwall. W H Gill was one of his primary backers, but the photograph of them taken that day is a fascinating study in contrasts.[240] Gill, born in 1885, glowers gruffly at the camera, hands in his pockets, his Victorian waistcoat tightly buttoned. Beside him, Churchill smiles insouciantly, a cigarette in his hand, a young man full of confidence and *brio*. Whatever political affiliations they may have shared, it is difficult to reconcile the natures of the two men.

When asked whether he would stand, Churchill replied:

> I am not perfectly acquainted with the facts of the case, and I must naturally hear what that case is before I decided whether I can go forward.[241]

Churchill and Gill
photo: Aberdeen Press and Journal

After lunch Churchill went to Tain and Invergordon with Gill, where he was introduced to a group of Easter Ross farmers, this being the group most in favour of his nomination and most likely to vote for him in large numbers, and he made personal calls to principal residents in the towns and villages.His supporters made positive noises: 'If there is any swing', one prominent Churchillian declared, beautifully channelling P G Wodehouse's Sir Roderick Spode, 'it is a swing to Churchill. The ploughmen are solidly with us'.[242]

Churchill was pressed on whether he required a unanimous invitation from the Executive, but said he couldn't make a definite statement. It would depend on the tone of the meeting, he said.

As it turned out, the tone of the Executive meeting that evening was not what he anticipated.

Rather, he was 'taken aback' by the plain-speaking of those who were against him.[243] He had, *The Scotsman* considered, expected unanimity from the Committee who had, after all, asked him to travel 2,000 miles to appear. Instead, he found an outspoken minority strongly favouring the National candidate and questioning his suitability. After an hour's debate, a vote was taken and the Executive was split eight to three. Voting for Churchill were: Reverend Sellar, presiding, Sir Robert Brooke,

Captain Tindal, W H Gill, James Scott, Mr F Macrae, Hector Forbes and General Macpherson.

Three voted against: Sir William Martineau, Captain Shaw-Mackenzie and Provost Macdonald. It is intriguing to know what persuaded Sir Robert Brooke who had, after all, resigned as Vice-Chair of the Association over the question of fielding an independent candidate, and had written such a passionate letter to the press only that morning, to vote in favour of Churchill.

The vote was not yet to adopt Churchill as a candidate, but only to recommend to the Association meeting the following day that he be adopted. Accordingly, the agenda for that meeting would have two items: firstly to consider whether or not to contest the seat at the by-election; and secondly, to adopt, if so resolved, Churchill as their prospective candidate. It was agreed that the press should be allowed to attend and 'as far as possible they should attempt to ensure that only members of the Association are admitted to the meeting'. This somewhat ambivalent phrasing would have repercussions but, for now, the Unionists had agreed the way forward.

MacDonald on the Stump

Churchill's putative opponent, Malcolm MacDonald, was also in Easter Ross during the day, where he addressed farmers from the auctioneer's rostrum at the sale ring in Tain. Belying suggestions that the area was Churchill territory, he spoke for twenty minutes without interruption and frequent applause. He addressed some of the key arguments that had been made against him. Firstly, to the idea that he knew nothing about agriculture, he argued that he had represented a mainly agricultural constituency for six years. To the charge that, as the Secretary for the Dominions, he would privilege their interests over those of British farmers, he offered a robust rebuttal.

MacDonald Address
photo: Aberdeen Press and Journal

If there were a clash between the Dominions and British farmers, it was his duty as Secretary of State to try to reconcile them but, should this prove impossible, his policy was home farmer first, Dominions second, foreigners last. Finally, there were suggestions that, as a Cabinet Minister, he would have no time to devote to his constituency. He stated that he'd previously been a Cabinet Minister and during that time had never allowed Cabinet duties to interfere with his constituency duties and he would not allow this to happen in future.[244]

Perhaps to test him further on the first argument, Colonel Cran of Tain asked what he thought about the subsidising of wheat causing a depressing effect on the value of oats.MacDonald demonstrated some degree of knowledge of the subject when he suggested that the root of the problem with the price of oats was the decrease in the horse population, and that the government must devise a policy that acknowledges that.[245] He was willing to go into the whole matter and try to get fair play for the oat producers.[246] The consensus was that MacDonald had performed well on his first test with the Easter Ross farmers.

MacDonald Meets a Group of Farmers
photo: Evening Standard

MacDonald and Churchill were billeted in the National Hotel, on the same floor, albeit on different wings, and it was perhaps inevitable that they would bump into one another at some stage in the campaign. Few, however, expected it to happen on the first night. They met in a corridor that evening, Churchill elegant in a grey lounge suit and MacDonald less so, in a russet-brown dressing gown with a towel round his neck, en route to the bathroom. Churchill quickly slipped round a corner in the corridor and the moment passed.[247]

The Liberals' seemingly endless quest for a candidate appeared – for a while, at least – to be moving towards resolution. In a statement issued that evening, Ranald Findlay announced that a candidate had been found and had accepted an offer to stand. Making a clear comparison with MacDonald, Churchill and McNeil, he said:

> It is clear that a candidate who is himself a Highlander, acquainted with Scottish and, in particular, Highland problems, would make the widest appeal. Accordingly we issued a confident invitation to Provost Roderick Smith of Stornoway to offer himself as the independent Liberal candidate and it is with great pleasure that I announce his willingness to go forward.[248]

Smith was a Ross-shire man, Findlay said, well-known and respected throughout the country:

> His entry into the election robs Mr MacDonald's sponsors of their panic weapon [that there is no other suitably qualified candidate]...We ask no more in this election than that Liberals should vote Liberal.[249]

However, matters may not have been as clear-cut as Findlay believed. When *The Scotsman* contacted Provost Smith about his nomination, he said he had not made a decision and was setting out for Dingwall that evening to discuss the matter. This prompted Dr Fraser Orr, Vice-Chairman of the Scottish Liberal Federation to insist Provost Smith 'gave us a guarantee that he would stand'.[250] Unfortunately, Provost Smith himself seemed unaware of any such guarantee.

The Liberals' search for a candidate, perhaps, was not yet over.

✡ ✡ ✡

Saturday, 11 January 1936

Snow on Snow, an Offer Followed by Another Offer, Goodbye Wentworth Day, Farewell SNP

Dingwall awoke to an overnight blanket of snow, a foretaste of things to come. Saturday, the *Press and Journal* declared, would be 'the most dramatic day of the amazing tangle that has developed since the seat became vacant'.[251] *The Scotsman* thought it 'doubtful if political feeling has ever run higher in this Highland town'.[252]

Churchill Speaks

Attempts by the Unionist Executive 'as far as possible' to ensure that 'only members of the Association are admitted to the meeting' were not wholly successful. *The Scotsman* noted wryly that the 'Whips of the rival groups must have been very diligent beforehand' and the Temperance Hall, which had been booked for the meeting because of its hefty capacity of 250, was deemed insufficiently large. The meeting was transferred to the town hall and, even there, the main hall and the gallery above were full. 'It could be safely assumed', *The Scotsman* recorded, 'that the Association membership must have been considerably augmented during recent days by those whose interest in the matter was sufficiently keen to induce them to put down the requisite shilling to ensure the right to vote at the meeting'. Easter Ross, it noted – 'the centre of the opposition to Mr MacDonald' – was especially strongly represented.

Captain Tindal, RN, chairing the meeting, suggested diplomatically at the outset that 'those who had crept in by mistake' should withdraw and a few did, but the hall remained packed. Randolph Churchill was asked to give his address first, which the *Inverness Courier* considered, to an extent, influenced the subsequent vote. It also noted the contrast in this treatment of Churchill to that afforded to MacDonald a week previously when, although he was known to be in the next room, he was not called to speak.

Churchill referred almost immediately to 'Central Office interference'. He had tried to discover the attitude of Central Office to his candidacy but received a 'somewhat evasive reply' from the Chief Whip, Lord Stonehaven (this being the 'Basingstoke telegram of 3 January'). Since then, he said, London and Edinburgh had made their intention all too plain. He referred to a criticism of him in *The Scotsman* for addressing his enquiries to Lord Stonehaven when, in matters of candidature, Scotland had the right of self-determination. But, he said:

> after the transactions of the last fortnight are we really to place any belief in their right of self-determination north of the Tweed? It is idle to pretend that there has been no interference from London in this matter. Repeated, sustained efforts have been made to induce your Association to endorse a candidature which is evidently repugnant to the majority of you.

This was a matter which needed to be resolved, he said, although he didn't give the impression that he would be overly disappointed not to be involved:

> Loath though I am to quit the sunny skies of Morocco, loath though I am to plunge myself for the third time in ten months into a hotly-contested fight, and though I doubt whether I am the most suitable man to bear your banner in the fight, I would be doing less than my duty had I not returned to consult with you upon this vital and urgent public question.

Describing himself, like Sir William Martineau, a 'mere Englishman', he said there would be no recriminations on his part if they decided he was not the right man to stand. Hector McNeil, the Socialist candidate, would later pick up on this curious passage, saying he interpreted it as the self-professed 'bad boy' of the Unionist Party making a tacit apology to Headquarters in an attempt to curry favour. Whether that is the case, or whether Churchill was merely seeking a way out of an adventure about which he seemed oddly ambivalent is open to conjecture.

He turned to the MacDonalds, being carpetbagged into the Scottish Universities and Ross and Cromarty divisions respectively:

> Scant regard would seem to have been paid to the interests of the constituency, to the interests of the party, or to the special needs of the localities in either of these choices.
>
> When the Universities vacancy arose, did any of its electorate think of Ramsay MacDonald as candidate? No. The suggestion emanated from London. Similarly who in the Ross and Cromarty Liberals thought of Malcolm MacDonald? Again, the happy thought was London's.

The subject of the MacDonalds would prove to be catnip for Churchill, something he would return to time and again in the campaign. He continued his attack:

> We were told that the two MacDonalds, representing National Labour, were indispensable to the National Government. That argument is a lie. It is a fraudulent, hypocritical, insincere, barefaced lie. What Labour do

they represent? Is there a single Trade Union which offered them its support? Is there a co-operative society which accepted them? Is there a single working class constituency in Scotland, England, Wales or Northern Ireland prepared to harbour them? No! These two men are probably more hated and despised by working class labour than any other two men in the Kingdom.

There is no such thing as a National Labour elector in this country. Let us therefore hear no more of this pleading that the National Government cannot be truly National unless it can extend high offices of State to men who are repudiated by organised Labour from one end of the Kingdom to the other.

This argument is more than lies. It is the manifestation of arrogant, overwhelming and presumptuous conceit. Of all things that the MacDonalds might have chosen to call themselves – Liberals, Socialists, Communists, Tories, Fascists, anarchists – surely National is the most laughable of all. Where was Mr Ramsay MacDonald in the war? Where were he and his son in the General Strike? National? Why, only recently they were international Socialists and Mr Ramsay MacDonald in an interview with an American newspaper only twelve or fourteen months ago, when he was Prime Minister of the National Government, said that he was still a Socialist. They are not Liberals, Conservatives or Socialists. They are want-to-get-into-Parliamentarians.

He continued his character assassination of Malcolm MacDonald, raising applause and cheers: 'Judged by the test of ability, [he] would not be included in the Cabinet. In a junior Ministry, yes; in the Cabinet, no. Judged on the test of patriotism, he is the last man to be in it.' He went on: 'Don't think I have any personal ill-feeling towards him'. Churchill paused, seemingly surprised by the outbreak of laughter. 'I repeat my words', he said, improbably. He continued:

I like to see young men get on, but I like to see them succeed on their own merits. Mr Malcolm MacDonald's inclusion in the Cabinet was a job, and the attempt to foist him on to Ross and Cromarty was a job upon a job.253 He is trying to use Ross and Cromarty to regularise his position, and the same is true of Mr Ramsay MacDonald in the Scottish Universities.

> Your interests are not being studied in the least. You are merely being commanded in the most high-handed fashion to allow yourselves to be used as the convenience and utensil of the MacDonalds' political appetites. The whole of this shabby transaction constitutes a fraud upon representative government.

Churchill will have known, from his experience in standing in Wavertree, that local party members would be concerned about appearing disloyal to the party and the National Government. Declaring himself (contrary to all evidence) a supporter of the National Government, he explained:

> It has been suggested that if you do not accept Mr Malcolm MacDonald, you will do Mr Baldwin a disservice. I am not aware of any public declaration by Mr Baldwin which could possibly lead anyone to suppose that he would prefer you to return Mr Malcolm MacDonald instead of myself.
>
> Indeed I must assume that as he is the Leader of the Unionist Party he would rather have a Unionist in the House of Commons. If you choose me as the official Unionist candidate, I do not doubt that our leader, Mr Baldwin will send me the usual letter of support which every candidate duly chosen by a local Unionist Association has the right to expect.

This is not true, as Churchill would have known full well. The Whip's Office had already made it clear that the leaders of the Unionist party supported MacDonald and Baldwin would be bound to support a man in his Cabinet. Indeed, the Financial Secretary to the Treasury, William Morrison, was due to speak on MacDonald's behalf the next evening.

Presumably aware of this, Provost Macdonald of Invergordon pressed Churchill on the matter, asking whether he would expect the support of Baldwin. At this point, Churchill obfuscated, replying he could not say definitely because Baldwin had not given any public declaration one way or the other. Perhaps he hadn't, but his party officials had made the matter clear, and the answer was not in Churchill's favour.

When he turned from politics to policy, Churchill's grand oratory became somewhat flatter and betrayed a less insightful view than Malcolm MacDonald. Nothing would remedy agriculture except a severe tariff on agricultural imports, he said. Quotas, marketing boards, and schemes for restricting production were unhealthy: the policy should be greater production. This is only partially true. In fact, under Secretary of State Walter Elliot, production had risen by around 15 per cent by 1936,[254] but the headline figure masked variations: as Malcolm MacDonald had previously pointed out, with oats, the issue wasn't production but demand, particularly in certain sectors. If demand diminished, increased production would achieve nothing.

Discussing the 'scandalously low wage of the farm servant', he said that the community, which might be persuaded to pay a little more for their food, would do so with less reluctance if they knew that a large proportion of the increase was to go in higher wages to the agricultural labourer. Why only a 'proportion' – large or otherwise – of increases should be passed to the low-paid workers, was not explained, nor to whom the remainder of the increases would go.

At this point, Sir Robert Brooke proposed the press and Churchill withdraw while the rest of the business was discussed. This was agreed, and for two hours the meeting debated the issues.

The motion to stand a candidate was moved by Hector Forbes and a motion against doing so was moved by Sir William Martineau. By a vote of 135 to 93, it was agreed that the Unionists would fight the election.

Reverend Sellar proposed, and James Scott seconded, that Churchill should be adopted as the candidate. General Pollock-McCall of Kindeacre proposed that he should not be adopted, and William Gibson, Invergordon, seconded.

By a vote of 160 to 47, Churchill was selected as the Unionist candidate.

An Offer is Made

Churchill was summonsed back to the meeting but he did not accept the news with quite the satisfaction the gathered membership might have anticipated. Instead, he offered an escape from the impasse in which they found themselves with regard to their National Government colleagues. Referring to the large number who voted against him, he suggested the 'main prepossession' in these people's minds was the fear of splitting the National vote and letting the Socialist in. Therefore, he suggested passing a resolution that a message should be sent to the Liberal Association, stating that he had been selected but was prepared to stand down, and the Unionist party was prepared to give its entire, united support to any National Liberal (not Malcolm MacDonald's National Labour) candidate they would care to suggest. 'That seems to me fair and reasonable', he said, before offering a warning:

> If our reasonable and courteous suggestion is not accepted we shall take off the gloves and have such a fight as has never been seen at any election in England or Scotland.

Some interpreted this as a sporting offer built on fair play. Others were more cynical, seeing it as an attempt to find a way out of a contest in which he had earlier seemed less than eager to engage. Ewan Cameron suggested it was 'probably a ploy to polarise the election between the two rivals'.[255] The *Manchester Guardian*'s dry account suggested a different ulterior motive:

> he only produced this noble offer after he had made sure that a majority of the meeting had accepted him as candidate. So he does not really seem to be anxious to compose the shattered Government front in Ross and Cromarty. What he wanted perhaps, was a good Sunday press, and he got it.[256]

Most suspected the Liberals would reject the proposal out of hand. However, a motion to do as Churchill suggested was passed unanimously and a letter was despatched immediately to the Liberal Association outlining Churchill's offer and giving the following rationale:

> [A] double advantage would be reaped in that the Liberals and the Unionists would be united in favour of a National Government candidate, and that it is extremely probable in those circumstances that the independent Liberal would [also] withdraw from the field.

They requested a response by 5 pm on Monday, and explained that if the proposal was rejected Mr Churchill would open his campaign forthwith.

At the end of the meeting, Churchill emerged into a thronged main street. He was seized by his admirers and carried shoulder-high along the street, the conquering hero bringing the town to a standstill. He wrote to his father later that it was the best speech he had ever made.[257] It was indeed impressive, and there was no question that Churchill could command an audience. He was a 'born orator', Winston S Churchill wrote, before going on to suggest this was as much a disbenefit as a benefit: 'because of the very facility with which he could speak extemporaneously, [he] failed to make the effort required to bring him true success'.[258] We can see this in his speech here, and in later speeches in the campaign. When on his hobby-horse, the MacDonalds, or indulging in low politics and political shenanigans, he was superb, with an orator's gift for the ready and witty phrase, able to rouse a crowd to righteous indignation. When pressed on policy matters, which required research and substance, he dithered and prevaricated.

Churchill is Chaired Through Dingwall
photo: Edinburgh Evening News

J Wentworth Day returned to London, well satisfied with the outcome. 'Ross and Cromarty may very well go down in history', he said, 'as the political birthplace of one who may become one of the greatest statesmen of the century'. However, perhaps conscious of Churchill's less than emphatic acceptance of his selection, he made clear:

> If for any reason Mr Churchill does not stand and Mr Malcolm MacDonald still does stand, we shall provide an independent Unionist.

Malcolm MacDonald, perhaps intentionally, missed the excitement in Dingwall, spending the day in Cromarty speaking to prominent locals. Meanwhile, he received a letter of support from Bassetlaw Division of the Unionist Association, where he had been the Member of Parliament until the general election. 'Having been for so long a member for this division, which is so largely agricultural, we…feel you will be fully acquainted with the requirements of our oldest industry', the letter read, reinforcing again one of the central arguments of the campaign, the importance of agriculture.

For the independent Liberals, Provost Roderick Smith finally reached Dingwall but, since no meeting of the group was planned before Tuesday or Wednesday, there was no further development. When asked if he would stand, Provost Smith offered the same answer as Randolph Churchill, saying he would gauge the tone of the meeting and decide from there.

Hector McNeil kicked off his campaign with a meeting in the evening in the same room that had seen the Unionist drama earlier, the news of which would have been greatly encouraging for the Socialists, since it offered a strong possibility of winning against a split opposition. The meeting was a deal less raucous than Churchill's but *The Scotsman* reported that the large audience was attentive and McNeil was encouragingly received.

'Make no mistake about it', McNeil said, 'there is only one question before you. You are going to be asked to pass a vote of confidence in or a vote of censure on the National Government'.[259] To laughter, he commented on the 'unusual aspects' of the campaign so far, and predicted 'more fur flying' before its conclusion. 'We will not fight on personalities but on principles', he said, immediately breaking his vow by calling Malcolm MacDonald a 'political remittance man' and Randolph Churchill an 'extremely nice fellow' but 'politically daft'. His aim was to ask Ross and Cromarty to 'censure the foreign policy of the National Government which has almost led us to war'. This offered a foreshadowing of the main political preoccupation of the next few years, with Neville Chamberlain's doomed policy of appeasement causing huge fissures in the previously solid National Government. Supporting McNeil were Malcolm Macmillan MP and Arthur Woodburn.

At a three hour private meeting in Perth, the Scottish National Party voted unanimously not to contest the by-election, citing shortness of time available to organise a campaign and the vast and scattered nature of the constituency.

As if Dingwall hadn't seen enough excitement for one day, at some time around midnight the most spectacular fire seen in the town for many years engulfed the Tulloch Street premises belonging to James Falconer of Pitlassie Farm. The bakery, including all its valuable machinery, was destroyed but the Fire Brigade – which was composed largely of Rover Scouts, aged 18 to 24 – managed to save the dairy and shop, accounting for some two-thirds of the property.[260]

Dingwall Fire
photo: Aberdeen Press and Journal

✲ ✲ ✲

Monday, 13 January 1936

An Elastic Membership, Support from Baldwin, 'Damn the Consequences' and Interloping Ploughmen

After the tumult of the weekend, the new week began with some newspaper editorials. The *Daily Mirror*'s *Cassandra*, maintaining a tone of indulgent bemusement, declared:

> I am offering a pound of acid drops to anyone who can explain what the blazes they are up to in the Ross and Cromarty by-election.
>
> To Mr Randolph Churchill, who has flown all the way from Morocco to be a candidate and then immediately offers to stand down for somebody else, I present the Corkscrew Trophy – the award of Super Careful Conduct.[261]

In a more sober reflection, *The Scotsman* addressed the behaviour of the Unionists. Out of 'resentment' at the 'high-handed' manner in which Malcolm MacDonald had been 'foisted on the constituency', the local Unionist Association had gone to the length of adopting a rival candidate,

Randolph Churchill, raising the prospect of an 'internecine struggle' between parties which supported the National Government. The paper conceded that not consulting the Unionist Association was 'bad management', but cautioned the Unionists would have been better advised to register a protest but not take the extreme course of adopting a rival candidate. While the Unionists' feelings could be appreciated, their judgement could not be commended.

Churchill's declaration that he had a good chance of winning was dismissed and he was accused of misleading his audience by supposing he would get a letter of credence from the Prime Minister or support from Central Office. Events a few hours later would bear this out.

Reflecting on Saturday's vote, the paper suggested slyly that the Unionist Association appeared to have a 'somewhat elastic membership'. This would be elaborated on by Sir William Martineau in explosive fashion later in the day. On the adoption of Churchill, the paper was dismissive:

> it passes comprehension that the young Englishman...can have any real understanding of the problems of a constituency like Ross and Cromarty.

It concluded by putting its weight behind the candidacy of Malcolm MacDonald.[262]

The Scotsman's doubts about Stanley Baldwin writing in support of Churchill were vindicated within hours, with a telegram from the Prime Minister to Malcolm MacDonald:

> Having been unanimously chosen by the Ross and Cromarty Liberal National organisation to contest the seat, in succession to their late member, you have my wholehearted support. I strongly urge Unionists, in the interests of the National Government, to support you as they did Sir Ian Macpherson.
>
> Scotland and the Highlands will surely realise that it is to their advantage to have you, yourself a Scotsman, in the Cabinet.[263]

The *Evening Standard* was quick to query the timing and method of delivery of Baldwin's support, coming so early in the campaign and through the instant medium of a telegram. It was 'carefully timed', it concluded, to arrive in Dingwall while the Liberal Association were discussing Mr Churchill's offer to stand down in favour of a National Liberal if MacDonald withdrew:

> Everyone knew that Mr Churchill's offer would be turned down. Mr Baldwin chose that moment also to turn Mr Churchill down.[264]

There is a discernible lack of personal warmth in Baldwin's communication but it was nonetheless unequivocal in offering government support to MacDonald and not Churchill. The Ross and Cromarty Unionist Association reacted with fury, sending a telegram to Baldwin, the tone of which suggested the mists had descended on them:

> [We] have learned with regret that you have sent a telegram in support of a candidate who is opposing the Unionist candidate, whom our Association has adopted in support of the National Government.
>
> We would respectfully point out to you that your action challenges the whole democratic structure of the Unionist party.
>
> We regretted at the time that our principles forbade us to yield to the pressure that was put upon us from London, but we always assumed that whatever decision we arrived at would be loyally endorsed by you.
>
> ...
>
> On Saturday, January 4, 1936, Sir William Martineau, our late chairman, went to London instructed on our behalf to interview the Co-ordinating Committee, with a view to finding a candidate acceptable to Liberals and Unionists. The candidate to whom you have now given your support, though he is a member of this Co-ordinating Committee, instead of waiting for its recommendations proceeded at once to accept the Liberal invitation. In our view, he thereby showed scant respect for the feelings of your followers or for the feelings of the Co-ordinating Committee.
>
> In these circumstances we can only express our astonishment and our regret at the course you have adopted.
>
> None the less, we wish to assure you of our support to the National Government and confidently believe that in Mr Randolph Churchill we have chosen a man who will convey that support to Westminster.[265]

Randolph Churchill, perhaps surprisingly, adopted a 'more in sorrow than in anger' tone. He was 'surprised' by Baldwin's letter of support for MacDonald. If, because of the 'political entanglements' in which he had involved himself, he was unable to support the official Unionist candidate, then 'I should have though he would at least have abstained from any discrimination'.[266]

Moral high ground duly taken, he said he would not be discouraged by this 'strange political development' (one which had been anticipated by the Scottish Whip's Office two days before) and would redouble his efforts 'albeit without my leader's aid' to rally the Unionist cause in Ross and Cromarty.

He would have the opportunity to demonstrate his redoubled resolve very soon because, as expected, the ten men of the Liberal Association's Emergency Committee rejected the Unionists' offer. A letter, signed by Dr Middleton and Alexander Macrae was despatched to the Unionists' headquarters:

> The members of the Ross and Cromarty Liberal Association, after due consideration and after interviewing Mr MacDonald and hearing his views – an opportunity which we regret your Association did not take advantage of – unanimously decided that they could best serve national and local interest by giving their wholehearted support to his candidature.
>
> We are satisfied that Mr MacDonald's adoption has widespread approval in the county, and we go forward firm in the belief that he will receive the support of all who put country before party and desire the continuance of National Government.[267]

Being accused, even implicitly, of not putting the national interest first would have been a stinging rebuke for the Unionists. They must have realised, though, that they were now in a most difficult position. *The Scotsman* declared that Baldwin's unqualified support of MacDonald would considerably influence Unionist thinking in the constituency. 'Neither Mr Churchill nor his supporters can be under any delusion on that score.' All the same, the paper referred wearily to the 'damn the consequences mood that had overtaken the local Association'.[268]

Churchill, the paper continued, seemed to have been infected by the

Association's militant spirit, too. It quoted Augustine Birrell's scathing analysis of Parliamentary candidates:

> Confidence is the badge of the tribe of candidates. How it is born, where it is bred, on what it feeds, save vanity, we cannot tell. Figures cannot shake it. It is too majestical to be affected by ridicule.[269]

This must have made chastening reading for Churchill. Disagreement and even distaste are emotions which candidates will be happy to provoke but, despite Birrell's contention, ridicule and scorn *can* do terminal damage to a reputation. It was becoming clear, though, that Churchill's entry to the race was proving controversial. Ramsay MacDonald, in a letter to Malcolm, said that he had lunched in the Athenaeum that afternoon and reported that 'everybody there is full of disgust with the Churchill candidature'. The common view was that he should be 'stamped out as a slug crawling on our public life'.[270]

This time, Churchill decided attack was the best form of defence, and he took to savaging the Liberal Executive. Their decision to reject his offer was 'another example of the lack of principle which has destroyed the [Liberal] party and which is today one of the most lamentable and sinister features in our political system'. It would increasingly be Unionism's duty to guard the integrity of representative institutions against interference by the Executive, 'now that they have been blatantly sullied by the Liberal party'. Declaring he would open his campaign forthwith he concluded:

> The ancient Liberal watchword, 'The price of freedom is eternal vigilance,' ought now to be 'The price of Liberalism is the patronage of the Tory party'.[271]

Clan Donald Stands and Fights

Malcolm MacDonald must have been most satisfied with the events of the day. It would grow even more positive that evening when a mass meeting at Dingwall town hall was so oversubscribed he had to conduct a further overspill meeting afterwards. William Morrison, 1st Viscount Dunrossil and Financial Secretary to the Treasury, addressed the assembly, reinforcing the National Government's support for his candidature. With him on the podium were Sir William Martineau and Captain Shaw-Mackenzie, who had earlier followed Martineau and Sir Robert Brooke in resigning from the Unionist Executive.

MacDonald opened by remarking that certain disinterested parties had suggested he was a Scotsman who had deserted Scotland until it suited him to remember it in connection with this by-election. 'What nonsense', he thundered.

> I was born on the shores of the Moray Firth. My home has always been there and is there still. Whenever I can get away from the South I am in Lossiemouth.

Referring mockingly to Churchill, he declared, to rousing cheers:

> And now there comes hot-foot from Africa someone who stands in the path and says 'you shall not go forward.' He says 'If you will retire I will retire.' When a descendant of the Great Duke of Marlborough comes to the Highlands to challenge a descendant of the Clan Donald, the MacDonald stands and fights.

From the audience, someone shouted, 'And we will fight with you'. MacDonald smiled. 'And the MacDonald will fight and win', he concluded, to even louder cheers.

He gave a spirited defence of the National Government. It had started as an experiment but in its first four years it had proved successful, principally because it contained leaders drawn from all three old parties:

> None of the old parties had a monopoly of virtue. There was some wisdom in each of their policies. This is a Government in which there has been a pooling of wisdom, in which Statesmen have not been restricted in action by party dogmas and prejudices which may have applied to affairs thirty years ago, but which no longer apply today.

He went on to list its achievements: the national budget had been 'hopelessly unbalanced' when it took office, and the 'whole credit of the country was strained'. Today, the budget was balanced, credit had never stood higher, emergency taxation had been almost entirely removed and every cut made in 1931 had been restored. Within four years, the government had expanded social services on an unprecedented scale. Slum clearance had massively expanded, facilitated by a concomitant increase in new house building.

To those who believed they should return to party government, he rejoindered:

> Whereas ten years ago party governments were flourishing in almost every country of any importance, today there is scarcely such a country where a party government is still in power. The fact is that it is an experience common to most great countries that mere party government is not strong enough to tackle the post-war problems. There are two alternatives. There is the dictatorship which suppresses freedom, and there is the government of national co-operation which is strong because it can preserve liberty.[272]

The split in the Unionist ranks was in danger of becoming a chasm. Captain Shaw-Mackenzie, in his resignation letter, was cutting about the local Association:

> My reasons [for resigning] are that I have been asked to remain loyal to an Association which is disloyal to our party leader's wishes, and at the same time utterly opposed to the dictates of my heart. No man can serve two masters and, being a loyal and free citizen, I reserve the absolute right to support any candidate who I honestly believe can benefit my country at the time.[273]

Next, Sir William Martineau rose to speak in support of MacDonald. He introduced a new allegation which, although not unexpected since rumours had been circulating since Saturday, was nonetheless shocking to hear on a public stage. Churchill's supporters, he said, had 'brought their wives and their daughters and their sons and their ploughmen [to the meeting on Saturday]. They were determined to win the vote even if these ploughmen had never been Unionists in their lives before'.[274] He claimed that some 60 farm labourers were brought in and made members of the Association by their employers, allowing them to vote. If this had not happened, he said, Churchill would have lost. Since the proposal to stand a candidate was agreed by a vote of 135 to 93, there is some truth in this.[275]

Martineau also rounded on the small batch of farmers from Easter Ross whom he blamed for the impasse: 'I particularly use the word small', he said, 'because it is small, although the people are big and have big voices'. They thought of their pockets before they thought of their country, he said dismissively.[276]

MacDonald's perfect day continued after he had concluded his public meetings. When he emerged to return to his hotel, a band of pipers was waiting for him and they escorted him along the snow-covered streets to the hall. Mirroring what happened to Randolph Churchill two days before, he was carried shoulder-high through the town. Even after he had returned to his hotel, a crowd of almost one thousand stood outside, chanting for him to appear. He came to the balcony and made another speech, to great acclaim.

Immediately after he had departed, cries rang out for Churchill to appear. Later, he did and proceeded to launch an attack on MacDonald. This was unwise, as he was greeted by a storm of cat-calls, boos and shouts of derision, completely drowning his speech. 'Go back to Morocco', he was told. 'Surely you are not afraid of free speech in Ross-shire?' he countered. At this point a piper struck up some lively airs, drowning him out completely. Finally, no doubt chastened, he was forced to withdraw.

There followed a slight altercation between the candidates' agents, with Churchill suggesting that the piper had been paid to play to disrupt Churchill's address. Reminiscing later, Alexander Macrae, secretary of the Liberal Association said, 'I was quite athletic, and I told Randolph I would throw him off the balcony if he said that again.'[277] Macrae then challenged Tom McDonald, Churchill's representative, to confront the piper and ask if that were true. McDonald did and – not entirely surprisingly, and equally inconclusively – the piper denied any such thing.[278]

In London, the Speaker of the House of Commons gave notice in the evening edition of the *London Gazette* of his intention to issue a warrant for a new writ for the Ross and Cromarty Division at the end of six days after the insertion of the notice. This meant that the first week of February would still be the most likely week for the by-election to take place. Three more weeks of high farce and low cunning would be required before the results were known.

* * *

Tuesday, 14 January 1936

The Politics of the Dunghill

As the day before, the candidates would have been rapt by the morning papers' leader columns as they ate their bacon and eggs. In typically robust style, the *Inverness Courier* gave its view on the Conservative meeting the previous Saturday. Referring to its leader the previous week comparing the rebel Unionists to the Bulls of Bashan, it suggested Saturday's meeting had added the 'cackling of geese and the crowing of a young cockerel' to the cacophony. Their reward was that the 'only organ of the gutter press published in Scotland' [the *Scottish Daily Express*] had given them its 'perfervid blessing'. The 'politics of the dunghill' which Churchill espoused was hitherto unknown in the Highlands and while the paper had no doubt the electors would show their contempt 'in emphatic fashion', they were filled with regret that this act of 'political infamy' should have been committed by people who called themselves Unionists.[279]

A second leader came from the *Dundee Courier*, which reflected on the amount of attention being bestowed on the by-election by an English press usually indifferent to Scottish and, in particular, rural Scottish affairs. The explanation was obvious, it declared: Randolph Churchill. It drew parallels with Churchill's previous sally into by-election politics, in Liverpool Wavertree where, despite declaring himself a supporter of the National Government, his standing as an independent split the National Government vote and handed the seat to the Socialists. 'In Ross-shire the same story is being retold', it warned. 'In the circumstances', it continued, 'It would be strange if Mr R Churchill's devotion to the National Government were not widely questioned and another motive sought for his actions'.

There were Unionists, the editorial continued, 'who frankly wish the break-up of the National Government and the reappearance of party government'. It said that Churchill claimed not to be one of them but, judged on his actions, not his words – 'patently wrecking tactics' – his purpose was surely to 'get back to the party basis'.

Why might this be the case, it pondered. There were frequent grumbles in the Unionist ranks about their lack of promotion prospects because of the 'composite nature of the government' which meant that members from other parties had to take places in government. 'Probably Mr Winston Churchill regards himself as one of those martyrs who have been sacrificed to make way for Liberals and Labourists', it concluded, suggesting that Randolph Churchill probably shared that view.

This explanation, the *Dundee Courier* believed, 'has the merit of accounting for the peculiar character of Mr Randolph Churchill's Ross-shire speeches'. His 'vitriolic fury' towards Malcolm MacDonald could not otherwise be accounted for. He had 'no hope whatever of victory' but his candidature could potentially ensure MacDonald did not prevail either. This was the real reason behind Churchill's decision to stand.

The local Unionist Association were 'now acting as the instrument in the Churchill vendetta against a member of the National Government', it concluded, describing them as 'muddled-headed, adhering as they did to Churchill's thesis that the true way of supporting a National Government is to vote against it'.[280]

There is some truth in what the *Dundee Courier* suggested. Winston Churchill, firmly in his 'wilderness years' period, was constantly plotting from the backbenches how to return to government. Only a few weeks before, he was holidaying in Marrakech with David Lloyd George and surveying from afar the disaster of the Hoare-Laval crisis and the subsequent appointment of Anthony Eden as Foreign Secretary, an appointment Churchill greatly deprecated. Martin Gilbert points out that, at this point, Churchill had been on the back benches for five-and-a-half years, and Lloyd George for thirteen. Churchill wrote to his wife Clementine: 'What a fool Baldwin is, with this terrible situation on his hands, not to gather his resources & experience to the public service'.[281] Winston was also acutely aware how Randolph's campaign could reflect on him. On New Year's Eve, when Randolph's plan first came to light, Winston wrote to Clementine:

> Randolph is of course wanting to fight Malcolm M but he won't be able to – because it would put a spoke in my wheel and nothing good for him.

He doubted Randolph would go through with it, he added. 'I do not think he would really when it came to the point.' Later, when it became clear that Randolph would indeed stand, Winston wrote to Clementine again:

> You will see how unfortunate and inconvenient such a fight is to me. 'Churchill v MacDonald.' If they get in, it would seem very difficult for Baldwin to invite me to take the Admiralty or the coordinating job [as Defence Supremo] and sit cheek by jowl with these wretched people. I therefore would greatly have preferred Randolph to damp it all down.[282]

Like the *Inverness Courier*, the *Dundee Courier* picked up on the 'vitriolic fury' of Churchill's speeches. Increasingly, it said, members of Churchill's entourage were becoming concerned about the intemperate way he spoke of MacDonald. In particular, the booing which had caused him to retreat from the balcony of the National Hotel the previous evening was caused, they felt, by the inflammatory attack he raised on MacDonald. They would, *The Scotsman* reported, take measures to persuade him to desist from focusing on personalities.[283] If they tried, it seems highly unlikely they would have made much headway. Churchill wrote in his autobiography: 'I could never brook authority or discipline'.[284] For a man of many faults, this may have been his gravest, because it meant he was incapable of reining in his behaviour.

The *Press and Journal* focused on the course of events which had led to the current situation and posed a 'simple question':

> Do we wish to see a National Government candidate elected and are we willing to risk a National Government candidate being defeated just because we are not united?
>
> Would it not have been better for the two Associations…to put their heads together and agree upon a candidate acceptable to both? That would have been a matter of courtesy.

But, the paper added, this was not done. 'Hence the absurd situation that has arisen.' The paper did not come out for either candidate but was critical of Churchill. Talking of his suggestion to the Liberals that both he and MacDonald stand down, it concluded:

> At first blush, that offer appears to have been sporting and even generous. Yet it does suggest that he may be more concerned with the personalities than with the principles involved.[285]

This leader column, although not overtly critical of MacDonald, appeared to cause consternation in government circles. In a letter to his son, Ramsay MacDonald suggested it was 'anything but helpful'.[286] He said that representations had been made to Lord Camrose, owner of the newspaper and, although Camrose could see 'no ground for complaint', Ramsay still felt his intervention would have a beneficial effect.[287]

Churchill had by now relocated to a boarding house in Strathpeffer (a village once home to Aleister Crowley, occultist and writer – the 'most evil man in Britain'), reducing the risk of further embarrassing meetings in the corridors of the National Hotel. He took to the press to take issue with the *Press and Journal*'s editorial the previous day. To their point that he had not said he was standing in support of the National Government he pointed out that he had said precisely that – and the *Press and Journal* had reported as much – at his adoption meeting on Saturday, and he had expanded on the theme several times since. Unsurprisingly, he also took issue with the editorial's suggestion that he may be more concerned with personalities than principles, to which he countered:

> The imputation of motives without any evidence and contrary to all public declarations is dangerous and unsatisfactory in public controversy.

He reiterated that he had made clear he would withdraw to make way for a candidate acceptable to both Unionists and Liberals. If the offer had been accepted 'I should now be in London and a National Liberal would be uniting under his banner Liberals and Unionists in a straightforward fight against the Socialists'. Instead, the Liberals had chosen a 'nondescript candidate'.[288]

As suspected, then, any attempt by his entourage to temper Churchill's language had failed. Churchill also reacted with anger to the claim the previous day by Sir William Martineau that 60 ploughmen had been brought to the adoption meeting to rig the vote. It was the other way around, Churchill insisted. They had been brought in by MacDonald's supporters but, when they heard the arguments, they decided to vote for Churchill.[289]

Churchill did receive a piece of good news, when Sir Robert Brooke, erstwhile vice-chairman of the Unionist Association, announced that he would speak in support of him in Dingwall on Saturday. Brooke had, unexpectedly, voted for him in the adoption meeting but this was still a surprise, given that he had resigned as vice-chairman over Churchill's candidature.[290]

Malcolm MacDonald spent the day canvassing in Cromarty, at the tip of the Black Isle. He was met outside the town by a party of supporters and a pipe band and was carried shoulder-high to the Victoria Hall. Two-one to MacDonald on the shoulder-carrying tally. Both he and his sister, Sheila, who addressed an overflow meeting at the same time as his address, were well-received.

MacDonald began by stating, 'How long I remain Dominions Secretary depends on you'. The Beaverbrook-owned *Evening Standard*, fervently opposed to the MacDonalds, made great play of this, inferring it meant he would immediately resign from Cabinet if he were to lose.[291] Ramsay MacDonald, writing to his son two days later, bemoaned Beaverbrook's 'malignant campaign'. The *Standard* had made a 'great cock-a-doodle-do of [the suggested resignation], commenting with unconcealed delight that that would mean then when you again contested a seat it would be as a very ordinary person who could not use his Cabinet position as a reason why people should vote for him'. He recommended his son should now 'attack, based on the achievements of the Government and the dangerous futilities both for home and foreign policy of Opposition Labour'.[292]

MacDonald then addressed the allegation that he had been parachuted into the constituency, giving a complete account of the communications and discussions that had been ongoing since before Christmas:

> I had not contemplated coming to Ross and Cromarty to fight a by-election until one evening I received in London a telephone call from the

North. A message was conveyed to me from local political leaders in the constituency asking whether I would like my name to be considered with others as a possible candidate. I agreed.

Sheila MacDonald Campaigning
photo: Aberdeen Press and Journal

He did nothing more until receiving a letter a few days later from Dr Middleton, asking to discuss the situation with him if he was returning to Lossiemouth for Christmas. This he did – the Lossiemouth Tea Party (26 December). 'It was not until after I had met the Liberal Association, and received the unanimous invitation from them, that I got in touch with any political headquarters in London', he said.[293] He also stressed that the Unionists were informed at each stage, and neither he nor the Liberal Association had made any commitment until his adoption meeting.[294]

His main focus for the day, however, was agriculture. In Munlochy, a village lying at the head of Munlochy Bay, he declared that the government had made a good start on dealing with agriculture, but still had work to do. He instanced areas where improvements had been wrought – wheat, mutton and lamb had been helped by the regulation of imports; no one could deny that potato farmers had benefited from National Government policy; without government intervention, oats would not be grown at all; regulation of beef imports and the subsidy scheme had prevented the cattle industry from collapsing long ago. More could be done for the cattle industry by adopting the approach taken by the Wheat Act, regulating imports and imposing a levy, which would provide sufficient funding to pay a subsidy to cattle farmers. It was unfortunate, he said, that some of the commodities in which the government had been less successful were those most important to Ross farmers, but he assured them of the government's commitment to address the issues. On farm servants' wages, he referred to the County Wages Committee in place in England and, without giving any pledge to improve it, suggested that the method of agreeing farm servants' wages in Scotland might not be as advantageous as the English approach.[295]

For the Socialists, Hector McNeil was on the opposite side of the constituency in Wester Ross, with meetings in Plockton, Stromeferry and Lochcarron. Winter had taken hold and the snowy roads were becoming difficult. They would grow more treacherous in the coming weeks and it would be Hector McNeil who endured the greatest privation. Perhaps for this reason a feature of his campaign was a pledge to improve the local transport infrastructure. The trouble, as he saw it, was that they were dealing with 'tyrannous landlordism', a phrase more commonly associated with Ireland but appropriate in Ross and Cromarty. There were no telephone or telegraph facilities after seven o'clock at night, he said.[296] Ambulances currently had to use hazardous roads or equally dangerous ferries. Thus, a new road would greatly assist those in need of medical assistance, and better roads would be of benefit to tourists, too.[297] A stretch of road through a deer forest near Kyle of Lochalsh could be brought up to modern requirements at the cost of only a few thousand pounds, he suggested.

Mrs Mackenzie, Crofter
photo: Dundee Courier

McNeil may have had a point, but he would have difficulty persuading some of the locals, judging by a photograph carried by the *Dundee Courier*, of the formidable Mrs Mackenzie, a crofter from Loch Broom, who was agitating against the construction of a new road from Inverbroom to Ullapool. She does not look like a woman to be crossed.

Following a meeting of the independent Liberals, it was reported that Provost Smith's candidacy was now a 'foregone conclusion'. Ranald Findlay rounded on his rivals, Churchill and MacDonald, saying that while they continued their 'discreditable scrapping', Provost Smith's stock was rising. He continued:

> Touring the Black Isle, we met many supporters in this reputed stronghold of the MacDonalds...There was abundant evidence of strong support [for us]. I was assured time and again that Mr Malcolm MacDonald has few friends in these parts. Mr Churchill has none, except a handful of big farmers.

He went on to suggest that 'unjustifiable influence' was being brought to bear on independent Liberals by MacDonald's sponsors. It was being intimated to them that a failure to return Mr MacDonald could precipitate a national crisis. 'Is this what four years of National rule has brought us to?' Findlay said. 'Is a Government which enjoys an unwieldy majority in Parliament to be shaken to its foundations if an English reject is not returned by a Scottish constituency?' Not only that, but he suggested efforts had been made to frighten off Provost Smith. 'They are hardly likely to be successful', he said.[298]

The *Evening Standard*, though, was not as convinced as Ranald Findlay that Provost Smith's candidature was assured. It contacted him and asked if he would stand: 'Mr Smith is a shrewd Highlander and he is also a chemist. I do not think the chemist in him has yet decided to become a politician', it reported, quoting Provost Smith: 'I must be satisfied that there is a reasonable chance of success'.[299] Given the Liberals' campaign to date, that would be difficult to prove.

Another unusual element entered the campaign when Harrington Law, son of the late Prime Minister Andrew Bonar Law, arrived in Dingwall, bringing the number of scions of great British statesmen in the constituency to three. He was not here to campaign; he was at pains to explain to the press but was in charge of a corps of cameramen from

British Movietone News who were taking pictures of this strange election.[300]

Even more oddly, a fourth son of a former, current or future Prime Minister would shortly be making his way to the constituency, with Stanley Baldwin's son, Oliver, a journalist, despatched to write on the campaign. With Ramsay MacDonald's daughters, Sheila and Ishbel, also campaigning for Malcolm, that brought the number of offspring of former, present and future Prime Ministers in the campaign to six, surely a record that is unlikely to be beaten.

✡ ✡ ✡

Wednesday, 15 January 1936

'Wiser, Safer and Better to Withdraw'

There was early morning intrigue with a set of footprints in fresh snow leading away from the National Hotel towards the edge of town. The press were quick on the scene, and the identity of the early riser was discovered – Malcolm MacDonald, making a film with Harrington Law.[301] From what remains of the film, it was scarcely worth losing an hour's sleep.[302]

For the first time in the campaign, the independent Liberals got their moment in the spotlight, although they would come to regret it.[303] After 'one of the most amazing meetings which this remarkable by-election has produced', Provost Smith – whose candidature was supposedly a 'foregone conclusion' – declined to stand and warned gravely about the future of Liberalism. The independents' campaign, inept until now, descended into chaos.

The meeting was presided over by Tom Mackenzie of Inverness, and Provost Smith began by asking those in the audience who classed themselves as independent Liberals to stand. Only around 20 per cent of the audience did. Why, at this point, the 80 per cent – effectively infiltrators – weren't expelled can be put down to either misfortune or incompetence, but the fact they were allowed to stay did not augur well for the future conduct of the meeting.

From the outset, Provost Smith was confronted by strong opposition. In particular, Sir Ian Macpherson's endorsement of Malcolm MacDonald was cited as a key factor in people choosing to stay with the National candidate. Provost Smith criticised Macpherson, saying he had supported 'an individual of a different colour to what he formerly represented'. The constituency had been Liberal for 80 years, he said, and surely someone local could have been found to stand in the election. Given that he lived in Stornoway, 120 miles from Dingwall, this seemed to implicitly exclude himself from what he viewed as the primary criterion, which may be deemed a peculiar strategy. He then said he wanted to ascertain the mood of the meeting. That may have been a further mistake as, one by one, the audience enlightened him. A suggestion was made that the Provost withdraw to allow the meeting to debate the issue more fully, and Provost Smith agreed. *Well, you would.*

Ranald Findlay tried to lower the temperature by reading out letters of support for Provost Smith, including from the party leader, Sir Archibald Sinclair, Ishbel Hamilton-Gordon, Marchioness of Aberdeen and Temair, and Sir Robert Hamilton, MP for Orkney and Shetland. The argument raged on. The view of Sir Ian Macpherson was raised repeatedly. One speaker pointed out that, since some of the dissenters were, by their admission, not independent Liberals, their views should be discounted. At this point, an audience member stood and advised that Provost Smith would be making a mistake if he went forward. 'There is no beating about the bush', he said. 'We are Liberals and we must take the best man, and I think the majority of us are going to support the National Government.' The chorus of boos and shouts of 'No!' at this point suggested the speaker was perhaps overstating his position. However, sensing the discord in the room, Tom Mackenzie stressed that only independent Liberals had been invited. He then asked those who supported the Provost to stand up. Of the 100 in attendance, only about two dozen stood.

Provost Smith was recalled and members of the meeting were asked, again, to stand if they supported the Provost. The same small cohort rose to their feet.

'That is a very honest position', Provost Smith said. The matter was for them to decide, not him. Ross-shire had been let down in the campaign, and if they decided to support either a Socialist or a Unionist (MacDonald and Churchill), then there was no need for him to go forward, but he thought there had been underhand activity in the ranks of the wider Liberal Party:

> There may be many independent free Liberals but I feel that a caucus has been at work and there has been a great deal of sabotage in the Liberal ranks. It seems an inopportune moment to stop that rot, and while I believe that Liberalism lives, I cannot see my way to come forward as Liberal candidate, because they are attempting to strangle Liberalism.
>
> It would be to my mind useless and unfair to stand and show a weakness in the Liberal ranks of this county which, I do believe, does not exist except as a momentary thing. I do not think Ross-shire is the place where the first fight should be carried out. Therefore, I must say for myself, I am not prepared to stand as a Liberal candidate in the election.

That seemed to be that, until Dr Stoner, visiting from Brighton, stood and declared that English Liberals would be astounded to see Ross-shire Liberals willing to be handed over from one political owner to another like a flock of sheep. Ranald Findlay took advantage of the resulting mood shift to reiterate the evidence of his canvassing in the county. Murdo MacDonald of Evanton then moved that Provost Smith should be invited again to stand.

All those who were not independent Liberals were asked to withdraw. Five minutes later, with the hall practically empty, Provost Smith thanked those who remained for having the courage of their convictions. But, he said:

> It would be fatal to Liberalism at the present time to come forward to test the feelings of the constituency. I feel it is wiser, safer and better to withdraw.

With that, the calamitous meeting was over.

In truth, the meeting was merely a dramatic representation of the chaos that had engulfed the Liberal Party for the past fourteen years or so, since the 1922 general election which marked, according to Ewan Cameron, the end of Liberal electoral dominance in Scotland.[304] By then, only the Highlands remained loyal to Liberal traditions and it was clear that even here, things were changing.[305] Increasingly, the Liberals were out of step with modern thinking. The Scottish Liberal Federation's manifesto for the 1935 general election had focused on small-scale localism at a time when wider efficiency and professionalism in local government – which suggested an opposite approach – was being pushed by other parties.[306] It found itself attacked from the right by Unionists defending imperial Britain's economic interests and from the left because it couldn't consolidate a working-class voter base.[307]

A Liberal Correspondence

Earlier, a different farce had played out between Dr Middleton, chairman of the local Liberal branch, and Ranald Findlay. Despite Findlay being in a hotel a matter of yards from the Liberal headquarters, where Middleton was based, they conducted a lengthy communication by mail, with around half a dozen letters being exchanged.

It began with Dr Middleton requesting to be allowed to speak at the meeting to explain his views on the impact that adopting an independent candidate would have on the future of Liberalism in the county. Findlay pointed out, reasonably, that Dr Middleton's views were already well known. However, he would allow him to make a statement at the beginning of the meeting, subject to a five-minute limit. This was not acceptable to Dr Middleton, who wanted to be able to speak at the moment he considered most expedient. Findlay held firm and reluctantly Dr Middleton accepted his decision, stating that the condition was unfair and regretting that a portion of the Liberal Association should deny the British right of free speech.

This petty exchange is instructive, not only in terms of the immediate by-election but also for the future of Liberalism. As with the Unionists, members of the Liberal executive had wound themselves into such a frenzy that entrenched positions were leading to a ridiculous level of intransigence and suspicion. Were that to be simply the by-product of the corrosive background to this by-election, it would scarcely matter – the rancour would fade with time – but it pointed to a wider malaise, one that would rupture the National Government and leave the Liberal Party an impotent husk within a matter of years. The world was shifting, and British politics was not changing with it. War and the issue of appeasement would bring these tensions – now boiling over in Ross and Cromarty – into the open across the country. Things would not be the same again.

Pigs, Talkies and Snow

In the National campaign, Malcolm MacDonald attended four meetings, twice at auction marts in Dingwall during the day and in the evening in Culbokie and Kinkell. The venues provoked the *Daily Mail*'s Percy Cater to reflect:

> I have never before heard a political speech delivered to the accompaniment of the lowing herd and the jolly obligato of pork on the hoof.[308]

MacDonald's meeting at Reith and Anderson's mart was favourably received but at Hamilton's mart, he faced strong opposition, not only from humans but from the animals being traded. At one point he was interrupted by some particularly loud grunting. 'That must be a member of the opposition', MacDonald quipped. When he turned and saw the offending animal was a pig he backtracked, wary of being accused of descending to Churchill's level of personality politics. 'I didn't mean that as a personal allusion to my opponents', he explained.

Asked a particularly complicated question on finance, he said, to much laughter, 'I am not sure you don't think I am the whole Cabinet'. Raising a round of applause, he continued, 'I can only do my part as one Highlander in the Cabinet, but I can't do miracles'.

One farmer, an elderly gentleman and an avowed socialist, was very vocal in his opposition to MacDonald, accusing him of having sold his party 'for a price to Baldwin and a Peerage to Macpherson'. He continued to heckle, barking statements rather than questions until the rest of the audience grew restless. Shouts of 'Put him out' rang out. MacDonald persevered and at the meeting, the protester came and shook his hand. 'But I still won't vote for you', he said.

Randolph Churchill was reported as having 'another quiet day', his campaign not due to launch until Thursday with a meeting at the farm in Fearn of James Scott, one of his principal backers. His main activity for the day was making a talkie film with Harrington Law, also at James Scott's farm.

Hector McNeil's difficulty with transport the previous day was nothing compared to his travails today. He became snowed up on the road between Loch Carron and Applecross, which includes the infamous *Bealach na Bà* viewpoint. *Bealach na Bà* is Gaelic for 'Pass of the Cattle', evidence of its origins as a drover's road. Single-track and with hairpin bends more often seen in Alpine retreats and gradients approaching 20 per cent, even today the road can be impassable in winter weather.

Hector McNeil's entourage found themselves unable to move in either direction because of the ice-bound roads and severe snow drifts. A snowplough was despatched but couldn't reach them. Eventually, they managed to return to Auchnasheen and thence to their base in Kinlochewe. It was a day of campaigning lost but an insight gained into the majestic but lowering beauty of the West Coast of Scotland.

Bealach na Bà
photo: Eilidh Carr

* * *

Thursday, 16 January 1936

The Lights Go Out, the Fog Clears, Snow Falls

The election continued to attract attention in England and in the national newspapers. Reflecting on a 'breathless day', the *Daily Mail* noted approvingly: 'What a pace we are living at in Dingwall'.[309] The *Daily Mirror* ran a cheeky leader column on the conduct of the campaign so far, wondering how much further it could descend into vitriol:

At this early stage of the battle the combatants have already reached what (we hope) must be their top notes in mutual recrimination. Forgive us for repeating a few of these electioneering phrases from local Press or competing candidates:

'Arrogant and presumptuous conceit. A lie fawning under a leaky umbrella. Politics of the dunghill. Casting a filthy trail. Chicanery. Conspiracy. Rank cowardice. Methods of the gangster.'

...

And the worst of it is there's so much time left.[310]

No, perhaps the worst of it is that it is impossible, from this distance, to know which of the candidates was being described in some of these comments.

Fresh from an afternoon spent with the curlers at Caberfeidh, Randolph Churchill arrived in Fearn for the inaugural meeting of his campaign later in the day.[311] Why he chose to launch in Fearn and not Dingwall was the cause of some speculation. The *Inverness Courier* considered it to be another example of the tail trying to wag the dog. The event could not be called an unmitigated success. The lights went out, literally. His speech was almost drowned out by overexcited hecklers. The speech of James Scott, his supporter, *was* drowned out. None of this had been expected in the home village of Scott, and supposedly a Unionist stronghold.

The village hall was filled with upwards of 200 locals, many of them standing at the back or perched on window ledges and even on the tops of cupboards. From the tenor of the comments, it was clear McNeil and MacDonald supporters had infiltrated the meeting. Before the lights went out, Churchill had already endured a good many interruptions and there had been occasional booing. This discord wasn't only from the audience, however, and several times Churchill was forced to turn and ask the people arrayed around him on the platform to stop talking, which must have been doubly irritating. *The Scotsman* considered Churchill 'handled a harassing situation remarkably well', overcoming giggling and loud talking in the hall. He was well equipped to handle such disruption. William Alison, writing in the *Evening Standard*, compared the approaches of Churchill and Malcolm MacDonald:

[Churchill] makes rousing speeches full of flowing phrases accompanied

> by waving arms. He is out to enthuse his audience, to encourage hecklers and challenge opposition. Mr MacDonald talks quietly and smiles benignly through his spectacles. He relies on persuasion rather than punch.

Churchill had been speaking for half an hour when the lights failed, plunging everything into darkness.

This was the cue for '[w]histles and shouts and roars of laughter', drowning out Churchill's words. Torches and flashlights were produced and aimed at Churchill. At one point he had up to twenty lights floating around him on the stage. He grabbed a torch himself and tried to continue. 'I have no doubt', he said, 'some of the interrupters will be much braver while they are sitting in the dark'. He had a hurried consultation with James Scott and someone was sent to investigate the fault. Churchill appealed to the audience's sense of proportion. Their sense of proportion seemed only to diminish.

'Surely a small electrical defect', he remonstrated, 'is hardly enough among what I was always told were the dour Scots to produce this extreme manifestation of whistling?' That, unsurprisingly, increased the noise from the dour Scots in the room. 'What are you afraid of? I am only going to tell you the truth. Let's have a little order.'

At this point, the lights came back on and Churchill reasserted some semblance of authority. At one point he paused 'for a full minute', surveying his audience, before saying:

> I am really not going to bother to strain my voice if you don't want to hear me. I probably have to make more than a hundred speeches, and I do not propose to speak at all unless I am listened to.

He continued in a much more reasonable atmosphere, even eliciting cheers and applause. *The Scotsman* noted approvingly that he managed the questions from the audience with skill. While largely addressing questions of agriculture, he did raise *The Scotsman*'s comment about him being booed from the balcony of the National Hotel on Monday because of the locals' distaste for personal attacks. He said that in the campaign he proposed to indulge in a good deal of plain talk to 'combat the humbug which was being sedulously put about as a substitute for argument' by MacDonald's supporters.

He further suggested the 'Lowland Press' was trying to imply that 'Highlanders will resent what are called personal attacks on Mr Malcom MacDonald'. But those papers did not print what he actually said, he noted, so he would say it again now.

> I pointed out that Mr Malcolm MacDonald had stated that he hoped that his election would result in a victory for the three parties who were united in support of the National Government. I proceeded to comment on the strange fact that this statement was made by a man who apparently belongs to no party at all.
>
> I further pointed out that when Mr MacDonald was in London he called himself a member of the National Labour party, in order that he could get a job, but that when he came down here to ask for your votes, so that he might have the qualification for discharging that job, he abandoned his party label. Now, will you please tell me what is personal about that? Why, it is not even an attack. It is a plain statement of fact.
>
> ...
>
> Of course, we know that the other side would rather have no controversy. Don't let them throw dust in your eyes. Don't be deceived by these mealy-mouthed pleas. I do not propose in this election to make any personal attacks on anyone, but I conceive it is my duty to place the facts before you.

As had happened before, having assumed the moral high ground, within moments he stumbled upon it, declaring this dangerous world was 'no place for political softies' and – without justification – talked about a 'shameful' record and 'squealing' against those who tried to reveal it.

The meeting hit another crescendo of discord when W H Gill rose to propose the vote of confidence. Gill received a good hearing but when James Scott rose to second the motion he was drowned out by a torrent of noise from the audience. Scott, a 'big broad-shouldered, fearless man' tried to continue but wasn't allowed to speak. Churchill intervened:

> I must say, as a mere Englishman, how shocking it is to all the traditions in which I have been brought up by my mother, who is a Scotswoman, to find this attempt to deny free speech in Scotland. I understood that

such a thing, though tolerated among the politically ignorant in England, was almost unknown in Scotland.

Scott tried to speak again but could get no further than seconding the motion. The Chairman put it to the meeting and quite a number raised their hands. Then he asked those who were against to show. Nobody did but when the chairman declared the motion carried unanimously there were shouts of 'No.' Thus, the meeting ended with the same rancour with which it began.

His words do give an indication of the approach that Churchill had decided to take in the campaign. He was there as what today we would call a 'disrupter'. His principal selling point, he suggested, was that he was 'not likely to truckle to authority'. He would be unafraid to champion Ross and Cromarty's interests, however unpopular that made him with the government. 'I do not pretend to be an expert on agricultural matters, but I do claim some talent for controversy and agitation.'

Churchill's problem was that he took his controversialism too far until it became destructive, not of his intended targets but of himself. Time and again, Churchill was warned by the newspapers, by the public, by his campaign staff that his approach to the campaign was alienating more people than it attracted, and yet his animosity towards the MacDonalds could not allow him to tone down the invective.

Elsewhere, Sir William Martineau became the official leader of the Unionist campaign on MacDonald's behalf. In response to Stanley Baldwin's advice, those opposed to Churchill's adoption were now taking active measures to support Malcolm MacDonald. 'The Unionists who are backing Mr Churchill are not to have everything their own way', Martineau said. He maintained that, although there had been an 'apparent majority' for Churchill at Saturday's meeting, he and his supporters represented 'a very real majority of Unionists in Ross and Cromarty'. Assisting Martineau in the campaign was the organising agent at Scottish Unionist HQ, Allan Beaton, and the two men had been canvassing in Alness, Invergordon and the Black Isle. By the end of the week, Martineau promised, there would be committees of Unionists working for MacDonald in every part of the county.

MacDonald himself found time away from the slog of the campaign to indulge in a bit of winter fun, with a snowball fight in which he managed a direct hit on one his campaigners, Earl De La Warr.

When he returned to the campaign, visiting the Council Chambers at Invergordon as the guest of Provost Macdonald and members of the Town Council, he said it had been a bewildering by-election to date but the fog was clearing. He also met local businessmen and spoke to a group of unemployed men. He then visited Cromlet grounds, where he met 80 workmen laying oil pipes for twelve oil tanks in an underground oil storage depot – later known to locals as 'The Tunnel' – which was being erected on the site by the Admiralty. He spoke also in Jemimaville and Cullicudden.

Transport remained a focus of Hector McNeil's campaign. Snow continued to affect his progress and he required the assistance of a group of young boys with shovels to clear a way for his entourage to visit Gairloch. Speaking in Melvaig, he noted ruefully: 'The outposts of the empire are as much in Ross and Cromarty as in Central Africa'.[312] More seriously, he claimed that around 1,500 voters were being disenfranchised by the distance they had to travel to polling stations and called for a change to the Ballot Act to allow for portable ballot boxes in rural areas. In many parts of the county, he claimed, people would have to pay eight to ten shillings for transport to their polling station, beyond the reach of many would-be voters. Meanwhile, electors in Torridon who had to wait two hours for him to reach the venue whiled away the time with an impromptu ceilidh.

Provost Smith returned to Stornoway, but it transpired the independent Liberals roadshow was far from over. During the day, Ranald Findlay issued a statement saying that the rank-and-file revolt against MacDonald among Liberals was genuine and there was still a strong desire to stand a Liberal candidate. 'Last night's meeting did not', he said, 'and could not, decide that the seat would not be fought. I am consulting today both with local Liberals and with party leaders'. Given that, after nearly three weeks, they were no closer to finding a candidate and that at the meeting to approve a candidate the day before only 27 independent Liberals turned up, one could only admire Findlay's tenacity. Calling the Liberals a '*valse triste* of politics', the *Daily Mail* painted a poignant picture of Findlay 'sitting lonely at his typewriter' in the National Hotel. 'Everybody thinks', it continued, 'he is hoping that his keyboard will give him a clue to a new champion'.[313] *The typewriter probably had about as much chance as anything else.*

The first odds on the election outcome made stark reading for all but Malcolm MacDonald, who was priced at 5-1 on. Hector McNeil was 5-1 against and Randolph Churchill was priced at 20-1. *No doubt he would find a way of blaming this on Conservative Central Office.*

* * *

Friday, 17 January 1936

A Blizzard Descends, a Stag Attacks, an Also-Randolph

There is a reason why politicians try, whenever possible, to avoid elections in winter. Ross and Cromarty woke to a widespread blanket of heavy snow. Even the Black Isle, often a meteorological anomaly while the rest of the county endures snowfall, was covered. Dr Middleton, assisting Malcolm MacDonald, was warned that snowdrifts would make it impossible for him to return to his home on the Black Isle and he had to remain overnight in Dingwall.[314] An inch of snow fell on Dingwall in an hour and snow continued intermittently throughout the day, gradually coalescing into the worst blizzard to hit the county in years. Snow lay thick on the mountains and glens and in the towns and villages.

The *Inverness Courier* began the day with two letters addressing Randolph Churchill's behaviour. They were not flattering. A letter from 'Mulbuie' took Churchill's 'unexampled insolence' to task, berating him for the content of his personal attacks and drawing parallels between the relationship of Churchills father and son and MacDonalds father and son. Winston Churchill's chequered Parliamentary career was drawn into question in the context of 'Want-to-get-into-Parliamentarians', casting Randolph Churchill's phrase back at him; Churchill's charge of nepotism against MacDonald Junior would hold greater weight if Churchill himself didn't trade on the family name; and if MacDonald was 'foisted' upon the constituency, did not the revelation that Lady Houston was sponsoring Churchill's candidacy suggest the same thing?[315] All three charges are probably good examples of 'whataboutery' but they had a ring of truth about them.

A second letter, from 'Clan Donald', described Churchill's campaign as 'ludicrous', drawing the parallel with his candidacy in Wavertree 'as an opponent of Socialism' which succeeded only in getting the Socialist elected. Churchill had come to the Highlands equipped, '[n]ot with much mature political experience, but that Churchillian bravado and impertinence which doubtless will sway some of the lighter heads in the constituency'. The county's task was 'plain and simple' and Randolph Churchill played no part in it.[316]

Not content with correspondence, the Inverness Courier carried another of its leader columns. Less vitriolic than previously – *What was there left to say?* – it nonetheless proceeded to skewer Churchill. Referring to his speech at Fearn, the paper commented that he was a man who, by his own confession, had little knowledge of agriculture and whose only assets were some talent for controversy and agitation. "If that is not humbugging the electors we do not know what is', it said, adding that knowledge of agriculture was exactly the skill that the electors of the constituency required.[317]

Perhaps sensing that his son's campaign was not going entirely to plan, Winston Churchill wrote to his wife, Clementine, suggesting it would be 'convenient' for him to remain in Marrakech as long as possible. 'Emphasise I am taking no part in Randolph's campaign', he explained.[318] Even his most doughty supporter was distancing himself, then. Indeed, it is noticeable how little support Churchill received during the campaign, which he fought almost single-handedly. This has caused Ewan Cameron to speculate, probably correctly, that people were warned off supporting him. Cameron suggests as proof that none of the usual right-wing clique that had formed around Winston Churchill, like the Duchess of Atholl or Bob Boothby, spoke in the constituency.[319]

Socialist Travails

Hector McNeil's heroic struggle against weather and topography continued. He told *The Observer* that at times his entourage had had to thread their way over sheep tracks, during which time the only life they came across was herds of deer. On one occasion his car was attacked by a stag.[320]

His itinerary was so upset by the road conditions he was generally greatly delayed in his speaking engagements. Travelling from Gairloch to

Ullapool, he was forced to make a 50 mile detour.[321] He described a hair-raising experience to the *Manchester Guardian* on a steep mountain road between Gairloch and Poolewe. They came to a halt once more because of the mass of snow in front of them, only for one of their cars to begin to slide backwards downhill. The road was a shelf cut into the mountainside, with only a parapet of turf on the far side protecting them from the precipice. If the car picked up enough speed to break through the parapet, they would have plunged into the loch below. Arthur Woodburn jumped out of the car and pressed himself against it, trying to slow its progress. He was pushed towards the parapet and planted his feet against the turf to maintain a hold and in this way managed to halt the car while the driver found a boulder to place under one of the rear tyres to use as a block. The whole party gathered bunches of heather to spread across the road so that the car's wheels might bite and, slowly, nerve-rackingly, they managed to extricate themselves and carry on their journey.[322]

McNeil finally reached his destination late into the night and it was a little before midnight before he finished his speech. To his credit, and to the credit of the electors, he addressed a large and receptive audience. Presumably to his great relief, his tour of the West concluded and he made his way back to Dingwall. Unfortunately for him, the worst of the snow had already preceded him.[323]

In his paper on the campaign, Ewan Cameron reported that MacDonald told his father he would focus his attention on Hector McNeil:

> From now on I shall take very little notice of Churchill and keep drumming the fact that the fight is between McNeal (*sic*) and me.[324]

This could be seen on the campaign trail today, when McNeil was the focus of MacDonald's addresses. MacDonald made two speeches, in Mulbuie and Maryburgh, both of which, despite the weather, were in front of large crowds. He declared that the fight was between him and McNeil. Any other candidates, 'however many they may be and however they describe themselves, would be also-rans'. A great peal of laughter arose when a voice from the audience shouted, 'Also-Ran-dolphs'.[325]

MacDonald had a great respect for his Labour opponent's ability, he said, but there were elements of his speeches which required clarification. He said he was in favour of farmers and crofters receiving a minimum price of 50 shillings per live hundredweight for meat. 'That is an admirable sentiment', said MacDonald, but what Ross and Cromarty's farmers and crofters would want to know was how he proposed to give it to them. The Labour Party, of which he was a member, opposed the National Government's scheme. Mr McNeil previously seemed to do so, too. MacDonald flourished one of McNeil's leaflets from the general election and read from it: 'But for tariffs and quotas the cost of living would have been halved.' So he didn't believe in subsidies a few weeks before, MacDonald said. How, when his party's policy was against subsidies, and he would be expected to follow the party Whip, would he go about providing the subsidy he now claimed to support? 'His declaration in favour of a minimum price of 50 shillings remains a mere pious sentiment', MacDonald concluded.

The Scotsman noted, admiringly:

> There is nothing flamboyant about Mr MacDonald's style, and his political capacity, courtesy, and modest bearing have favourably impressed his fellow Highlanders.[326]

Matthew Halton, the Europe correspondent of the *Toronto Star*, also picked up on MacDonald's manner. Comparing him to Randolph Churchill ('he has personality, wit and oratorical ability; but he's a bit venomous'), Halton considered MacDonald hadn't half the personality, but 'he is sane, courteous, intelligent, without his father's vanity and sentimentality; and he is able. He is pretty certain to win the seat'.[327]

Support from Brazil

'Mr Churchill had a comparatively quiet day', the *Press and Journal* reported, again. He had spent the afternoon 'attending to his correspondence, including many congratulatory messages, one of them from a young woman in Brazil who wanted his photograph'.[328] It is perhaps unsurprising that the vain Churchill might have released that particular titbit to the press.

Afterwards, he arrived in Tain with a loudspeaker and addressed an open-air meeting in the snow. *The Scotsman* noted the effect of this

Churchill Meets Some Farm Hands
photo: Aberdeen Press and Journal

'modern electioneering device' with its 'long-range capacity'. It concluded: 'Before the contest is over [Churchill's] voice will be heard booming in the villages and the glens'.[329]

Whether that would be a good thing or not, the paper did not say but, perhaps stung by Churchill's criticism that they had accused him of personal attacks when he had done no such thing, they concentrated on the 'constitutional niceties"' which were being widely debated in the campaign:

The deferential respect [Churchill] is paying here to constitutional purity… would probably carry much greater conviction among quiet-thinking people in the county if it were not common knowledge that, as a rebel Unionist, he deliberately flouted the decision of the Wavertree Unionist Association himself last year, and through his independent candidature helped to make a temporary gift of the seat to the Socialists.[330]

The contrast being suggested by *The Scotsman* between the 'modest' and 'courteous' MacDonald and the rebellious, intemperate Churchill is clear for anyone to infer.

Although Churchill's activity may seem less frenetic than the other candidates, he had a strategy. In a letter to his father, he wrote, 'I have not attempted to organise the West Coast, but am concentrating all my efforts on the 20,000 voters in the East'. This seemed a sensible approach, and it is debateable how much the efforts to reach those in the West by MacDonald and McNeil actually achieved. Churchill went on. 'The electorate, as a whole, are by no means as dour as I had anticipated. The Highlander is a very different cup of tea from the Lowlander.' It is probably fortunate that this opinion remained out of the public domain for the duration.[331]

Randolph might have felt less sanguine had he seen a telegram sent to Winston Churchill that day by Brendan Bracken on the progress of the by-election: 'Randolph's prospects very doubtful. Socialist win probable. More stags than Tories in Cromarty'.[332] Winston, already resolved to remain aloof from his son's campaign, was no doubt further persuaded that Marrakech was the place to be.

Meanwhile, the independent Liberals' psychodrama showed no sign of abating, as they continued their search for a candidate – any candidate – who would be willing to stand for them. It should be noted, however, this was not entirely unusual. I G C Hutchison pointed out that, during the 1920s and 1930s, the Liberals did encounter great difficulty in finding candidates, and then in funding them.[333] During the day, Ranald Findlay and Dr Stoner of Brighton, a 'strong Liberal sympathiser', were seen to head out on a 'mysterious mission'. In Dingwall, there were 'whispered hotel conferences', one of which was so secret that it took place behind locked doors. The *Dundee Courier* discovered that telephone calls had been made to London.[334] All of this activity pointed to the conclusion that there would indeed be an independent Liberal candidate after all. But who?

Two new names emerged. Captain A R McDougal of Lauder was well-known in Scottish Liberal circles and had contested Roxburgh and Selkirk at the general election (inevitably losing). At the invitation of Ranald Findlay, there was talk he might arrive in the constituency the next day. The *Press and Journal* considered McDougal, who had written a number of pamphlets on agricultural problems, to be the likely candidate.[335]

The second name to emerge was Dr W S Russell Thomas of London, who contested (and lost) Central Aberdeenshire in the general election. However, Thomas said he had not been asked to stand and the *Press and Journal* thought his name had cropped up 'as a result of a misunderstood telegram'.[336] Given the way their search had gone so far, a betting man would imagine Thomas was now a shoo-in for the role.

While, as the *Press and Journal* described it, 'the flickering torch of independent Liberal prospects in the Ross and Cromarty by-election still lives', there was, of course, a central contradiction in their approach. The whole reason the independent Liberals were exercised in the first place was that an outsider was being foisted on them. Now, in their increasingly frenetic search for a candidate, they were in danger of doing exactly the same thing.

The day was ended by news which, although no one could know it, would have considerable repercussions for the by-election. The first intimation that the King was ill had come early in the day, with the *Edinburgh Evening News* reporting that he was confined to his room with a cold. 'It is not regarded as in any way serious', it said.[337] However, at 11.15pm, a bulletin was issued by the King's doctors, Sir Frederic Willans, Sir Stanley Hewett and Lord Dawson of Penn:

> The bronchial catarrh from which his Majesty the King is suffering is not severe, but there have appeared signs of cardiac weakness which must be regarded with some disquiet.[338]

What impact this might have on the by-election nobody could yet ascertain.

✡ ✡ ✡

Saturday, 18 January 1936

White-Out, Black-outs, Three Acres and a Cow, Then Disaster

During the weekend a snowstorm hit all of Scotland that was particularly severe in the North. In some areas, over a foot of snow fell and snow drifts of six feet were reported. Roads were blocked and telephone and telegraph communications were affected by fallen wires. Power was lost in many areas. An Aberdeen trawler ran ashore between Roseharty and Fraserburgh and the crew had to be rescued. There were many road traffic accidents. Rescue missions were launched for people who had gone missing as they tried to walk home.[339] As any sensible Scot knew, this was weather for staying indoors.

A little importunate weather was not going to deter the actors in this strangest of by-elections, though. It is true that Hector McNeil, exhausted by days of trudging through snow in the west of the constituency, retreated to Glasgow for a prearranged preaching engagement, but his campaign continued without him. Barbara Woodburn, wife of Arthur, was canvassing in Dingwall, while Arthur spoke to a gathering in Garve. During his talk, he briefly mentioned the illness of the King and an audience member proposed they

Mrs Woodburn
photo: Aberdeen Press and Journal

should stand to sing the national anthem. They did.[340]

The Scotsman began the week with another editorial examining the two Scottish by-elections. Opinion was settling, it thought, and it was likely that on polling day the electors would rally to the National Government candidates. Nonetheless, it suggested Malcolm MacDonald may have a stiff fight in Ross and Cromarty. Support traditionally granted to Sir Ian Macpherson would now be split three or four ways, to the likely benefit of the Socialist candidate.

It recognised the dilemma faced by the independent Liberals in this, traditionally Liberal seat. If, as they did, they saw themselves as the body representative of Scottish Liberalism, then they would feel it incumbent on them to stand in the election. 'They may well feel that it would be nobler to go down fighting than not to fight at all'.[341] Alas, even at this early stage in the campaign the runes were certainly casting themselves in just such a configuration.

Saturday was another challenging day for the independent Liberals, a 'fiasco' according to *The Scotsman*. Early that morning Ranald Findlay stated that Captain A R McDougal of Lauder would be their candidate (as he had previously, with Provost Smith). McDougal was due to arrive in Invergordon on Monday, where he would be adopted in private before beginning his campaign that evening.[342] Before the day was out, however, Captain McDougal had changed his mind. 'The independent Liberal moves have become so mystifying that one can venture to say little more than that at present Capt McDougal's name has been eliminated', *The Scotsman* explained wearily.[343]

It is perhaps a pity that McDougal was lost to the campaign. A farmer and politician, he was a deep thinker on agricultural policy. Arguing in 1931 against state subsidies or doles, he suggested instead that:

> rents must come down instead of taxes on food prices going up. We farmers have the best markets at our doors; shackled by landlordism, antiquated leases and sporting rights, we must irrevocably remain a depressed industry. [344]

His points were still valid in 1936 and remained valid until the war changed the agricultural industry.

Ranald Findlay's list of possible candidates was 'diminished, though not yet exhausted', according to *The Scotsman*. Even if they should finally obtain a candidate, it would 'scarcely be other than an anti-climax to the involved manoeuvres of the last fortnight'.[345] However, the *Dundee Courier* believed this juncture marked the end of the independents' search for a candidate.[346] Later, the *Sunday Pictorial* offered an explanation for Captain McDougal's change of heart. 'I cannot find the time', he said.[347]

And, with that, the independent Liberals were back where they started.

Randolph Churchill demonstrated his exuberant spirits by joining a snowball fight outside the National Hotel. 'It was not his opposition to the National candidate which accounted for his participation', *The Scotsman* suggested, 'but rather the Churchillian disposition to sail into battle if it is not a "private fight"'. Bus drivers and conductors and press men were among the combatants, and 'Mr Churchill seemed to enjoy himself immensely'.[348]

Glamour and Fury

After these exploits, the greatest political excitement of the day was created later by Randolph Churchill's open meeting in Dingwall town hall. The hall was full within minutes of the doors opening and hundreds were unable to gain admission, being forced to wait until the conclusion of the meeting when Churchill would come outside and address them. 'The youth of Dingwall', declared *The Scotsman*, 'female and male, was well represented in the audience' for Churchill's first large-scale public campaign meeting, attracted by the 'unusual element of glamour' he brought to proceedings.[349]

It proved to be a rambunctious occasion, Churchill alternately infuriating and delighting the audience, basking in applause and battling jeers. The most confrontational moment came when he launched a personal attack on the 'strange activities' of the 'remarkable' Sir William Martineau:

> He presided over a meeting which unanimously rejected Mr MacDonald. He indicated to Conservatives that he had in mind a very suitable Unionist candidate, and when pressed for his identity coyly admitted that it was no other than his own son. This, mark you, was many days after the Government had indicated that they would like to see Mr MacDonald returned for Ross and Cromarty. Then he went to London, charged by his own Association to interview the Co-ordinating Committee and ask them to propose an alternative candidate whom the Unionist Association could support. As soon as he reached London the conversion came upon him. None can tell by what charms and blandishments he was induced to change his mind and abandon the trust imposed upon him by his Association. Suffice it to say that he telegraphed his resignation and threw in his hand.
>
> He then returned to Dingwall and used all his influence to reverse the decision which he had previously supported, and did all in his power to 'pack' the meeting to carry it his way. I advisedly say 'pack,' because he wrote to the newspapers and encouraged all patriotic Unionists to come along to the meeting, even if they were not members of the Association in order that they could vote me down and vote for the candidate they had already twice rejected. [They had, in fact, rejected MacDonald three times.][350]

The audience was already uneasy by this point. Martineau was well-known in Dingwall and this sort of low-personality politics was uncommon in this most conservative constituency. Churchill now went too far, claiming that Martineau had become the lone Unionist 'sugar daddy' of Malcolm MacDonald. There was an immediate uproar. Boos rang out and shouts of 'No personalities' went up. A couple of minutes elapsed before he could proceed. A wily political operator, however, Churchill managed to win back the audience. He asked if they were not to be allowed to have some good-natured fun in this election. 'I have some facts to give', he said, 'and I hope that a few sensible jokes will make the facts all the more palatable'. He claimed the right to have a few wisecracks, 'particularly on a Saturday night'. This sort of bluff bonhomie, the 'I'm just an ordinary bloke you'd like to spend an evening in the pub with', helps people seem more relatable, even though the truth of their natures is entirely different.

It was becoming a freak election, Churchill said, made so by the National Government candidate. This was the trigger for his next character assassination, inevitably of Malcolm MacDonald. 'I am afraid I have got to make one or two observations about Mr Malcolm MacDonald', he said, 'and I appeal to anyone who is squeamish to leave the hall'. When in London he called himself a member of the National Labour Party but now he was in Ross and Cromarty he styled himself a National Government supporter. 'Does he still believe in Socialism?' Churchill asked.

Referring to the Covenant of the League of Nations and the collective peace system, Churchill said he subscribed to those doctrines. Where did MacDonald stand on the collective peace system? 'He was a member of the Cabinet which endorsed the Hoare-Laval peace plan, under which aggression was going to be made extremely profitable'. Sir Samuel Hoare, who negotiated the disgraced plan, was 'compelled to resign by the force of public opinion'. Why did MacDonald not resign? he asked. Did he have no pride?[351] No, he was 'party to the iniquitous transaction' which would have handed over nearly one-half of Abyssinia to Mussolini's Fascists.

> Did Mr MacDonald say this was a breach of the League West Covenant? Did he say that aggression should not be permitted to pay? Not at all. I thought the Liberals cared for the League of Nations. Perhaps I am wrong. Perhaps all they care about is pleasing the Central Office of the Conservative Party.[352]

On agriculture, which MacDonald had been promoting heavily as a key campaign issue, Churchill went on the offensive. A levy system was the only hope of making cattle-raising competitive without the consumer having to pay an exorbitant price. But MacDonald was a member of a government which made that impossible because our hands were tied by the trade agreements we entered into with the Argentine.

> It is very easy for Mr MacDonald to come here and promise a levy. Why did he not support it when he had the opportunity?

He again burnished his rebel credentials. 'I don't want to represent Mr Baldwin in the House of Commons', he said, 'I want to represent Ross and Cromarty'. Asked if he would accept the government whip he said he would, but added:

> I shall regard my first duty as being to my constituents, my second duty to the Unionist party, and my third to the Government. You don't want your representative to be a mere voting machine.

He heatedly denied having anything to do with the distribution of leaflets in the constituency containing an attack by Lady Houston on Ramsay and Malcolm MacDonald. A persistent heckler said the men who distributed them were paid at Churchill's office. Churchill rose angrily:

> There are evidently some people here who are disposed to believe any lie which they think will injure me. That is the sort of propaganda stuff that is pushed out to deceive people like you.

He spoke about 'filthy insinuations' being made. When one of the men accused of distributing the leaflets was brought on stage, he roundly denied being in the pay of Churchill's campaign. As it happens, in her biography of Lady Houston, Teresa Crompton confirms that the payment had originated with her and therefore, by extension, her candidate Churchill.[353]

When he had finished his speech in the town hall, Churchill went outside to an open-air meeting at the National Hotel. He refused a car and rushed down the High Street, at times sliding on the frozen snow like a schoolboy, followed by a crowd of one hundred or so, all shouting and laughing. From a wooden box in the street, Churchill spoke into his megaphone for half an hour, bareheaded despite the falling snow.[354] Finally, as *The Scotsman* described it as a 'bout of heckling ended one of the liveliest political Saturday nights in the history of Dingwall'.[355]

Two letters, in different newspapers, offered contrasting studies of the election campaign. First, in the *Press and Journal*, a letter-writer styling himself 'Dependent on Agriculture' stressed the importance of agriculture to Ross and Cromarty and bemoaned the weakness of the government's interventions to date:

> The ploughman's vote will be for Mr Churchill on the question of agriculture, not on the question of the ethics of the election. That is a minor point to most of us, although so much importance has been given to it in the Press.[356]

In truth, this letter sounds entirely bogus. The formality of the language and the fact it simultaneously raises the question of ethics and declares that ethics are of minor interest suggests that careful thought went into the planting of this particular idea. It is not beyond the realms of possibility that the letter was written by Churchill, or at least originated in his offices.

Highland Tradition

A letter in *The Scotsman* from 'Old Fearnite' offered more insightful fare:

> To those who really know the traditional Radical political sympathies of Easter Ross, the mixed reception accorded Mr Randolph Churchill at the first meeting of his campaign at Fearn will occasion no surprise.[357]

Easter Ross was particularly fertile land, he wrote, comparing favourably with the best in the Lothians. Apart from the fishing villages around the coast, agriculture was the main industry; the bulk of the population comprised ploughmen and agricultural workers. He went on:

> For generations there has been a strong Radical tradition, dating back from before the time when agricultural workers got the vote and the Collings campaign for three acres and a cow.358 At this time, the clearances in the neighbouring county were still in living memory and, consequently, landlordism was highly unpopular, giving an added touch of bitterness to the conservative radicalism of the residents. I can remember in the nineties witnessing similar political stormy scenes in the same hall where Churchill spoke.
>
> Looking back over more than forty years, I cannot but think that the one or two Easter Ross farmers were singularly ill-advised in bringing this brilliant scion of the house of Marlborough to open his campaign amidst such surroundings. The action reveals a total lack of knowledge of

political tradition in, apart from politics, a strongly conservative county, and an equal lack of psychological understanding. Big farming interests are represented by few voters as compared with the agricultural workers.

The odds against Mr Randolph Churchill are heavy indeed.

The letter raised an important historical point for this Highland constituency. Over many years, there had been protests across the Highlands against landlordism and the iniquitous rents and conditions imposed on crofters. Skye was a particular hotbed of activism but disputes arose across the Highlands, including Easter and Wester Ross and Dingwall. By the 1880s, there was a growing feeling that crofters and cottars in the Highlands were a special case because of the history of the clearances. T M Devine explains that 'Gladstone argued that the people had a historic right to the land which had been expropriated from them by commercial proprietors in the eighteenth and nineteenth centuries. The crofters had suffered a profound injustice, which should be redressed by parliament'. The Third Reform Act in 1884 granted the franchise to all male householders and an unintended consequence of this was that, in 1885, the Crofters' Party, the political wing of the Highland Land League, won five Parliamentary seats, including Roderick Macdonald in Ross and Cromarty. Land was becoming a significant issue. A Royal Commission was established to examine the condition of crofters and cottars and reported in 1884, leading to the Crofters' Holding Act in 1886, which curtailed landlord powers and provided small tenants with security of tenure and fair rent charges. Initially, there was a strong feeling that the Act did not go far enough, in particular, because it gave only minor concessions to crofters' demands for more land and did nothing to alleviate the condition of cottars or the landless. This led to ongoing unrest across the Highlands, what became known as the Crofters' War, which Devine describes as an 'effective political campaign for crofters' rights with a high-profile series of acts of resistance, of which the refusal to pay rents and the "trading" of old lands were the most significant'. Over time, the Act was reassessed and generally considered to have been favourable, but unrest continued well into the 1890s, as described by 'Old Fearnite'.[359]

His skewering of the sensibilities being exhibited by Churchill and his small entourage – blithely coming in and using techniques and arguments alien to the constituency – very accurately summed up the hubris of their entire campaign.

Malcolm MacDonald was making a better fist of things, showing a clearer understanding of Ross-shire politics and community. In a meeting in Ullapool, taking Hector McNeil's campaigning issue of the importance of developing tourism by improving roads and building hotels, MacDonald agreed that greater efforts could be made to improve tourism. He would, however, 'deplore it' if the Highlands were to become a 'mere playground or health resort for visitors from the South'.[360] Tourism should only be seen as a sideline from their main activity.

Depopulation of the area had to be checked and prosperity returned, he said, but that should be facilitated through a revival of fishing and agriculture. Road development and improvements were essential not for tourists, but for fishermen, crofters, farmers and farm servants. One wonders what he would think of the North Coast 500, the modern marketing of the 516-mile round journey through the north of Scotland as 'one of the world's most beautiful road trips'.[361]

Disaster

The meeting in Ullapool was a great success but disaster was about to befall MacDonald. At the end of the meeting, a large crowd gathered outside the hall and he was hoisted shoulder-high once more (three-one to MacDonald) and, led by a brace of pipers, a procession made off through the streets. As earlier in Dingwall with Randolph Churchill, some good-natured snowballing began. There was a small element of opposition to MacDonald among the crowd but *The Scotsman* was at pains to record that 'there was no suggestion of unfriendliness in the exchanges'.[362]

However, while he was hoisted on the backs of his supporters and holding on to their shoulders, MacDonald was hit full in the face by a snowball. Unable to protect himself he was struck in the right eye and his spectacles were broken, the splintered glass cutting his nose and entering his eye. He was taken to a nearby hotel where Dr Middleton provided immediate first aid while they waited for the local GP, Dr Wallace, to arrive. Wallace dressed MacDonald's injured eye and, although in pain and suffering shock, MacDonald embarked on the 40-mile trip back to his hotel in Dingwall, arriving just after midnight. This must have been a fraught and painful journey, the freezing and slippery roads making driving difficult and the inevitable jolts and judders in a car without modern suspension would surely have caused incessant pain to his eye.[363]

At this point, it was decided to summon an eye specialist from Inverness and, a little after two in the morning, MacDonald was inspected by Dr Theodore Chalmers. His diagnosis was that the cornea had sustained a few abrasions but there was no sign of serious damage. MacDonald was moved to St Margaret's nursing home in Inverness, accompanied by his sister, Sheila. On Dr Chalmers' recommendation, it was agreed he should remain there for two days and would not resume campaigning until a few days later.

The campaign would continue, of course, and an impressive roster of speakers had already been lined up, including Colonel John Colville MP, Under Secretary of State for Scotland; W J Anstruther Gray, Unionist MP for North Lanark; Earl de La Warr, Parliamentary Secretary to the Board of Education and chairman of the National Socialist Party; Geoffrey Shakespeare MP and Sir Murdoch Macdonald, Liberal National MP.

MacDonald issued a statement apologising to electors on the West Coast for missing the arranged meetings. Quoting Andrew Bartin in the old Scots ballad, he said:

> I am a little wounded but not slain
> I will but rest a while, then rise to fight again.[364]

Although MacDonald was now seemingly incapacitated for some days, news of the King could potentially render that insignificant. On Saturday morning, it was reported that the anxiety described the previous evening still persisted. By afternoon, his 'cardiac weakness and the embarrassment of the circulation' had slightly increased and was giving cause for anxiety. No change was recorded in a statement at 10 pm. By Sunday evening, there was still no change in his condition although a meeting of the Privy Council had been called for Monday. This, according to *The Scotsman*:

> should not necessarily be regarded as an indication that there is any grave change or that any such change is expected in the King's condition, but rather as meaning that the King's illness is likely to be prolonged.

Counsellors of State would be empowered to act for His Majesty during his illness.[365]

The *Edinburgh Evening News*, too, was keen to offer an upbeat assessment of events. While it was reported that oxygen had been administered during the night to the King, it stressed that this had been done on various occasions in the past few years.[366] All the same, although there was little concrete news, it was evident from the way the press was reporting the issue that the matter was serious.

Then, at 9.25 pm, a statement was published: '*The King's life is moving peacefully to its close*'.[367]

✡ ✡ ✡

Monday, 20 January 1936

Convalescence, Death and Mourning in Minus 17

At 9.30 pm the previous evening, five minutes before the statement announcing the approaching death of the King, and just after the Bow Bells signal on the wireless, there was silence until 9.37 pm. Then listeners were advised that an announcement was to be made at 9.38:

> This is London. The King's Life is drawing peacefully to its close...All stations of the British Broadcasting Corporation will now close down until 10pm, when a further announcement will be made.[368]

After a twenty-minute silence, a choir sang the 23rd Psalm and then a clergyman spoke: 'We invite you to join in a recollection and prayer for our King', he said, and a full religious service followed.[369] The country went into mourning.

The King's death was recorded at midnight. We now know that he was euthanised by his physician, Lord Bertrand Dawson, partly to ease his suffering but also to ensure the news could be announced by the morning papers, rather than the 'less appropriate evening journals'.[370]

Aside from the death of the King, the by-election was being massively compromised by the weather. The brutal storm of the weekend continued and, if anything, intensified during Monday, afflicting most of Scotland with, it was generally agreed, some of the worst weather in a generation. On Sunday, a temperature of minus seventeen was registered at Kintore in Aberdeenshire. Throughout the North, prolonged showers of sleet, then snow and, later in the day, heavy rain fell on roads and countryside already inches deep in frozen and compacted snow. Later, gale force winds blew in from the north, making driving conditions exceptionally hazardous. Motorists were reduced to using sledges. Practically every water pump in the village of Inverallochy, near Fraserburgh was frozen. The Dundee to Blairgowrie train disappeared and was finally found stranded ten miles from Dundee, its progress blocked by fallen telephone poles. Several sheep were killed in Lewis when the roof of a partially built school blew off and the walls collapsed on them.[371]

Still, the campaigners campaigned.

Malcolm MacDonald continued his convalescence in the Inverness nursing home. He had a telephone installed by his bedside and in the morning he was in contact with the Dominions Office in London for twenty minutes on 'important matters'. Unable to use his eyes, he dictated his election address.[372] A wireless was also installed.[373] Ironically, this enforced privacy may have been a boon for MacDonald. In a letter written four days previously, his father, Ramsay MacDonald, had asked him if he was still dependent on a telephone in a room open to the public. 'It is very awkward if that be so', he went on, 'because I might want to give you some information of urgent importance and should like to hear from you how things go and what is happening without the delay of postal delivery'.[374]

Meanwhile, his tour of Wester Ross went ahead in his absence, with Dr Middleton leading the team of campaigners on a series of engagements scheduled to last the rest of the week. MacDonald's sister, Sheila, was canvassing in Dingwall and in the evening she addressed a women's meeting in the Temperance Hall. The *Dundee Courier* considered she roused them to a 'tumult of enthusiasm' and was becoming the 'personality of the election'.[375]

For the Socialists, Hector McNeil held meetings in Munlochy, Avoch and Cromarty, raising the issue of meat purity. No doubt, he said, people would want to buy home-produced meat as much as possible, but they were challenged by being unable to tell its provenance. He was therefore proposing that all meat should be properly graded and that shops should clearly distinguish between home- and foreign-produced meats.[376]

Judging by the lack of reporting on his activity, Randolph Churchill appeared to be having another of his quiet days. Perhaps he was busy canvassing support of a different kind, such as the hagiography which appeared in the letters column of *The Scotsman* that morning, from someone named 'Majority', extolling the virtues of the Churchill clan:

> Why is it that a great and distinguished family like the Churchills never seem to get the support from the British public which appears to be their due, considering the immense and valuable service to the State which so many generations of them have given? It appears to me that the public distrust brilliant figures or are shy of placing their faith in men of courage and outspokenness. The great Duke of Marlborough had a tremendous struggle to attain the supreme command of the Army to which his talents entitled him...Lord Randolph suffered a great rebuff while Mr Winston Churchill has always lacked the support which his great gifts and foresight demand. Now Mr Randolph Churchill has inherited the enmity of the public which seems to follow his line. He is dubbed a 'young man in a hurry.' It appears to me to be a cause of concern that there are not more young men of his calibre in a hurry. Mr Winston Churchill has often been taunted with his change of party, but Emerson, by his interpretation of inconsistency, has given the answer to that taunt when he said 'a foolish consistency is the hobgoblin of little minds'.[377]

The desire to pepper their prose with allusions to great literature is a feature of a certain class of politicians, from Randolph Churchill in the 1930s to the present day. The grand display of learning often conceals an acute paucity of thought. Again, one is left to muse on the identity of the writer 'Majority' who seemed so concerned by the serial slights inflicted on the Churchill clan and ~~on~~ Randolph in particular.

By far the most significant movers of the day were the independent

Liberals, as their seemingly forlorn campaign to find a candidate took one final, wholly unexpected turn, with the announcement that a candidate had been found who had agreed to stand.

The Scotsman maintained its tone of world-weary detachment in describing the travails of the independent Liberals:

> Nothing can now be regarded as very surprising in this by-election...but the appearance on the scene of Dr Thomas at least ranks with the more remarkable episodes of the contest. He was almost smuggled into the county.[378]

Town Crier
photo: *Aberdeen Press and Journal*

Suspicions were first aroused in Dingwall early in the morning, when a run of small handbills was printed by a local printer, announcing that Liberal candidature meetings would be addressed by Dr Russell Thomas and Richard Ellis tonight in Invergordon, Evanton and Alness. Announced by a bellman, the handbills were distributed in the deserted and snow-covered streets of Invergordon.[379] 'Come in your thousands', the bellman yelled optimistically to a town with a population of 1714.[380] Later in the morning, Ranald Findlay was reported to have travelled to Dingwall through the middle of a storm.[381] Something did seem to be happening.

A group of thirteen independent Liberals met in private. Three of the thirteen were 'visitors from outside the constituency' and only three were electors.[382] The meeting lasted just two minutes and Ranald Findlay emerged to tell the waiting reporters that Dr W S Russell Thomas had been adopted as their candidate for the election. Thomas's name had cropped up before, at the same time as Captain McDougal's name was being touted as the likely saviour, but this had been thought to be an error.[383] Now, he had been adopted. There was a sense of desperation surrounding the proceedings. The *Daily Mail*'s Percy Cater was scathing, describing the adoption event as 'the most secret public meeting that I have ever known'. He described the removal to Invergordon as 'the retreat from Dingwall'. It was, he said, 'carried out in blinding snow, which made the retreat from Moscow like something on the films'.[384]

Dr Thomas was an old-school Liberal of the Welsh firebrand variety. He had figured in a similar scenario during the recent general election when he stood as an independent in Central Aberdeenshire in defiance of the wishes of the main body of the Liberal Association. He was soundly defeated by Sir Robert Smith, the sitting Unionist member, coming third behind Labour and seeing the Liberal share of the vote drop by 21 per cent. In the 1931 election, he lost in Ilford, Essex, again coming third behind the Conservatives and Labour, and seeing the vote share drop by 22 per cent.[385]

Dr Russell Thomas
photo: Creative Commons

Dr Middleton was furious, issuing a scabrous statement aimed at Ranald Findlay:

> To the intense surprise of the Ross and Cromarty Liberals the general secretary of the Federation made his appearance in Dingwall and, without the slightest consultation, either with myself or the local secretary, proceeded to attempt to cause a division among the Liberals of the county.
>
> After what can only be described as hawking the independent Liberal candidature around, he at length secured a possible nominee. But the meeting which was held for the purpose of adopting him was a fiasco. It can only result in permanent harm to the name of Liberalism, not only in Ross and Cromarty, but over the whole country.[386]

Speaking to reporters in Invergordon, Findlay offered a resolute defence of his decision:

> The tactics adopted by the supporters of the National candidate at last Wednesday's meeting at Dingwall stiffened the resistance of loyal Liberals. It is high time we got back to clean politics. The Liberal campaign opens tonight according to schedule.[387]

Since the campaign had already been running for some eighteen days, the independent Liberals' schedule appeared to have had built in quite a significant contingency.

Nonetheless, they were now in the campaign and, in abysmal weather, Dr Thomas held the three meetings as promised. Between 40 and 50 attended at Evanton but, *The Scotsman* noted, the audience was not greatly enthused by the doctor's 'fiery Welsh eloquence'. Perhaps, it ruminated, the crushing cold inside the hall and the blizzard outside had a dispiriting effect.

'I do not want to enter into personalities', Dr Thomas said. 'I am not here to indulge in the mud-slinging which has been going on', he continued, before loading his sling with a handful of mud and taking aim. 'I won't say much about Mr Randolph Churchill. He stands for nothing except the recklessness for which the Churchills always stand.'[388] He went on:

> Liberalism is a great faith, often greater than its professors. Sometimes those professors are weak, and like dogs will turn away with their tails between their legs, but it is they who are at fault, not the Liberalism. Two schoolboys have been hammering at each other for weeks past, one of them adopted by an Association which has belied the name of the Liberal Party. You have a Liberal Association which adopts a man who, in the past, was devoted to Socialism. That sticks in my gullet. That man is no better than a camouflaged Tory.[389]
>
> I am not a Scotsman. I am a Welshman, first cousin to the Highlander and we, as Welshmen, have Liberalism running through our veins, and you in this election must decide that this National ramp [a swindle or a scam] is a farce and nothing more than political jobbery.[390]

So the independent Liberals were finally in the campaign, and 'on schedule'. Alas for them, their schedule coincided with an enforced and almost immediate cessation of activity. The front page of *The Scotsman* that morning contained a small box on the right-hand side bearing the headline 'Death of the King'.[391] News never appeared on the front page of *The Scotsman*, devoted as it was to small ads. This was an early indicator of the enormous impact the King's death would have across the country for the next week. Theatres and cinemas closed. Shops kept their blinds down. Many citizens wore mourning black.

In this mood, it was inevitable that the by-election campaign would have to be halted. Malcolm MacDonald's agent contacted the agents of the other candidates to call a truce in campaigning, although the by-election, by law, would have to continue as normal.[392]

And so, it seemed that everything was about to come to a halt.

✡ ✡ ✡

Tuesday, 22 January 1936

Car Crashes, a Scandal, a Writ and a Truce (Supposedly)

It is probably fair to say the prospect of a truce would have offered a welcome respite to Hector McNeil and his Socialist colleagues who, throughout the campaign, appeared to fare worst in the inclement weather. Late Monday and the early hours of Tuesday saw them reach their nadir. *For now, anyway.*

The storm continued unabated and conditions remained dangerous. In places, snowdrifts were so deep that even after a full day's effort snowploughs could not cut a path further than a few miles, leaving many towns and villages cut off. There was a complete breakdown of bus and telephone services in Moray and Banff. Telegrams had to be sent by bus or train to Perth to be forwarded. In Speyside, snowploughs proved wholly inadequate against drifts formed by a 60 mph gale, gusting to up to 80 mph. Further snow fell during the day, although there was a thaw later. Even that left the roads in a dangerous condition.[393]

Through this, Hector McNeil and his colleagues continued to wage their campaign. Heading back to Dingwall from the Black Isle in a raging blizzard, McNeil's car was held up near Munlochy by a deep snowdrift. Two horses had to be hired from a nearby farm to release him.

Meanwhile Arthur Woodburn's party drove their car into a ditch on the road to Cromarty. By chance, Randolph Churchill was passing on his way to a meeting and sportingly tried to free their vehicle but all efforts failed. Churchill carried on to his appointment but telephoned Dingwall to arrange help. Woodburn trudged three miles through the blizzard to find a house from where he could make a telephone call. One or both of these telephone calls proved fruitful and a crane was sent out to retrieve the car and its freezing passengers.

On returning to Dingwall around midnight, Woodburn and his entourage learned that McNeil was missing. Although frozen and in poor spirits, the men formed a search party and set out with shovels and refreshments. Unfortunately, they quickly became trapped in a 5 ft snowdrift from which it took three hours to extricate themselves. They returned to Dingwall, defeated, and found McNeil recently arrived, safe and well. Had they known it, the two groups were only about 400 yards apart.[394]

McNeil's ordeal was not over, however. On arriving in Dingwall, he was advised that early next morning he, Randolph Churchill and Dr Thomas were to travel to Inverness to meet with Malcolm MacDonald in his nursing home to discuss the possibility of a truce in the by-election. That gave him only two or three hours of sleep. They arrived at St Margaret's Nursing Home around midday and the four candidates argued for two hours without reaching a consensus.

Sheila MacDonald noted in her diary how heated this meeting became. From downstairs, she could hear Randolph Churchill's voice getting louder and louder. When he emerged from the meeting he exclaimed, 'Malcolm is an obstinate pig', before rushing out. The meeting had turned into a brawl, with Churchill interrupting Malcolm three times before Malcolm could finish reading his draft statement. Churchill then accused Malcolm of 'making political capital out of the King's death'.[395]

The candidates could agree that campaigning should cease, but the length of the truce was in dispute. MacDonald wanted it to hold until after the King's funeral the following Tuesday, while the others thought this too long. In a leader entitled 'A Scandalous Report', the *Inverness Courier* lambasted the political machinations at play during and after these discussions.

Outside the Nursing Home in Inverness
photo: *Aberdeen Press and Journal*

While they were taking place, a rumour began to circulate that, although the other three candidates were willing to proclaim a truce until after the late King's funeral, Malcolm MacDonald had disagreed. 'There is not a vestige of truth in this report', the paper stated. Indeed, it was 'the precise opposite of what actually occurred'.[396] The other candidates rejected MacDonald's proposal to extend the truce until after the funeral. They instead suggested a truce of two or three days, plus the eve and day of the funeral. MacDonald refused to agree to this arguing it was wrong to electioneer during a period of state mourning. He issued a statement, which made no reference to the other three, leaving them to make their own arrangements. They did so, stating their truce would last until Saturday.[397] When they became aware, however, that public opinion was strongly against campaigning at this time they recanted and fell in line with MacDonald's proposal. The *Inverness Courier* offered no suggestion about who was responsible for spreading the rumour about MacDonald but considered it was 'discreditable in the extreme that such a lying and scandalous report should ever have been circulated'.[398] That may be so, but it does seem in keeping with the tenor of the campaign, and it is hard not to look at the various actors in the drama and leap to a conclusion as to whence the disgraceful report may have emanated.

All four candidates remained keen, however, that the public should have as much opportunity as possible to question them and hear their arguments. Therefore, they contacted Sheriff-Substitute Gillies to request that the election be postponed to as late as the law would permit. Gillies consulted with Sheriff-Principal Mackintosh in Edinburgh, who agreed to extend the date. Consequently, the writ was issued in Dingwall that afternoon, fixing the date for nominations for 31 January and the poll on 10 February, the latest possible date.[399]

Meanwhile, the animosity between the *Inverness Courier* and Randolph Churchill took full form in that morning's paper, with a letter from Churchill attacking the *Courier*'s leader-writer and the *Courier*'s dogged responses. In a letter dated 17 January, Churchill chided the paper, 'You are really very hard to please'. On the accusation that he admitted knowing little of agriculture but agreed he was adept at controversy and agitation, which the *Courier* had described as 'humbugging the electors', he asked how the paper would have responded had he switched the two around so that he knew about agriculture but had no talent for controversy. This is a deflection: by suggesting the opposite claim would be an example of humbugging, the original claim could not also be.

He chose to answer only one of the questions the paper had put to him in its previous leader – whether he believed it was humbug to suggest that Highlanders would resent personal attacks on Mr Malcolm MacDonald. 'No, Sir, I made no such suggestion', he wrote. 'What I did suggest was that it was humbug to pretend that I had made a personal attack on Mr Malcolm MacDonald.' He also denied that he had engaged in mud-slinging, focusing 'chapter and verse, upon his public record'.

He turned to the paper's leader writer, whom he described as 'virile and outspoken'. And who he accused of selecting 'inelegant phrases' ('filthy trail' and 'dunghill') that 'bespatter[ed]' his leader column. 'While I myself would not drape my political thoughts in the verbal instruments favoured by your leader-writer', he wrote, 'I am the first to salute him as a forthright and outspoken campaigner'. This is a particularly snide – and spectacularly spurious, not to mention hypocritical – example of tone policing, using the tone of an argument to dismiss its relevance.[400]

The *Inverness Courier* was having none of it. They published Churchill's letter in full but used their leader column to rebut it. While commending Churchill for his good humour and – unlike some of his supporters who had boycotted the paper – his willingness to engage with them in debate, it said his letter demonstrated how, with 'all the skill and bonhomie of the astute controversialist' he carefully picked only one of the many points the paper had raised against him in their leader and then, just as carefully, avoided the actual point at issue, which was that as someone who admitted he knew little about agriculture, he was unfit to represent an agricultural constituency. The paper took issue, too, with Churchill's reiteration that he had not made any personal attacks on Malcolm MacDonald. It pointed out clearly and concisely what was personal about Churchill's attack:

> [N]o more offensive charge could be levelled against a public man than to declare that he called himself a member of any political party in order that he could get a job.

Churchill's letter, they went on, showed that he could conduct a controversy with good humour and courtesy but 'it would redound to his own credit if he would conduct his election campaign in the same spirit'.[401]

The truth of the matter was, though, that Churchill didn't understand the culture and the community he had become immersed in and was treating the campaign as though he were still at Eton or in the Oxford Union.

Meanwhile, arrangements for the funeral of the King were being finalised. A special order was made by the Privy Council for the proclamation of King Edward VIII across the nation. The terms were notified to Sheriffs of the shires of Scotland and Lord Provosts and Provosts of all Royal, Parliamentary and Police Burghs, with copies of the proclamation and the Order of the Council. Cromarty, Dingwall and Invergordon would read the proclamation at noon on Friday, 24 January.[402]

Let the truce begin.

✡ ✡ ✡

Wednesday, 23 January 1936

When is a Truce Not a Truce? When is a Woman Not a Woman?

With the political truce seemingly holding, the *Press and Journal* considered that Dingwall 'hardly knows itself after the political hotch-potch of the past three weeks'.[403] No meetings were taking place but Randolph Churchill was in Tain and district, calling on supporters and fulfilling a tea party engagement.[404] There appears to be a fine line between 'calling on supporters' and campaigning. In truth, campaign teams remained at work and the truce seemed confined to an absence of public meetings. Dr Thomas was in Invergordon and Herbert McNeil had returned to Glasgow. Malcolm MacDonald remained confined to bed in his nursing home. His eye, though improving, was still inflamed and painful. His intention, eye permitting, was to return home to Lossiemouth on Friday and from there travel to London for the funeral of the King. In this lull, the *Press and Journal* reported:

> [I]t will now be practically impossible for any of the candidates to visit

every portion of the widely scattered constituency as they had originally intended.[405]

Whether this was a disappointment or a relief to the villages and hamlets on the periphery was not considered.

The Role of Women

Willa Muir, in an almost contemporaneous article from 1937, talked about the place of women in Scotland, working class and middle class alike:

> [A] woman's place is still considered to be the actual home. A Scotswoman at a mixed public meeting or on a mixed committee feels that it is not her 'place' to let her voice be heard, and she will not risk speaking up unless she has something very urgent to say.[406]

Sheila MacDonald
photo: Creative Commons

Ishbel MacDonald
photo: Creative Commons

The roles of Sheila and, later, Ishbel MacDonald (plus Marjory Gordon, Morag Edgar, Barbara Woodburn and Katharine Elliot, who we will meet shortly) in Malcolm's campaign are instructive. There were occasions when it was clear they were speaking to women-only gatherings – Sheila on 20 January and 1 February, for example – but on most occasions the meetings were mixed. At that time, this was unusual, particularly in the Highlands of Scotland. It is evident, though, from the high number of letters Malcolm MacDonald received at the end of the campaign which referred to, for example, the 'splendid efforts' of Sheila MacDonald,[407] and 'the splendid advocacy of your charming sisters'[408] that the MacDonald sisters were gifted and personable campaigners.

Barbara Simpson of Hilton in the parish of Fearn, wrote to Malcolm MacDonald to say she had voted for him, having made up her mind 'when Miss Sheila was on her rounds'. She said that she was 42 years old and a mother of nine and it was the first time she had gone to a polling booth, 'so that I will remember my Vote No 366'. She received 16/- per week in groceries from the Parish and 'not one of the bairns is able to get employment and for myself I have worked hard all my life but now I am like a Broken Doll between operations & illness'.[409] It is letters like this, clearly written from the heart, which give a sense of how Sheila must have impressed the locals.

Lest she should let the 'Personality of the election' epithet go to her head, however, Sheila was firmly put back in the woman's place – the home – by the *Dundee Courier*, which recorded, under the heading 'Miss Sheila as Housewife', news that while her brother Malcolm was recuperating at home she would 'become the housewife for the Lossiemouth party. Instead of making speeches to big political gatherings, as she has been doing, she will make scones, cook dinners, and attend to all other household duties'.[410]

You can almost hear the harrumph at breakfast tables throughout Angus as *patresfamilias* gesticulated towards the article and read it aloud to their spouses, braying 'quite right, quite right. Don't want the gels getting ideas above their station'.

Sheila MacDonald, later Lochhead, became a social worker with a particular interest in prison reform, on which she wrote a monograph, *Outside In: A Study of Prison Visiting*. She worked as a classifying officer in Wormwood Scrubs Prison and later became a prison visitor and served as a magistrate. For three years she was chairwoman of the National Association of Prison Visitors.

Ishbel was more politically active than Sheila. She had been Ramsay MacDonald's official hostess in Downing Street during both his spells as Prime Minister and was elected to the London County Council for Bow and Bromley ward in 1928 and again in 1931. When her father formed the coalition government, although Ishbel did not join him in National

Labour she had the whip removed and sat as an Independent Socialist. When Stanley Baldwin called a surprise general election in 1924, Malcolm MacDonald, who had been selected as Labour candidate for Bassetlaw in Nottinghamshire was already engaged on a speaking tour. Ishbel stepped in and campaigned on his behalf and, in an election where nationally the Conservatives scored a massive victory, she reduced the Bassetlaw incumbent's majority to just 1,449, prompting a 'surprised and delighted' Malcolm to suggest his presence would not have improved on the result. That said, she later wrote in an unpublished memoir that she hated the 1924 election and had 'hated every election since'.[411] Perhaps unsurprisingly, then, in 1935 she bought a public house in Buckinghamshire.[412]

These two women, plus Marjory Gordon, Morag Edgar, Barbara Woodburn (or Mrs Arthur Woodburn, as she was called in all the contemporaneous papers) and Katharine Elliott (similarly, Mrs Walter Elliot) battled prejudice and entrenched views to help ensure women's voices – not only theirs but the female electors of Ross and Cromarty, who outnumbered the male – were suitably heard. *We owe these pioneers a debt of gratitude.*

✡ ✡ ✡

Friday, 24 January 1936

Long Live the King (Until December, Anyway) and a Still Small Voice

Cromarty, Dingwall and Invergordon held proclamation ceremonies for the new King, Edward VIII. In Dingwall, sleet fell before and after the ceremony but fortunately held off for the duration of the proclamation. All shops and businesses were closed and a huge crowd gathered in front of the Townhouse. The Seaforth Highlanders and the Territorials were represented, as were the Girl Guides, Boy Scouts, Boys' Brigade and over 700 school children. At noon a cannon was fired from Mitchell Hill and a fanfare was sounded by a lone bugler.

Sheriff Gillies read the proclamation from the balcony, the same text being pronounced across the country, after which the National Anthem was sung and hearty cheers resounded for the new King. A second fanfare and another cannon shot concluded a brief but memorable ceremony.

They would do it all again in December for George VI after the abdication of Edward VIII. *Long live the King.*

Among those on the balcony were Sir Hector Mackenzie of Gairloch, acting Lord Lieutenant, John Stirling of Fairburn, Convenor of Ross County Council, Viscount Tarbat, Lady Marjory Mackenzie and Provost John Macrae, alongside local magistrates and members of Dingwall Town Council, members of Ross County Council and officials of the Town and County Councils.

In addition, because of the by-election, Malcolm MacDonald, newly released from his Inverness nursing home and his sister Sheila, along with Randolph Churchill, Dr Thomas and Alex Matheson, representing Hector McNeil, were in attendance.[413]

Impressions of the Contest

The *Edinburgh Evening News* took advantage of the truce to analyse the campaign progress. It was written by a 'Special Correspondent' who was someone with a long connection with the constituency.[414] He deprecated some of the 'sensational daily newspapers' which had worked up the by-election until, 'like the Loch Ness monster and the Dornoch Church case, it had assumed the proportions of a "stunt"'. Descriptive writers, he said, had been dumped in the constituency with instructions to work the 'job' for all it was worth. The result was that trivial happenings were being magnified and events that in themselves would have 'no bearing whatsoever on the result' were being presented in such a way as to make them appear important.

He referred to the candidature 25 years before of the long-standing member, Sir Ian Macpherson. His initial election, he explained, was by no means guaranteed and he was certainly not the most popular of candidates. 'History is merely repeating itself', he concluded, pointing out that although Macpherson's initial majority was narrow, he became a popular Member. Nonetheless, the embittered feelings that followed Macpherson's election 'were more in evidence than anything I have seen during the present political mix-up'. If that is the case, then the Liberals of the 1910 vintage must indeed have been remarkably obdurate.

He regretted the lack of consultation with Unionists before MacDonald's candidature was agreed but suspected this was only part of the reason for the revolt by the Easter Ross farmers which catapulted Churchill into the fray. The genesis of their discontent could be traced a few years back to the visit of a farmers' deputation to London, which aimed at bolstering agriculture. Ramsay MacDonald was among those who 'gave that deputation short shrift'. We were seeing the product of that in Ross-shire now, where 'the fathers themselves have eaten sour grapes and their teeth are set on edge'.[415]

The so-called revolt, he thought, should not be taken too seriously because at the ballot box, the power of these big farmers counted for very little. Their selection of Randolph Churchill showed:

> [A] woeful lack of vision and understanding, which is just in keeping with their usual everyday conduct. The truth of the matter is that these big farmers have ceased to become farmers and are now mostly dealers in the stock market, and they want the Government to spoon-feed them. But there is also an undercurrent of personal jealousy in the matter, which cannot be enlarged on here.

The most regrettable feature of the campaign, he thought, was the 'pathetic efforts' of the Scottish Liberal Federation to save its face.

> Candidate after candidate, realising the hopelessness of the situation… refused to go forward and in the end we [got] a stranger who possibly knows as little about Ross-shire…as the Conservative candidate.

He predicted that they were 'riding for a very big fall'.

Commenting on changes in the political environment, he suggested, the 'old Radical wing of the Liberal Party…has now gone over almost solidly to Socialism'.

An important pointer to the election result would be the vote in Wester Ross. Here, the older electors were conservative in their Liberalism just as they were conservative in their religion. Wester Ross people seldom moved away from the old traditions. The key to the election, though, was the 'still, small voice' of the average Highland voter, who did not relish clever platform 'slogging'. While he might listen to it and appreciate a point made, it would never influence his vote. By eschewing personalities and focusing on political issues, Malcolm MacDonald was making headway and gaining confidence.

The special correspondent predicted a narrow win for MacDonald over McNeil, with both Churchill and Thomas struggling to save their deposit.

The Dornoch Church Case

The Dornoch dispute arose when Provost John Murray, an elder of the Evelix congregation, was suspended because he allowed his two daughters to sing and dance at home on Christmas Eve. His name was struck off the roll when he declined to appear before the Kirk Session to explain himself. The decision was confirmed by the Northern Presbytery but there was a feeling they had acted unconstitutionally. The case went to a private conference in Glasgow in May 1936.[416]

The *Toronto Star*'s Europe reporter, Matthew Halton, travelled to Ross-shire during the campaign and he mused:

> I remembered that away up north of Dingwall there was a town called Dornoch where the people were reputed to be so holy that on Sunday they closed even the churches.

He was warned off going there, he wrote, because he would be stuck for two days because the trains didn't run there on a Sunday and nobody in the town could be hired to transport him. He went anyway, and talked to Provost Murray:

> He himself is as pious a man as I have met for some time – as I talked to him I felt the cold hand of Calvinism blotting out warmth and life and the sun – yet he was expelled from his church because he allowed his children to smile on Christmas Eve.

A 'lassie' at the hotel told him:

> Don't you go away and say we're all like that. It's only the Wee Frees and the Free Willies who won't even take a tram ride on Sundays.

Later, seeing three sailor boys being waved off by their girls, he wrote:

> They were unashamed of love: by their actions it was plain that the Scots may regard Calvinism as a good enough theory of the universe, but not as a pattern for living.[417]

There's a whole book in that last sentence.

* * *

Tuesday, 28 January 1936

Four Candidates and a Funeral

On the day of the King's funeral, the letters page of the *Inverness Courier* was replete with communications by candidates and agents breaking the truce by writing about it, as the argument about the scurrilous rumours to the effect that Malcolm MacDonald had not wanted to observe one rumbled on. First off was Arthur Woodburn, agent for Hector McNeil, who wished to dissociate the Socialist campaign completely from reports that any candidate was against declaring a truce. All four candidates agreed to one, he said, adding that the National Executive of the Labour Party had also suspended all political meetings nationally until after the funeral. Saying that McNeil had also been a victim of the whispering campaign, he joined the paper in pleading that it should cease.

The editor, in reply, said he had been unaware of any whispering campaign against Mr McNeil and was glad to have given Mr Woodburn the opportunity to expose it publicly.[418]

Ranald Findlay, author of the next letter, did not receive such a sympathetic response. Stating that he had been present at the discussion between the candidates about holding a truce, he confirmed that the report MacDonald had resisted was indeed 'scandalous'. 'But what a pity', he continued, 'you should seek to make capital out of it on behalf of the National Government candidate'. The meeting was confidential, he said, and the description the paper gave of the proceedings was misleading and unjust to the other candidates. On behalf of Dr Thomas, he wished to protest strongly against the insinuations in the article. And asked that his letter be published in full 'lest your report (no doubt published in all good faith) should mislead the electors of Ross and Cromarty'.

The editor welcomed Mr Findlay's confirmation that the report was scandalous but confessed himself unable to follow the reasoning of the rest of his letter. Because the meeting was (according to him) confidential, Mr Findlay seemed to suggest that the *Courier* should not have sought to expose the lies in the report about MacDonald's preference. In such a scenario, Mr MacDonald would have to suffer from those lies rather than have them contradicted. 'This may be your idea of fair-play', the editor said, but it 'is certainly not ours'. He went on:

> The independent Liberal candidate did not agree to Mr Malcolm MacDonald's suggestion for a truce until after the late King's funeral... he proclaimed instead a truce of only a few days' duration, and... subsequently he fell in with Mr MacDonald's original suggestion. From these facts the electors of Ross and Cromarty are quite capable of drawing their own conclusions – and it is not our fault if these conclusions are more favourable to Mr MacDonald than to Mr Findlay's belated candidate.[419]

Finally, referring to his letter the previous Tuesday and the *Courier*'s leader in response, Randolph Churchill re-entered the fray. He probably shouldn't have. The area of contention between them, he suggested, appeared to have 'appreciably narrowed'. Reminding them of his reasoning that Malcolm MacDonald said he was National Labour in London and National Government in this campaign because in London he wanted a job and in Ross and Cromarty he wanted votes, he challenged the paper:

> You, Sir, indignantly repudiate my explanation. Perhaps, then, as you have already taken so much upon yourselves in this election, you will supply me with a more creditable and acceptable explanation than that which I have offered. If you can do so I shall have the greatest pleasure in withdrawing mine in favour of your own. Until you do so, it is not unnatural that mine should be considered to hold the field.

The editor repeated verbatim the words that Churchill had used in his accusation of MacDonald and repeated his contention that this was 'a specific charge of a most offensive kind, which Mr Churchill knows is not true'. He continued:

> We wonder what he would say if we declared in the same definite and emphatic manner that Mr Winston Churchill left the Conservative Party for the Liberal in order to get a job, and that he subsequently left the Liberal Party for the Conservative in order to get another job. There would be much more justification for such a charge than for the charge which Mr Winston Churchill's son makes against Mr Malcolm MacDonald, but we have never made it and do not make it now. We merely point the moral to Mr Randolph Churchill.[420]

Ouch!

Back in the real world, the King was laid to rest and ceremonies took place in churches across the country. Malcolm MacDonald attended the funeral in Westminster Abbey. The other three candidates attended a public memorial service in Dingwall town hall. Presumably, all had their minds on the next day and the resumption of hostilities.

✡ ✡ ✡

Wednesday, 29 January 1936

In the Country of the Blind

The *Press and Journal* reported on the resumption of hostilities by calling it the busiest day since the campaign started and the most lively. Given some of the days already experienced, this seemed quite a statement. 'Hostilities' was the appropriate term, it said, because 'the election is becoming a real wordy warfare'.[421]

The Scotsman, too, noted the 'increased virulence' of the campaigning. 'There can be little sympathy', they sniffed, 'with the methods of personal abuse that have figured too prominently'.[422]

As ever, it was Randolph Churchill who was at the heart of most of the vituperation. By a baleful coincidence all too common in this campaign, he was addressing a meeting of townswomen in the Burgh courtroom in Dingwall while, next door, Sir William Martineau had called a meeting of loyalist Unionists. Some of these Unionists entered Churchill's meeting by mistake. Referring to Martineau's meeting, Churchill said:

> These people are merely a handful of county snobs who can be got at from London. If you want to find the biggest collection of snobs in the county, go and watch them coming out.[423]

He had moved from insulting candidates and politicians to turning on the electorate, an approach guaranteed to misfire.

Martineau's meeting saw 60 Unionists from all over the constituency agree that a Coordinating Committee should be formed, with equal representation from the Liberals, to manage the remainder of the campaign and to stress the fact that those loyal to the National Government formed the majority, even if the minority were more vocal. It was agreed that Mrs Munro-Ferguson, Provost J E Macdonald, Sir William Martineau and Captain Shaw-Mackenzie should represent them on the new committee. If Randolph Churchill had been capable of embarrassment, then he might have blanched at the news that Lady Middleton, his cousin, had sent a letter of support for MacDonald and apologised that she and her son were unable to attend the Unionist meeting.[424]

It was market day in Dingwall and, in addition to his townswomen's meeting, Randolph Churchill made another visit to the market. Entering the rostrum, he took the gavel and sold a few animals. After he had sold one heifer, another was brought in. 'Here is the brother of the previous animal', Churchill said, provoking hearty laughter from the farmers at the city boy's confusion. The auctioneer tactfully moved proceedings on. Churchill read a letter from Mr Peter Robertson, a well-known

Churchill at Dingwall Mart
photo: Aberdeen Press and Journal

Ross figure, who had suggested that in the interests of national solidarity all the candidates should withdraw except for MacDonald. Churchill was furious:

> That is disgraceful and disreputable propaganda and one of the most improper things in my experience of politics. It is deliberately designed to make party feeling out of the national loss and Mr MacDonald, when he read it, must have said, 'Please preserve me from my friends'.[425]

That led Churchill to his favourite subject once more, and he resorted to a further attack on Malcolm MacDonald. He was 'the most junior of all Cabinet Ministers and the one who has the least backing in the country', he said. It was an indecent spectacle to see a Cabinet Minister saying that he would use his influence in the Cabinet to give concessions to his constituents. Indecent, and also groundless, since everyone knew he was in no position to grant such concessions. MacDonald, he went on, had been party to the government's disastrous Ottawa Agreement of 1932.[426] With a startling lack of awareness for a man who had flown 2,000 miles into the constituency from Morocco at the behest of a group of farmers, he went on:

> I cannot understand how a man who has spent all his holidays in Lossiemouth has begun to take an interest in your affairs only during the past three weeks. He must have seen foreign barley on the quays of Lossiemouth and what has he done to stop it? Really, little good comes out of Lossiemouth.[427]

This attack on the government's approach to agriculture was part of a concerted campaign, however, and one the rebels felt sure was gaining traction. *The Scotsman*, conversely, was suspicious of Churchill's motives for expounding these arguments: 'criticism of the Government's agricultural policy', it said, 'is a better excuse for opposing the Government candidate than objecting to Mr MacDonald on personal grounds'.[428]

All the same, Churchill couldn't stop himself from attacking MacDonald. Later, he went to Muir of Ord, a town which, according to the *Press and Journal*, had a reputation for 'rather exciting meetings no matter who is the speaker'.[429] Accordingly, Churchill faced a sometimes angry audience, especially when talking about MacDonald. 'Keep off personalities and tell us your policy', he was heckled.[430] Undaunted, he returned to his theme of MacDonald's impotence in government: as Dominions Secretary, he said, MacDonald was paid £5,000 per year, but 'if he was to say, "We must shut out these Canadian oats. They are ruining the Ross-shire farmer," he would not remain in office another day. He would be compelled to resign'. It was, felt the *Inverness Courier* (far from his greatest fan), 'freely stated afterwards that had Mr Churchill continued in his attacks on MacDonald, he would have stood a good chance of being chased out of Muir of Ord'.[431]

His comments about MacDonald's difficulties in shifting government policy may have been true, but Churchill could not explain how, as a backbencher, he would be any more successful. With the audience increasingly vexed, Churchill stopped speaking and invited questions, claiming he had to leave to speak at another engagement, then abruptly departed. The meeting was truly a mixed affair, Churchill at times getting a fair hearing and at others being heckled to the point of outrage. Nonetheless, the *Press and Journal* felt he comported himself well, and his 'strong voice enabled him to keep command of the situation'.[432]

Making up for Lost Time and Making Progress

For the independent Liberals, Dr Thomas was making up for lost time, compressing 85 meetings into the next ten days.[433] He attended the Dingwall market at the same time as Randolph Churchill but his reception was 'rather indifferent'.[434] He appealed to the 'small man' for support and said the big farmer, the man with multiple farms, might have benefited from the government's policy of subsidies, but the industry rank-and-file was as badly off today as ever they were.

How well the 'small man' was disposed to support him was very much open to question. The *Inverness Courier* reported that when he began to speak at the Auction Marts, most people left and those who remained continued to discuss their business in private groups. They paid no attention to Mr Thomas, who fled after five minutes.[435]

Hector McNeil was carrying on quietly and making progress, with six meetings during the day. Speaking at Fearn, he demanded Malcolm

MacDonald's resignation as Dominions Secretary if he was earnest in his attempt to represent Ross and Cromarty. 'There is absolutely no use electing anyone who is not prepared to devote himself entirely to this Division for the next five years', he said.

Fighting Speech of the Day

MacDonald, though, had the best of the day's campaigning. Making his return to the campaign after his eye injury, he gave the 'fighting speech of the day', according to the *Dundee Courier*.[436] While in London, he had been examined by Sir Stewart Duke-Elder, the eminent eye surgeon and this turned out to be most fortuitous because Dr Duke-Elder found that small pieces of glass were still embedded in his eye and, had they not been removed, these could have caused significant damage.[437] The eye was making a good recovery, he was told, although there would be scarring for some time and, in truth, MacDonald could still see very little out of it.[438]

Speaking in the town hall in Dingwall, he gave a barnstorming account and received an enthusiastic reception. He began by analysing and critiquing the policies of Hector McNeil and then Dr Thomas. 'There is another candidate', referring to Churchill, which drew laughter. 'What does he stand for? He stands for the policy with the strongest possible expression of personal antipathies.' Churchill had confessed there was nothing else keeping him in the campaign, MacDonald said. If another candidate had emerged, not only would Churchill have withdrawn but he would have supported the new candidate wholeheartedly. MacDonald summed up:

> He agrees with the National Government; he agrees with my policy; but he cannot stand me. His whole original contribution to the election is a nightly hymn of hate.

Declaring that the urgent problems of the next few years could only be resolved by cooperation between all parties, he summed up the alternatives facing the electors:

> The Labour candidate cries 'Vote for me and I will give you revolutionary

> Socialism'; the anti-government Liberal urges, 'Vote for me and I will restore free trade in Britain, with all its consequences'; the Unionist candidate shouts 'Vote for me and I will give the longest string of insulting adjectives against the MacDonald clan that has ever been heard in Ross and Cromarty'.

MacDonald was asked why he left the Labour Party. 'I was turned out of the Labour Party in 1931', he explained, adding:

> The whole of the Labour Cabinet decided that the financial crisis was so serious that a policy of additional taxation and drastic cuts must be put through.439 The very authors of that policy turned me out for supporting the Government which carried it through.[440]

Colonel John Colville MP gave an 'earnest and thoughtful address' that 'made a deep impression' on the *Inverness Courier*. The various trade agreements with foreign countries had been beneficial overall, and Scottish unemployment had dropped by 85,000 from a peak of 362,00 in 1931. Canadian oats only accounted for 7 per cent of the total in the country, although there was still work to be done here. Negotiations were in place to secure a substantial reduction in imports from Canada. The man who would lead those negotiations was, of course, Malcolm MacDonald. 'He is the only man among the four candidates who could get within miles of the Canadian representatives', Colville said.[441]

Moving a vote of confidence in MacDonald, Major Munro-Ferguson said that one of his assets was the equanimity with which he had borne the 'hatred and malice'.

> It is the American blood in Mr Churchill. It is America calling for him, I tell you. American politics are his *force majeure*. He speaks of purity in politics. He will find that purity of which he speaks in the land to which he half belongs.

This, it must be said, is coming close to the sort of *ad hominem* attacks for which Churchill was to forcefully deprecated, along with a side-serving of racism. But the Major continued: 'Mr Randolph Churchill said at the beginning of the campaign that he would take the gloves off. He is fit even to turn out stark naked'. To laughter, the Major continued that this was a most unedifying spectacle. Churchill had done himself infinite harm and MacDonald infinite good.

> Never in my life – and I have taken part in a good many political campaigns – have I seen such a vendetta as that with which that broth of a young man is pursuing a real statesman.[442]

Afterwards, MacDonald was followed to his hotel by a cheering crowd where he addressed them from the balcony.

Lord Strathcarron (previously Sir Ian Macpherson) had already embarked on his health cruise but was playing his part in the campaign vicariously through the medium of film, the 'latest form of election propaganda'. A National Government film van was circulating in the constituency showing three features. In the first, Stanley Baldwin warned of the dangers of Socialism. The second depicted the industrial revival wrought by four years of National Government. The third film was specially shot for the campaign, featuring Lord Strathcarron seated at his desk and addressing his former constituents.

It was a terrible blow to give up the old county, he said, although the peerage had presumably assuaged some of the pain. The electors could make no better choice than Malcolm MacDonald, he continued, with his wide knowledge of practical affairs and interest in agriculture. 'He is the best man to represent your great county', he concluded.[443]

Finally, it was reported that Mrs Morag Edgar, a Gaelic speaker, had embarked on a long tour of Wester Ross, addressing her audiences in Gaelic with the slogan *An Guaillibh a Choile*, which the *Press and Journal* translated as 'Highlanders shoulder to shoulder'.[444]

✡ ✡ ✡

Thursday, 30 January 1936

Blackshirts and Many, Many Meetings

Today was a fast day in Dingwall, with business activity reduced to a minimum, shops closed and services being held in churches.[445] The candidates escaped the 'Sabbath-like' calm of the county town and made off into the wider constituency.[446]

Presumably unaware of the fast day, the British Union of Fascists (BUF) chose today to make their unlikely entry into the drama of the Ross and Cromarty by-election. The *Inverness Courier* bore the news with stoic reserve: 'After the many excitements produced by the election', it said, 'Ross-shire will not be surprised whatever happens'.[447] Wearing the full Blackshirt uniform of forage cap, black shirt, black riding breeches and top boots, R A Plathen appeared in Dingwall and introduced himself as the Inspecting Officer for the BUF. [448] The *Inverness Courier* reckoned that he would 'have no Blackshirts to inspect in Ross-shire unless he takes them into the constituency with him'. That was exactly what he was planning, according to the *Dundee Courier*. Plathen was here to 'organise and arrange meetings' and a party of Blackshirts was arriving from Edinburgh to help him.[449] Plathen remained coy, however, on whether the BUF were planning to stand. 'You will have to wait until tomorrow [when nominations close]', he said. Into this void of information, rumour began to insinuate itself. Sir Oswald Mosley (the leader of the BUF) was going to be the candidate, it was suggested. By evening, though, an official statement came from BUF headquarters in London stating that there had never been any question of Mosley or any other Fascists standing in the election.[450] The *Inverness Courier* surmised that:

> The Blackshirts have been scenting a battle from afar, and have evidently been unable to resist the temptation to get to close quarters with the combatants.

It wasn't anything more, it concluded, than a 'picturesque interlude'.[451]

Picturesque it may have been, but it would not do to be complacent. The Battle of Cable Street was still nine months distant and the BUF were not yet four years old. [452] They were a rump organisation with no more than a few tens of thousands of supporters and, as they became more right-wing, they lost popular support. They were, though, supported in high places, notably by Lord Rothermere, proprietor of the *Daily Mail* and a Nazi sympathiser.

By coincidence, today was the third anniversary of Adolf Hitler's accession to power in Germany. He celebrated by taking the salute of 25,000 *Sturmabteilung* in a torchlight procession beneath the balcony of the Chancellor's Palace in Berlin. In a statement, Hitler said:

> The world must know that Germany will remain peace-loving so long as her honour is not touched, but whoever thinks they can touch our honour will see that we can oppose them.[453]

It is a standard trope of tyrants to begin with messages of peace and harmony. The façade does not last long. He continued, his words taking a more militaristic edge:

> We are without fear and without hesitation in standing for our people. We will take up any fight forced on us and take any decisions which must be taken.[454]

To reinforce that, on this day a new law was announced which authorised the German military to use arms to enforce any order for the surrender of arms or to disperse demonstrations or to enforce obedience.[455] *Kristallnacht* was still two-and-a-half years away, but the descent into military dictatorship was already happening in plain sight.

To be fair to Randolph Churchill, he was one of the first people to discern the menace posed by Adolf Hitler. In July 1932, aged 21, he went to Germany to cover the general election and spent time with Hitler's entourage. He reported on his experience in the *Sunday Graphic* and concluded:

> Nothing is more foolish than to underestimate the intensely vital spirit that animates the Nazi movement. Hitler has no detailed policy. He has promised all things to all men...The success of the Nazi party sooner or later means war."[456]

In October 1933, after Hitler had taken power, Churchill wrote in the *Daily Mail*:

> Hitlerism spells WAR...At the present moment Europe is drifting towards war with far greater certainty than in the year 1913. Britain's position is immeasurably less secure than it was in 1914.[457]

Given that Churchill was warning against Hitler even before he came to power – when most commentators were still dismissing him as delusional – he showed himself to be remarkably prescient. Of course, for people like Churchill and his father Winston, and the Duchess of Atholl (who was responsible for *Mein Kampf* being translated into English) opposition to Hitler had as much to do with his potential threat to the British Empire as any anti-fascist leanings.[458]

On the campaign trail, Churchill was expounding on his usual line. In Tain, he alleged Malcolm MacDonald was becoming 'very rattled'. Instead of countering Churchill's arguments, MacDonald sought 'to retire behind a smoke-screen of insincere persiflage'. He explained that his offer to withdraw from the contest did not support accusations of personal antipathy towards MacDonald:

> My offer was made with a desire to heal the gap among supporters of the National Government, as the Unionist Association had already twice rejected the suggestion that they should support Mr MacDonald. It was clearly a necessary condition of the offer that he should not be the candidate.

He continued:

> [The] 'great and powerful Cabinet Minister' unable to counter Churchill's arguments, was 'compelled to reply in a plaintive mew that I have used a 'string of insulting adjectives' against the MacDonald clan.

Not so, he said:

> I have never abused the MacDonald clan, though it has been necessary for me to pass a few strictures upon the political record of two gentlemen who bear its name.

The essence of what he says is true, but the snideness of his delivery was off-putting to his audience and yet Churchill remained incapable of reining in his excesses. On the contrary, he doubled-down. Returning to the point of personal antipathy, he said:

> These are the only adjectives I have used to describe Mr MacDonald – amiable, young, able, likeable, want-to-get-into-Parliamentarian, remarkable, unique.
>
> It is true that I have further described his record as being 'distasteful to Unionists,' his political affiliations as 'nebulous,' his views and principles as a matter of considerable conjecture,' his candidature as 'nondescript' and 'novel,' and his following in the country as 'non-existent.' This appears to exhaust my vocabulary as far as adjectives are concerned.
>
> He had better pull himself together.[459]

Like all the candidates, Churchill was on a conveyor belt of meetings. Later in the day, he spoke to a packed Fortrose town hall; so crowded that some adventurous locals caused a 'mild sensation' when they climbed through a window. This was his sixth meeting that day, Churchill told the audience, and he had another in Cromarty in an hour. His voice was already hoarse and he had difficulty speaking at times. The meeting went well, however, until a very abrupt departure, when he walked off stage saying he had promised he would not be late in Cromarty.[460]

Hector McNeil addressed meetings in Garve, Achnasheen and Gairloch. Although he had scrupulously avoided being dragged into the personality politics infesting the rest of the campaign, he did deride the National Government representatives in the campaign – an Anglicised Scotsman, an Englishman and a Welshman – for coming to Ross and Cromarty to solicit support while the government they supported refused to acknowledge its obligation to the county and its unemployed. The government was giving preferential treatment to England, he said. Under the new Unemployment Act (1934), England paid a penny per head contribution towards able-bodied maintenance while Scotland was 'bled dry' to the extent of 3s 3d.[461]

For the independent Liberals, Dr Thomas renewed his attack on political jobbery, an argument that was by now, apart from the fringes of

Unionist and Liberal supporters, largely lost. Turning to policy, his focus was on Highlands depopulation, his remedy for which was taxation of land values to bring much-needed land to the market at rents that smallholders could pay. Not until rents were reduced could farm workers expect fair wages. Subsidies went into the pockets of the few and the smallholder and the worker did not benefit.[462] This was essentially a recapitulation of twenty-year-old Liberal doctrine.

Land taxes were taxes on the value of land, regardless of any buildings or other improvements made. The tax burden therefore fell on the landowners. Land value taxes were mainly espoused by Henry George in the nineteenth century, and the proposal formed a key strand of Lloyd George's 1909 People's Budget. Seen to impose new taxes at an unprecedented level on Britain's wealthy, the budget was unsurprisingly unpopular with Conservatives, and the Conservative-controlled House of Lords threw it out, creating a major constitutional crisis. Two general elections were held in 1910 as a result and the Parliament Act 1911, which abolished the power of veto of the House of Lords, was introduced. One of Lloyd George's strongest supporters was Winston Churchill, and it is likely that, on this matter at least, Dr Thomas may have had support from Randolph.

Dr Thomas was aided, if that is the correct word, by a letter of support from Sir Archibald Sinclair MP, leader of the Opposition Liberals in the Commons. 'The keen and determined Liberals have found in you a worthy champion', he wrote. 'Your acceptance of their invitation will evoke a grateful response from Liberals everywhere. You will fight to win. Good luck.'[463] As paeans go, it was hardly of the same scale as those received by Malcolm MacDonald by everyone from the Prime Minister down; and betokened a (wholly realistic) pessimism in Liberal circles. The final 'good luck' is almost on a par with *Morituri te salutant* (We who are about to die salute you) in its fatalism.

Indeed, only that day the latest commendation of Malcolm MacDonald came from Sir John Simon, leader of the National Liberal party, who wrote:

> There is no one in public life better qualified than yourself to bring a fresh mind and an informed judgement to the handling of current questions.[464]

And the day before Sir Godfrey Collins had written to MacDonald personally from the Scottish Office, declaring, 'your zest, your balanced judgment (*sic*) and vigour have been invaluable'.[465]

The man himself had finally embarked on his interrupted tour of the West. While his sister Sheila – seemingly now relieved of her housekeeping duties – canvassed in Avoch and Munlochy, Malcolm addressed meetings in Laide, Poolewe, Melvaig and Gairloch. In the latter venue, he inveighed against the notion put about by the independent Liberals that they were standing against him because he had fought against Liberalism all his life. That was, indeed, a curious line of attack as it was false and could be easily disproved. MacDonald noted that during the six years he had been in the Commons he had always cooperated with the Liberal Party. Indeed, it was because of such cooperation that the minority Labour government remained in power from 1929 to 1931. Subsequently, he supported the idea of Liberals joining the National Government. He had worked closely with the retiring MP, Sir Ian Macpherson. A great deal of government legislation could be seen to have been influenced by Liberalism. 'I should have thought that if any candidate is deliberately fighting against Liberalism in this by-election', MacDonald concluded, 'it is the newcomer who is opposing the unanimous choice of the Ross and Cromarty Liberal Association'.[466]

In the morning, nominations for election had to be submitted. It is quite a thought that, with all the action which had so far come to pass, none of the actors had yet been official candidates. Tomorrow, that would change.

Would anything else?

✡ ✡ ✡

Friday, 31 January 1936 Part One

Inverness Courier vs Randolph Churchill, Round Two: 'An Odious Campaign'

Showing more persistence than sense, Randolph Churchill fired a new letter at the *Inverness Courier* and received the same truculent response. In a letter dated 28 January (the day of the King's funeral and therefore during the supposed truce), he reasserted his charge that when in London

Malcolm MacDonald proclaimed himself National Labour to obtain a job, while in Ross and Cromarty he was a National Government man because he was seeking votes. This line of attack had led to a vicious response from the *Inverness Courier* editorial the last time he used it. Today was no different.

Churchill said he would not respond to an allegation that his father left political parties twice to secure jobs because he was quite capable of looking after himself. Having said he wouldn't, inevitably he did. His father, he said, had fully explained his decisions on the two occasions he crossed the floor in the Commons and changed parties. 'The position of Mr Malcolm MacDonald is scarcely analogous', he went on. 'He professes two allegiances at the same time' – the National Government and the National Labour Party. 'Moreover, he has not offered a single word of explanation for this admittedly remarkable fact.'

Even the paper's powers of advocacy appeared bankrupt, he claimed, because it had proved unable to provide an alternative explanation for MacDonald's position to the one he had laid out.

> However much, Sir, you may look down your editorial nose, I will not allow myself to be deterred from expressing my genuine opinions. I am, however, still prepared to withdraw my explanation if, after further cogitation, you should chance upon a method of extricating Mr MacDonald from the dilemma on which he has impaled himself.

'The more letters Mr Randolph Churchill addresses to us the better pleased we shall be', wrote the paper's editor in response.

> For in every letter which he writes to us, as in every speech which he delivers, he makes it more and more evident that his election campaign in Ross and Cromarty is actuated solely by personal animus of a particularly virulent and contemptible kind.

The editor agreed that the positions of MacDonald and Churchill were scarcely analogous because 'MacDonald has not changed his party affiliations on two occasions and got jobs in consequence'. On the contrary, along with many Labour Party members, he joined with Liberals and Unionists in 'sinking party differences'. Turning again to the Bible, he ended with the *Book of Proverbs:*

As a dog returneth to his vomit, so a fool returneth to his folly, [for] a lying tongue hateth those that are afflicted by it.[467]

That wasn't the paper's last word, however – far from it. Once more, it devoted a leader column, 'An Odious Campaign', to the vexed issue of the Englishman. Now the truce was over, it said, electors could see Churchill's campaign was the 'vilest and most despicable' ever to disgrace a Scottish political contest. From the day he was adopted as a candidate, Churchill had made clear his antipathy towards Malcolm MacDonald and he had continued to attack him 'with an animus, a disregard for the truth, an unfairness, and a spleen which are as discreditable to himself as they are insulting to the electors'. Election contests in the Highlands were characterised by 'hard fighting with clear weapons' and Churchill had departed from that high tradition, descending 'to the use of poison gas'. He had used his letter – which it noted, reprovingly, had been sent during the truce – to continue his feud and to repeat his lies about MacDonald. Wondering what his supporters made of 'their candidate's poisonous campaign', it enumerated the reasons why those supporters might wish to pause and take stock:

Could MacDonald have split from his party and joined the National Government merely to 'get a job'?

Was a person capable of bringing such an 'odious charge' worthy of their support?

Did MacDonald have no right to seek their votes because he was a Cabinet member?

Were their fellow Unionists – those who were following the party line – really, in Churchill's terms 'the biggest collection of snobs in the county'?

In their inmost hearts, were they not sick of Churchill's 'crude impertinences'?

In summary:

Did they lack the moral courage to dissociate themselves from him and all his poisonous ways?[468]

This was a savage attack, suffused with moral indignation and turned, at the last, against those people in the constituency who continued to support Churchill.

The paper was:

> totally unable to understand how anyone calling himself a Unionist or anyone having the interests of the country, of the constituency, and of the Highlands at heart can contemplate it with equanimity.

There was no possibility that Churchill would be returned as a Member, it predicted, but cautioned of the 'very real danger' that he might enable the Socialist candidate to win.

It noted that Churchill said at his adoption meeting that the National Government's majority was so large that the loss of a single seat would be of no account. This was a 'facile argument', not least because losing Ross and Cromarty, a seat which returned a National Government candidate in the last election with a sizeable majority, would mean the failure of a Cabinet minister to gain re-election. This would 'have a serious effect on the Government's prestige, especially abroad'.

'But perhaps this is what Mr Randolph Churchill is aiming at', it suggested, 'for he makes no secret of his antagonism to the League of Nations, and was in fact foisted on the constituency very largely by the efforts of a newspaper [*Daily Mail*] which is one of the League's bitterest opponents in this country'.[469]

The *Inverness Courier* had, until now, firmly aimed its ire at Churchill's vindictive traducement of the two MacDonalds, but now it was suggesting a wider agenda. There is merit here. We have already observed the extent to which Churchill's campaigning zeal had been burnished by a desire to see his father once more in government – even if that meant the downfall of the National Government and a return to party politics. The political ambitions of the Churchills trumped everything, and in this Randolph was an able deputy to Winston. Randolph's son, Winston S Churchill, noted that during Winston Senior's 'wilderness years', which we were currently in, Randolph remained loyal to his father and 'made himself his lieutenant in all his political battles'. Principal of these was their crusade to awaken the British people to the dangers of German militarism and to strengthen Britain's defences in the hope of preventing the war they both so clearly saw coming.[470] And, of course, both men were highly critical of the League of Nations, Randolph dismissing it as a 'grand tea-party'.[471]

As we have already discussed, both Churchills were quick to see the German threat and ahead of national (even international) thinking on disarmament and rearmament but, reading the speeches and utterances of Randolph Churchill in this campaign can it be said that he was fighting for a greater truth, that he was genuinely interested in the needs of the electors of Ross and Cromarty (or Wavertree or Toxteth before them)? The *Inverness Courier* had it right. Churchill was causing turmoil in the constituency without any regard for the impact he was having on it. In this, he was displaying a classic public school sense of entitlement.

In his autobiography, he referred to an occasion when, at Eton, he managed to get early sight of the questions for the entrance exam for Oxford because the same paper was used earlier for pupils in Harrow, one of whom, his cousin, obligingly shared the questions. He mused:

> I have always wondered since whether it was tantamount to cheating. I don't think so. If the authorities were so stupid as to publish the papers at Harrow some hours before they published them at Eton, it would surely have been negligent on our part to omit taking advantage of this. We would have been as foolish as the examiners.[472]

Deep down, the man's dealings were dishonest.

The *Inverness Courier*'s leader set the tone for another day of bitter campaigning.

✡ ✡ ✡

Friday, 31 January 1936 Part Two

Nominations, Much Skidding, Several Ditches and 'Beating the Air'

Nominations opened at 10 am and closed at midday and, in addition to the four known candidates, no new names emerged. Such had been the nature of the campaign that the *Press and Journal* suggested 'the only last minute surprise has been that there was no last-minute surprise candidate'. Although they did not stand, the BUF stated that they would arrange a series of propaganda meetings during the remainder of the campaign.[473]

What they hoped to gain from this is unclear. It is a matter of satisfaction that the BUF made virtually no impact in Scotland. The only time Mosleyite candidates stood for election, in municipal elections in 1937, they achieved nothing.[474] Reasons for their failure to realise a foothold north of the border include a lack of understanding of Scottish political dynamics – including nationalism and the role of religion in Scottish cultural life, poor organisation and vigorous opposition from anti-fascist groups.[475]

Malcolm MacDonald, accompanied by Dr Middleton, Sir William Martineau (in a deerstalker) and his agent Alexander Macrae, was the first to appear at Dingwall Sheriff courthouse, only five minutes after nominations opened. Dr Thomas followed, with his nominator and seconder, Angus Finlayson and Ronald Mackay, both of Dingwall. A bruised and battered Hector McNeil, fresh from yet another road incident, was third to arrive, accompanied by nominator and seconder, Alex Matheson and Peter MacRae, both of Dingwall. As he exited, about twenty minutes before nominations closed, he was passed on the stairs by Randolph Churchill and the two younger candidates nodded at one another.[476] Churchill, accompanied by Hector Forbes of Culloden, Reverend Sellar and T H Burns, submitted his papers and emerged outside for photographs, where he almost became the latest casualty of the campaign after slipping on ice.[477]

Candidates
photo: *Aberdeen Press and Journal*

That Hector McNeil made the nominations at all was fortuitous. His ill luck was 'becoming proverbial', according to the *Daily Telegraph*. The previous evening, about 1am, on his way back to Dingwall on a particularly poor stretch of road between Achnasheen and Garve, his car skidded on a mixture of ice and snow. It hit a bridge parapet before zigzagging across the road and crashing into a telegraph pole, which was partially dislodged but did not collapse. 'It was as if somebody had hit our tail', McNeil told the *Telegraph*. Had they not hit the pole they would have careered down a steep hillside and sustained even greater damage. As it was, Hector McNeil suffered an injury to his left wrist and Barbara Woodburn, a passenger in the rear, was so shocked she remained in bed for all of the following day. They jacked the car up and managed to heave it back onto the highway, where they proceeded on their journey to Dingwall. To compound their misery, they then endured a puncture near Strathpeffer and did not reach their hotel until 5 am.[478]

The Scotsman's 'special correspondent' recorded his experience of being driven across the same roads that night, often at speeds no more than five miles per hour. 'It's a' richt, sae lang as we keep on the road', his driver assured him. 'Considering that at times we were moving along ledges cut out of the mountain-side, with a sheer drop of many feet below into the dark, sinister waters of a loch, I thought that as a delightful confirmation of the fact that the Scottish characteristic of under-statement and canniness still exists', he wrote.[479]

Malcolm MacDonald remained determined to make his way through the county. With the roads to the west hazardous, he took a train to Kyle of Lochalsh, from where he was driven around in a fish van by James Mackenzie, a local fisherman and fish merchant.[480] He spoke in Torridon, Kinlochewe and Lochcarron, staying at Kyle overnight. In Torridon, he repeated his point from earlier in the campaign that the county's inefficient roads were a key issue affecting the revival of agriculture and fishing. He then went on to prove it on the way home by, like Hector McNeil and at roughly the same time, being involved in a traffic accident between Gairloch and Dingwall. His driver was forced to swerve to avoid an oncoming lorry and they ended up in a ditch. Nobody was hurt. Completing the hat-trick of incidents on the night, Morag Edgar, the woman campaigning for MacDonald in Gaelic on the western shores, also crashed but she, too, emerged unscathed.[481]

Going for the topers' vote, Randolph Churchill declared that he thought the duty on whisky was too high and he would use his influence to have it reduced by 2/6 in the budget. (He suggested at one point during the campaign that he was a teetotaller[482] – he most certainly was not: by the 1960s he was an alcoholic with cirrhosis of the liver, had suffered five minor heart attacks and was under doctor's orders to give up drinking, which he did apart from a pint of lager and a couple of glasses of wine per day.)[483]

He also spoke more meaningfully at Invergordon on the urgent need to rebuild the British battle fleet and increase the size of the British cruiser and flotilla strength. 'The new German navy, in the construction of which our Government has acquiesced in defiance of the Treaty of Versailles, will renew the strategic importance of Cromarty and Invergordon', he claimed.[484] Unsurprisingly in this military location, his argument was well received. This was a subject about which Churchill had previously expressed great concern, and he had written about it consistently in his journalism for the *Sunday Dispatch*. His interest was sincere.

Dr Thomas visited the villages of Balintore, Shandwick and Hilton and expressed himself horrified by the disgraceful conditions of the villages; lack of ventilation and water supply being the outstanding problems. This was not a problem exclusive to Ross and Cromarty: by 1939, it was estimated that half of Scotland's housing stock was inadequate.[485] The nationwide depression and its impact on the fishing industry were to blame, he said. 'If I am returned to Parliament', he vowed, 'I shall raise my voice on behalf of rank-and-file workers of the county who are being exploited by landed monopolists'.[486]

With nominations now closed, the *Press and Journal* took a moment to consider the practical choice facing the electors. 'Snow and sensations have filled the constituency with liveliness', it said, but now was the time for the 'natural shrewdness of the electors' to have its innings. The issue was clear: 'the electors have to choose between supporting the Government and administering a rebuke to it'. This was the difference between serving their own best interests and 'beating the air'. The prosperity of the constituency depended on agriculture and it was suffering from the effects of the depression. How that could be alleviated was at issue.

The free trade policy of the Opposition Liberals and the anti-individualist doctrines of the Socialists were unsuited to an agricultural constituency and should be discounted, it said. Mr MacDonald, meanwhile, had recognised the need for a revision of agricultural policy, in particular the terms of the

Ottawa Agreement and, as Dominions Minister, he was in a position to take a leading part in formulating the government's future agricultural policy. Therefore, only through MacDonald could the 'opinions of the constituency pull their weight at Westminster'. The prospects of Randolph Churchill were left unconsidered.[487]

The *Dundee Courier* also reflected on both by-elections currently underway in Scotland. Polling for the Scottish Universities seat closed today, although the result would not be known until Monday. However, the betting was 'emphatically' on Ramsay MacDonald winning the seat.

Considering the Ross campaign, it said:

> [It] would be difficult to name a bye-election (*sic*) in which so many persons have appeared…only to vanish as quickly as they appeared. At one stage the onlooker received an uneasy impression that the rugged northern shire was not a constituency but a carcase which the vultures from far and near had discovered in the uncanny way of vultures.

It suspected, now things had settled down, that the battle was between MacDonald and McNeil, with the other two candidates 'mere diversions'.

'One by one', it said, Dr Thomas's predecessors as prospective candidates 'came to Dingwall, sniffed its political atmosphere, and precipitately retreated'. While admiring his strength of character, the paper dismissed Thomas's chances. It was even more dismissive of Churchill: 'the amount of noise he has been able to make since the contest opened is out of all proportion to his actual importance in it'. He was about the best specimen of the 'cub politician' seen in recent years, possessing 'impudence without limit and an almost unique gift for offensive personalities'. He was standing, it concluded, 'to carry on the feud between the house of Churchill and the house of MacDonald'. Ramsay MacDonald had 'committed the unpardonable sin of excluding Mr Winston Churchill from office when he formed the National Government and Mr Churchill remains in the shade because the National Government continues. Think of the outrage of it!'.[488]

Again, it concluded that a vote for the National Government was required.

✡ ✡ ✡

Saturday, 1 February 1936

The Fitba, Socialist Halfwits, Fresh Snow, Copious Hot Air and the End of the ILP

As Randolph Churchill sat down to read the morning newspapers, he would probably have been heartened to read a letter in *The Scotsman* from 'Farmer', discussing the by-election, only until the final sentence.

The farmer was a Unionist from Easter Ross – that is, the grouping who were integral to the machinations which had brought Churchill to the county in the first place. He had not yet made up his mind how to vote but in the recent general election, he voted for the National Government because he saw it as important that they won. However, that election had given them their mandate and now the people of Ross and Cromarty were 'quite entitled to press our own case more strongly'. Malcolm MacDonald knew nothing about Ross-shire (this seems a little harsh since, from his home in Lossiemouth, on a fine day he could see the county's eastern coastline) and appeared to know little about agriculture (again, somewhat harsh). Moreover, having two MacDonalds in the Cabinet was too many.

Churchill must have been waiting for the punchline. Unfortunately, it came: 'I do not approve of much Mr Churchill is saying and doing'.[489]

For once, the 'gladiators in the political arena'[490] were not the primary attraction of the day, with Ross County making a rare appearance in the second round of the Scottish Cup. Hector McNeil was among the crowd but probably attracted few new supporters with his laboured slogans written on homemade placards urging them to put Ross and Cromarty 'right back' on the map by putting Hector 'forward'.[491] These puns would presumably have worn especially thin by full-time, by which time Ross County had lost 5-0 to St Bernard's of Edinburgh.

It was into this dejected crowd, departing the stadium at the match's end, that Randolph Churchill found his way with his loudspeaker van on his return from a meeting with fishermen in the Black Isle. He expounded on agricultural policy, and the fans' mood, though downbeat, was not vindictive. One heckler, however, managed to rankle Churchill sufficiently for him to lose his temper, turning on the man with a remark about 'imbecility and Socialist halfwits'. After answering questions, he said he would answer only two more. Inevitably, someone asked a third question, which Churchill ignored. 'Answer the question', shouted the crowd repeatedly until Churchill shouted back at them: 'If you mugs think you can bully me you're mistaken. Goodnight'. Amid a storm of booing and having presumably lost more votes than he had gained, he jumped off his box and pushed his way through the crowd.[492]

His mood may already have been darkened by his experience earlier in Avoch. Writing to Malcolm MacDonald, Captain Shaw-Mackenzie reported: 'I gather Churchill did not have it all his own way at Avoch', He explained: 'They are queer people there, very poor and v. much in debt to the Banks on their boats. They want left poor devils'.[493]

Only Nine More Days and They Would be.

The *Daily Mail*, however, was talking up Churchill's chances. MacDonald's management, it claimed, was 'very worried' about Churchill's advances in the past week, noting a 'very perceptible change in the temper' of his meetings. His message, it thought, was appealing to the 'hard-headed and overwhelmingly agricultural constituency'. The paper also pointed out that there were more women voters than men in the constituency and Churchill, a 'wonderfully popular and attractive young man' would undoubtedly command 'a huge proportion of the women's vote'.[494] The implication, then, was that fickle females could turn the campaign to Churchill's advantage.

Churchill also published his election address – a document which candidates produce to lay down in detail the policy areas on which they intend to campaign. He stated he would support the National Government in 'all patriotic policies making for the national weal'.[495] That certainly left the door open for policy areas where he could claim otherwise. Churchill's address is instructive in terms of his personal, as well as his by-election preoccupations. 'There is no National Labour organisation in Ross and Cromarty', he said.

> All the wire-pulling of the political machine in London has, therefore, been brought into play in a disreputable intrigue to procure Liberal and Unionist backing for this nondescript candidature [of Malcolm MacDonald].

Unsurprisingly, he concentrated on agriculture, declaring his support for levies on foreign foodstuffs and using the proceeds to subsidise home producers. Furthermore, he promised to be vigilant against exploitation of these benefits, ensuring they were shared among those most in need in the farming community. He also declared the need for a long-term plan for the fishing industry.[496] There was no question that was needed, he added. Christopher Harvie noted that the fishing industry was so bad even the Cabinet used the word 'tragedy' to describe it in 1934.[497] One wonders, though, about the success of any potential mitigation: in 1935 a Herring Board was created to assist the industry, undoubtedly a good thing, but since it was based in London one must be pessimistic about any practical impact.[498]

However, it was when he turned to wider policy matters that Churchill's address was of greatest interest. He talked at length about the British Empire, foreign affairs and national defence. These – particularly India, the League of Nations and rearmament – were subjects he wrote about regularly in his journalism and were the nub of his (and his father's) growing dispute with the Unionist party and Baldwin's leadership. Much of this would crystallise in the next three years into the argument about appeasement.

Supporting Malcolm MacDonald, James Henderson-Stewart, National Liberal MP for East Fife addressed a meeting in Dingwall and reflected on his by-election campaign in 1933, when a 'certain Press magnate' (Lord Rothermere) took a leading part in a vituperative campaign against the National Government, with assistance from Randolph Churchill. 'The same circus arrived in Cupar as turned up at Dingwall', he said. The same arguments and personal attacks were promulgated. Churchill attacked the same two men, father and son MacDonald. 'It is not for me to advise Mr Churchill', he said, a sure sign that he was about to do so, 'but I do suggest that when next he enters a Scottish constituency he should remember that he is among gentlemen, who expect the conduct of a gentleman'.[499]

As well as Lord Rothermere, that by-election had been sullied by the intervention, once more, of Lady Houston, who again bankrolled attempts to unseat the National Government candidate. She sent her acolyte, J Wentworth Day to campaign and he certainly threw all his energy into it.

Lady Houston, being somewhat paranoid and certain the government were spying on her, refused to use telephone or telegrams and so, during the campaign, Wentworth Day travelled up and down from Fife to England numerous times on the overnight sleeper. He spoke at countless meetings and, after speaking at sixteen open-air meetings in one (February) day, he succumbed to double pneumonia. His efforts proved in vain (as they always did) because the government candidate won easily.[500]

As an aside, the novelist Eric Linklater stood for the National Party of Scotland in the by-election but performed disastrously polling only 3.6 per cent of the vote. He later lampooned the campaign in his wonderfully funny novel, *Magnus Merriman* which includes thinly veiled caricatures of Ramsay MacDonald and Lady Houston.[501]

Malcolm MacDonald was still touring the West, taking in eight meetings, while his sister Sheila was 'rallying the women', with his other sister Ishbel due to arrive on Monday. The talkie van featuring the films by Stanley Baldwin and Sir Ian Macpherson had arrived in Dingwall and, as something of a curiosity, stoked a great deal of interest.[502] Dr Thomas, however, was not impressed. He alleged the sound of the films was audible a mile away and called it a 'low and degrading method of electioneering'.[503]

Dr Thomas also published his election address, in which he expressed his 'horror and resentment' at the action of Liberals in supporting MacDonald. He criticised the National Government, which was dominated by Tories who were the enemies of progress and the friends of vested interests. 'Even the Abyssinian crisis was unscrupulously used by them to obtain a mandate from the country for another five years of social inactivity', he wrote. On the League of Nations, he promised to support it and 'place the whole of the influence and power of this country behind it so that the peace of the world can be ensured and a lead given to break down barriers which are ever a menace to our society'.[504] He condemned those Nationals who had no use for the League of Nations and were not willing to maintain an efficient army, navy and air force. He would press, he wrote, for a world conference to break down economic, national and tariff barriers, quotas, artificial exchange restrictions and other interferences with the exchange of goods and services between nations.

He was opposed to the Ottawa Agreement and similar accords because they tended to corner specific markets – the main excuse for the aggression of 'fire-eaters like Mussolini'. On the home front, he promised to press for greater self-government in Scottish local affairs and wanted a scheme of national development and reconstruction to relieve unemployment. To that end, he proposed a 'New Deal' that could be promptly inaugurated in the Highlands. Land settlement would be an important element of this.[505]

Hector McNeil spoke at meetings from Ardgay to Balintore and referred to the contradiction of Malcolm MacDonald being Dominions Secretary while trying to promote local agriculture. Imports from the Dominions had increased enormously, he said.[506]

Away from the by-election, a decision was made which would, in a few short years, have ramifications for the Labour movement. At the Scottish Divisional Conference of the Scottish Independent Labour Party in Glasgow, a proposal to rejoin the Labour Party was rejected, with only three votes in favour.[507] The ILP was drifting into oblivion.

Meanwhile, the foul weather continued unabated. Throughout the weekend there was fresh snowfall in Dingwall, although the West had not been affected by heavy snow for some time. However, many roads still showed traces of the blizzard from a fortnight ago, with long stretches ice-bound and dangerous.[508]

But the show must go on.

✡ ✡ ✡

Monday, 3 February 1936

Blizzards, More Ditches, Deer Aplenty but no Highland Bulls

'Wester Ross seems fated to get its politics mixed with snow', said the *Press and Journal*.[509]

When MacDonald and McNeil had conducted their western tours before the truce they did so through a blizzard. Now, MacDonald had returned and was joined by Randolph Churchill and Dr Thomas, and the blizzard conditions returned with them.

One week before election day, the candidates were, as often as not, up

MacDonald Examines His Tyre Chains
photo: Daily Mirror

to their necks in snow rather than electioneering. Armed with wheel-chains and spades, they made their way through the desolate and treacherous countryside.[510] Malcolm MacDonald, when he arrived in Dingwall that evening from a day in the West, was reportedly sporting hair that was dishevelled by the blizzard and clutching a hot water bottle.[511]

The first to come to grief during the day was Randolph Churchill. He cut off at Braemore to take the Dundonnell road to Aultbea but was soon held up in a snowdrift through which it took over an hour to cut a passage. Later, he came upon his loudspeaker van in a ditch and helped to drag it out. A few miles later his car slid into a ditch and it took another two hours to release it. At this point, the engine froze and he had to take the loudspeaker van to his engagement in Aultbea, normally a two-and-a-half hour journey which had taken six-and-a-half. When he reached his destination, a search party had already been dispatched to find him. The good news was that when he finally managed to speak he received an excellent reception.[512] 'The hard life up here', Churchill said later to the *Daily Mail*, 'has bred a race which does not ask to be pampered. It only asks for a fair opportunity to win its daily bread from the soil and from the sea'.[513] *Ever the politician.*

Dr Thomas's sojourn was even more eventful. First, he encountered two calves stuck in a snowdrift in the middle of the road and it was only after some difficulty that the animals were extricated to allow him to proceed.[514] Later, he was spotted by *The Scotsman*'s correspondent at an isolated schoolhouse in Strathkanaird, a few miles from Ullapool, coat off, digging a way out for his car which had slipped part-way down a bank and was in danger of sliding into oblivion. Eventually, with the aid of a few crofters who had turned up for his meeting, he heaved the car back to the road and the doctor adjourned with his helpers to the schoolhouse for his speech. He 'packed an amazing number of words into a ten minutes' speech, delivered at express speed', noted *The Scotsman*, not entirely complimentarily.[515]

On his way to the event, *The Scotsman*'s correspondent – who was revealing a penchant for poetic description – wrote of crossing deer forests on the journey from Garve to Ullapool, where herds of stags and hinds:

> nosed disconsolately on the inhospitable slopes, searching beneath the snow for nourishing fare, and groups of them standing about not many yards from the side of the road, their noble heads cocked suspiciously as our car advanced, made a magnificent picture in this setting of rugged grandeur softened by the vast expanse of snowy white in the background.

Dr Thomas passed the same scene on his way to the meeting, since he referred to it in his talk, albeit in a more prosaic fashion:

> I passed hundreds and hundreds of deer today, grazing on what would be the most productive cattle-raising land in this country, and not one black Highland bullock did I see.

While there was some applause, most seemed to take this bizarre notion as a joke, laughing merrily. Perhaps it was because deer forests were entirely customary at this time. Back in the 1880s, with crofters' disputes still raging and after several bad winters, particularly 1882/3, many of the big sheep farms were badly affected by the depression and there was, according to T M Devine, 'wholesale conversion of sheep farms to deer forests'.[516]

Thomas's meeting was attended by eight electors, plus a few girls and boys corralled to expand the audience. This was hardly surprising, given that most of the populace lived in crofts in the glens and would have needed to plough their way through deep snow to reach the schoolhouse. As it was, he was lucky to have this many; these were the people who had helped extricate his car from the banking. He was politely received, as was the custom in this area of Ross-shire, but he struggled to make any impact. One crofter said:

> We do not know Mr MacDonald from Adam, but he is supported by Sir Ian [Macpherson], and we don't think he would do wrong.

Dr Thomas rejoindered: 'I am sure the people of Ross and Cromarty will not be as easily deceived as you'.

'Ah weel', said the crofter, 'you are too late in coming on the scene, and you have not a ghost of a chance'. Polite they may have been, but the people of Ross and Cromarty were also wholly honest.

Dr Thomas was also the recipient of perhaps the strangest question of the campaign. 'If you were in the middle of the Sahara desert and you had a well of water and a barrel of beer, which would you drink from?', he was asked. Perhaps aware of the tensions in these parts between those of a temperate disposition and those fonder of the grain, he took the diplomatic approach. 'In the circumstances, the water would be the healthier option', he said.[517]

Sir William Martineau reacted furiously to an article in the *Scottish Daily Express* attributing to him the view that MacDonald was beaten and Hector McNeil would win. 'I have said no such thing at any time', he thundered. He had not troubled to deal with most of the misrepresentations made against him so far but this was so serious a response was required. He was convinced that Unionists would rally to the National cause and MacDonald would surely triumph.[518]

The Scotsman's correspondent seemed to agree, noting that during his travels through the west of the county, MacDonald's earlier campaigning appeared to have made a favourable impression.[519] MacDonald continued to receive heavyweight support. He addressed three meetings in Easter Ross, assisted by MPs Geoffrey Shakespeare and James Henderson-Stewart.

In a meeting in Cromarty, Henderson-Stewart made a strong attack on Socialism and all that it stood for. Declaring that only MacDonald or McNeil could win the election, he asked whether the audience could support the Socialists who had 'dragged down the country into the mess of 1931 or the National Government who had led it out of it?' A vote for a 'Welsh Liberal' or a 'London Conservative' was only ever a vote for the Socialists. Henderson-Stewart also spoke alongside Sheila MacDonald in the Gordon Memorial Hall in Rosemarkie and both received rousing receptions. Geoffrey Shakespeare spoke in Tain, and appealed to electors not to break the National Government front, which was the 'envy of the world'.[520]

Malcolm MacDonald was the latest candidate to publish his election address, declaring immediately:

> I am no newcomer to the Highlands. I was born amongst the fishermen and agriculturists of the Moray Firth. My home has been amongst them ever since.

He explained the government's plans to restore prosperity to the Highlands, with its Illegal Trawling Act to protect inshore fisheries and plans to revive wider fishing industries. The government was developing a policy for the national revival of agriculture, although it was far from complete. He also addressed any doubt about any conflict of interest between his Cabinet role and a constituency MP's role:

> There should be no misunderstanding about my position as Dominions Secretary. Whilst anxious to strengthen the British Empire by an extension of the Dominions' external trade, that must not be achieved at the expense of the home produce. The efficient home produce should have first place in the home market.

He explained proposals for smallholders and agricultural workers, such as unemployment insurance and an inquiry into farm wages. It was a broad-based address, clearly cognisant of the wide range of political views he had to bring on board.[521]

McNeil on Agriculture

During the campaign, Hector McNeil was covered less than any other candidate by the newspapers, presumably because the press was overwhelmingly supportive of the National Government and it wasn't in their interests to give too much publicity to the Socialist cause. His speech in Dingwall, however, was more fully covered than most. Before a crowded town hall, he was supported by Provost Macrae of Dingwall, presiding, Malcolm Macmillan, MP for Western Isles and Reverend James Barr, MP for Coatbridge. Returning to his well-worn theme that MacDonald could not be Dominions Secretary and local MP for an agricultural area, he unveiled a new epithet:

> Mr MacDonald has become the Dr Jekyll and Mr Hyde of parliamentary life...I challenge him publicly to pledge himself to say to these competitors

– 'You cannot come into our market until every ounce of British beef has been marketed and you can only come in at prices not injurious to the home producer'.522

Because of his official duties, McNeil explained, MacDonald had to persuade Parliament to guarantee an expanding market for the Dominions. That inevitably came at the expense of areas such as this. 'Ross and Cromarty is to be slaughtered to make a Roman holiday for the Dominions', he said. He gave some examples:

> We imported 177,500 tons of oats from the Dominions and Colonies as against 500 from foreign competitors. Frozen beef, we took in 112,000 tons as against 37,000 tons of foreign frozen beef. Mutton and lamb shows the same conclusion. We bought 271,000 tons from the Colonies as against 64,000 from foreign competitors. Moreover, these oats, this frozen beef, this mutton and lamb, these are the cheapest commodities. Foreign beef, for example, shows twopence a pound higher than the Dominions. It is these people who have so burst the market for home farmers that prices have tumbled almost steadily for the last four years.[523]

Although Randolph Churchill had identified the same issue, McNeil went on, he could not accept the Unionist's remedy of a levy on imports, to be used to reimburse home farmers. 'What does this mean?' McNeil asked.

> It means what it always meant that once more the Tory Party are going to ask the poorer sections of the community to buy the cheapest beef at a dearer price, so that the well-off section of the country can have their contribution, enabling them to put the dearest beef at a cheaper price. Poverty is being asked not to subsidise the farmer but to subsidise their best-off customers. The people who can afford to pay that economic price must be made to pay the full price themselves.[524]

The way this could be achieved was through an import board which could control what came into the country. This produce could then be marketed wherever there was a need and at a suitable price which would not injure the home farmer. Labour would see to it that 'neither the middleman nor the landlord will be allowed to steal the improvement of the farmer and leave the ploughman and the farm servant as badly off as they have ever been'.[525] Labour was the only party in this contest who would stand against these vested interests.

It was an impressive speech, well received, detailing clear points of divergence between the Socialists, MacDonald's National Government and Churchill's Unionists. McNeil admitted after the campaign (as did MacDonald) that he revised heavily on agricultural issues in advance of meetings, so concerned was he by the questions that farmers directed to him.[526] His speech in Dingwall clearly showed the benefits of that endeavour. He came across as serious, informed and passionate.

The biggest news of the day, of course, was not in Ross and Cromarty but further south, with the declaration of the result of the Scottish Universities by-election, in which Ramsay MacDonald prevailed with a resounding majority of 7,539 while the Socialist candidate lost his deposit. Unsurprisingly, Randolph Churchill reacted with hostility. 'That caitiff [contemptible or cowardly] decision makes it all the more necessary for Ross and Cromarty to vindicate the rights of democratic government', he huffed.[527]

Ramsay MacDonald's success would have 'beneficial repercussions' in the contest in Ross and Cromarty, thought the *Dundee Courier*. Although entirely different, the two contests had one thing in common: the attempt to import prejudices into them. Personal attacks had 'furnished the main material of the hostile electioneering'.[528]

For the *Inverness Courier*, too, this was a 'good omen'. It was more than a 'triumph over the malign forces which have ranged themselves against the MacDonalds', it was a portent which would be 'acclaimed by all who value the decencies of public life in this country'. Ramsay MacDonald, they said, had faced the same 'floods of poison gas' as Malcolm but had 'trampled upon the poison gas throwers and all their poisonous works'. It only required a victory for Malcolm MacDonald next week 'to complete the rout' and 'purge British politics of the most degraded form of political warfare which had ever defiled them'.

Perhaps aware of the strength of its words, it went on: 'If we write strongly on this matter it is because we feel strongly'. It then turned away from Randolph Churchill and addressed, in distinctly racist terms, the candidacy of Dr Thomas and, for the first time in a so far exemplary campaign, its standards of probity slipped. Under pressure from the rebel Unionists, the independent Liberals had sought, too, to pull an anti-MacDonald 'rabbit' from the hat. It was only after all the Scottish rabbits had run away that they found themselves a Welsh rabbit. 'And there is nothing so indigestible as that!' it said, absurdly. It adapted an old rhyme:

> Taffy was a Welshman, Taffy was a thief
> Taffy came to Ross-shire to steal a leg of beef.

Truly, the paper was on safer ground when it stuck to scripture. The leg of beef, it said, straining its analogy beyond breaking point, was 'as many as possible votes' being taken away from Malcolm MacDonald. The leader concluded by stating that any vote given to either Churchill or Thomas was a vote to further the poisonous campaign against MacDonald.[529]

In the wider world, a couple of news items had resonances with elements of the campaign. In America, President Roosevelt, still at odds with the Supreme Court, astonished Washington by recommending that Congress repeal three major pieces of legislation which supported his Agriculture Amendment Act, legislation which the Supreme Court had declared illegal (see 6 January). The Bankhead Compulsory Cotton Act, the Kerr Smith Tobacco Act and the Potato Act of 1935 should all be repealed, the President said.[530] This demonstrates the massively high stakes at play when it came to agricultural reform and support for farmers. The glib answers by people like Dr Thomas need to be seen in the context of the American Dust Bowl and fraught attempts to alleviate suffering in impoverished rural communities.

In his election address, Randolph Churchill alluded to the need to rearm the country in light of the international situation. Under the terms of the Treaty of Versailles, German rearmament was forbidden but, with Hitler in power, this was happening regardless. Everyone knew it, but not necessarily the extent, and hawks like Randolph Churchill and his father were in the vanguard of protestors that not enough was being done. The *Dundee Courier* reported today that after a 'vast programme of rearmament', by December Germany would be turning out 4,000 planes per annum and had already nearly reached parity with British airpower. Compared with Germany, British expansion plans, announced in May 1935, through which ten or eleven new squadrons had so far been created (with the rate of expansion now at about one new squadron per week) were lagging behind.[531] Germany's armed forces, meanwhile, including conscripted men, would reach 1.6 million by the end of the year. This was the point when the threat of Germany was becoming very real.[532]

✡ ✡ ✡

Tuesday, 4 February 1936

Fishing Trawlers, a Case of Misgendering and a Bit of Browbeating

'At the risk of being suspected of hyperbole, I must say that returning to Dingwall this afternoon gave me something of the feeling Arctic explorers experience when they return to their base after a spell in the snowy waste.' So wrote the eloquent 'special correspondent' of *The Scotsman*, whose descriptions of the natural world of Ross and Cromarty were equally as diverting as his pronouncements on the by-election campaign. This was, by general agreement, the most severe winter experienced in Wester Ross in many years. Snow blanketed the glens and mountains, and for miles around herds of deer were the only living things to be seen. The roads, for weeks treacherous, were in places completely impassable. The end of the Dundonnell road at Braemore was completely blocked and the mail van had failed to turn up two days in succession.

It was for this reason that the intrepid Dr Thomas borrowed a rowing boat and rowed across Loch Broom – a distance of around a mile – for his planned meeting at the crofting township of Ardindrean. Afterwards, he hired a fishing trawler to take him to his next meetings in Aultbea, Inverasdale and Poolewe.[533] On his way, he would have passed north of Gruinard Island; unpopulated since the early years of the century (but not yet subjected to its anthrax experiment). It's a wonder he didn't choose to stop there, on the off chance of finding a recalcitrant crofter. Nobody could doubt the dedication of these candidates.

Malcolm MacDonald also took to the water, crossing to the tiny village of Applecross by a small fishing trawler called *Shamrock*, owned and piloted by Duncan Macrae, a fisherman-crofter from Lochcarron, and son of John Macrae, the Lochcarron Bard.[534] This was the first time any political candidate had set foot in the town in 25 years and the first time that a Cabinet minister had visited. The minister's wife invited everyone to the manse to hear MacDonald speak, putting on a spread for them to eat.[535] Virtually the entire village turned out.

Some spoke no English and H F Rankin of London engaged them in Gaelic. Rankin had written to MacDonald on 28 December 1935, when news of his likely candidature first broke, offering to assist in the campaign: 'What about a canvass among the Ross-shire Crofters?' he suggested.

I could work up my Gaelic to saturation point and be prepared to hail them in a friendly way and help to overcome their shyness.

Having had previous experience of canvassing for Ramsay MacDonald in Seaham (MacDonald's old seat), he also offered to stop off in Edinburgh and 'put in a week or so among the Professors and students there' for the Scottish Universities by-election.[536]

Later, in Alness, MacDonald brandished a leaflet produced by Randolph Churchill's election offices, entitled 'Rather Shabby'. 'It is certainly an appropriate title', MacDonald said, calling it a typical example of the methods employed against him 'in a certain quarter'. The leaflet suggested that, during the campaign, MacDonald had been trying to evade the collective Cabinet responsibility for the disastrous Hoare-Laval pact. It quoted MacDonald in Ullapool: 'Sir Samuel Hoare was entirely and solely and iniquitously to blame for the Hoare-Laval debacle'. MacDonald said he had never used the word 'iniquitous' in any context, not even about his opponents, and he would certainly never use it against a close friend and, until recently, colleague. The word 'iniquitous' does indeed, sound suspiciously Churchillian. 'The quotation is an invention', MacDonald declared. 'It is a travesty of what I said.' His opponents, finding nothing in his genuine statements from which to make capital, were reduced to invention. He explained that, when Hoare brought the proposals to Cabinet, nobody liked them, but in the circumstances felt compelled to put them forward, with the proviso that all three participants – Italy, Abyssinia and the League of Nations – would have to approve them. 'I share responsibility for the decision', he said. 'We are a Cabinet of human beings' he added to explain that mistakes are and always will be made.

MacDonald and his sister Sheila were now joined by their younger sister, Ishbel, to create a genuine family affair. He was also boosted by an oddly worded message of support from Lady Astor: 'I feel certain that the women of Ross and Cromarty will vote for you to a man'.[537]

Ishbel MacDonald and Lady Wallace
photo: Dundee Courier

Randolph Churchill had meetings in Lochcarron, Plockton and Kyle of Lochalsh. Of these, Lochcarron was by far the most fiery. When speaking to a meeting about the Scottish Universities by-election in a place as small as Lochcarron, Churchill could scarcely have anticipated having an ex-Moderator of the General Assembly of the Church of Scotland in his audience. But that is exactly what happened, and the man in question, Dr Lachlan MacLean Watt, took great exception to Churchill's dismissal of the Universities' by-election result as 'shameful'.

'Shame, shame', interrupted Dr Watt. 'I am one of them', he shouted, meaning that he was one of the electors in the by-election, 'and I am not ashamed'. Churchill, sensing trouble, said, 'I did not say you were ashamed.'

Dr Watt replied, 'Thank God I never will be'. He turned and addressed the audience: 'We are entitled to vote where our conscience directs us, without being called cowards and recreants'.

Churchill denied calling Dr Watt – or anyone – a coward and at this point, the exchange subsided until questions at the end of Churchill's talk. Dr Watt asked the price of barley. 'Twenty-five shillings', responded Churchill. What was the price last year, Dr Watt continued. Churchill was not a man to conceal his irritation well. 'I don't have the figures', he replied. 'But I will look into it and send them to you. If I were to ask you the price of barley in 1641 I don't suppose you would know.'

The argument continued until Churchill began to lose his temper. Raising his voice, he said, 'I am not going to be hectored, or bullied, or browbeaten by any gentleman, however pompous and offensive. If you are not prepared to be civil…'

At this point, Dr Watt rose and, turning to the audience once more, said, 'I leave it to the meeting to decide who is doing the browbeating'. This stirred the audience, who cheered and clapped. Dr Watt continued. 'Don't call us names – Scottish people will not be dictated to'. Churchill tried to regain control, suggesting it was time for the doctor to end his cross-examination. 'I have the right to ask questions', Dr Watt replied. Churchill again called for restraint, referring to the doctor's 'extraordinary display of truculence'.

Once more, Dr Watt rose to his feet and objected: 'Object as you much as you like', said Churchill. 'You have no right to speak to any taxpayer like that', replied Dr Watt.

'The gentleman can object until he is blue in the face', Churchill said wearily. At this point, he asked for further questions from the audience. After having endured fifteen minutes of this argy-bargy, nobody dared and, with great relief, Churchill declared the meeting closed.[538]

The *Daily Telegraph* reported a couple of days later that this argument had not improved Churchill's chances in a community where the ex-Moderator had an 'immense prestige'. Its reporter encountered Churchill supporters in Dingwall who read reports of the meeting 'a little ruefully'. One person who was 'in close contact with local feeling' suggested the argument could result in a 'swing of at least 700 votes to Mr MacDonald'.[539]

Hector McNeil was the final candidate to publish his election address, offering a bold socialist platform in support of redistribution of wealth. Specifically for the Highlands, he said he would demand a government enquiry as a preliminary to the formulation of comprehensive schemes for economic and social improvement of the North. He proposed new industries for Ross and Cromarty to boost its economy, including the preparation of cod and halibut oil, hydro-electric schemes and the creation of tourist traffic through building roads, hotels and hostels.

On the stump, he declared that his party's policy sought to 'secure a proper distribution of plenty by a wise planning of the nation's economic resources, which necessitates the ownership and control of the land, the financial machine, and other basic industries and services by the community'. He went on:

> In a country like ours, which is predominantly industrial, the prosperity of agriculture depends on the ability of the town population to buy what is produced on the farms, and so we find agriculture in most of its branches has shared the general economic depression of the last few years.

Declaring that 'the needs of the mass of the people of Ross and Cromarty have not within the last 25 years been effectively voiced in the House of Commons', he vowed to bring forward the county's problems as 'vital living issues'.

The record of the two previous minority Labour governments, he said, demonstrated that his party had a sympathetic appreciation of the special difficulties of agricultural communities.[540] The address was largely based on the manifesto Labour had produced for the 1935 general election, entitled *Socialism and Peace*. That manifesto was, as Simon Heffer explains, essentially a blueprint for the Labour government that would take office in July 1945.[541] After years of disarray, Labour were beginning to consolidate a new vision.

McNeil was boosted by a letter of support from Clement Attlee, Labour's leader in Parliament. Attlee observed that, although the general election had been only a short time before, the National Government had 'forfeited any claim to the confidence of the country'. It had cynically tried to assist Italy to plunder Abyssinia. Its promises of social reform were unreliable – the school leaving age, for example, would not be raised until September 1939. The only immediate part of its programme which was progressing was increased armaments. 'It is not surprising' concluded Attlee, 'that a Government of this character is represented by a candidate [MacDonald] who professes to be a Socialist, is adopted by Liberals, and seeks the support of Conservatives'.[542]

* * *

Aboard the fishing vessel *Shamrock* bound for Applecross
L to R: Mr Smith, Malcolm MacDonald, Dr Middleton, Unknown,
Duncan Macrae, H F Rankin, Neil Ferguson, Unknown
photo: Dr Charles Ferguson

Campaigning in the 1936 Ross and Cromarty By-Election
L to R: Unknown, Neil Ferguson, Mr Smith, Dr Middleton,
Malcolm MacDonald, H F Rankin
photo: Dr Charles Ferguson

On the fishing vessel *Shamrock* preparing to sail to Applecross
L to R: Unknown, Unknown, Dr Middleton, Unknown,
Malcolm MacDonald, Mr Smith, H F Rankin, Neil Ferguson
photo: Dr Charles Ferguson

Near Loch Carron
L to R: Neil Ferguson, Dr Middleton, Malcolm MacDonald, Mr Smith
photo: Dr Charles Ferguson

Campaigning in Loch Carron
L to R: Gordon Newson?, Sheila MacDonald, H F Rankin, Neil Ferguson
photo: Dr Charles Ferguson

Campaigning in Applecross
L to R: Dr Charles Ferguson, Malcolm MacDonald, Mr Smith, Mrs McLeod, Dr Middleton, H F Rankin; Rev McLeod, Dr Ron McLean
photo: Dr Charles Ferguson

Campaigning for Malcolm MacDonald
Dr Charles Ferguson and Sheila MacDonald
photo: Dr Charles Ferguson

Campaigners
L to R: H F Rankin, Sheila MacDonald, Dr Charles Ferguson, Neil Ferguson
photo: Dr Charles Ferguson

Wednesday, 5 February 1936

The Sabbath, Oats and Adolf Hitler

Given that Ross and Cromarty was a stronghold of the Free Church of Scotland it was inevitable that religion would intrude on the by-election campaign at some point and, even though the candidates – as *The Scotsman* described it – had been 'scrupulously careful to refrain from raising controversy over matters that concerned personal religious belief and observance', it is probably only a surprise that it took so long.[543] It is also surprising that Randolph Churchill was not the one to invoke the wrath of the Wee Frees.

On this day an article appeared in the Scottish Protestant League publication, *The Vanguard*, entitled 'Warning to Ross Protestants', alleging that Hector McNeil supported the opening of cinemas on the Sabbath Day and suggesting that 'Rome ruled the Glasgow Corporation', where McNeil was a Labour councillor. McNeil's agent, Hugh MacCalman, sought an interim interdict to prevent the publishers from sending copies of the publication to ministers of the Free Church of Scotland and the Free Presbyterian Church of Scotland in Ross and Cromarty, which was their stated intention. Ross and Cromarty took religious observance seriously, of course, and the Sabbath's day of rest was strictly observed. The accusations, according to MacCalman, were 'false, calumnious and malicious' and were calculated to prejudice McNeil's chances in the by-election. The truth, he continued, was that McNeil had voted against a proposal for Sunday showings in Glasgow's cinemas. The charge that the Roman Catholic Church dictated Labour Party policy was also untrue.[544] Hector McNeil later said the article also implied he supported playing games on Sunday. That wasn't true either – he had voted against a proposal to open Glasgow's municipal golf courses on Sunday and they remained closed on the Sabbath now.[545] McNeil's self-vindication seems highly likely, given that he was a Divinity student. Sheriff Welsh granted an interim interdict.

McNeil, meanwhile, was at market day in Dingwall and, like Churchill, MacDonald and Thomas before him, took his place at the auctioneer's rostrum. Happily for him, he did not confuse the sex of any of the animals under his hammer. Asked about Randolph Churchill, he said, 'He is quite a nice fellow, but as an agriculturalist he is a joke'. Someone in the crowd piped up, 'Give him a chance, he's only 24!' To laughter, McNeil replied, 'I'm only 25, and I don't expect he will make up the intelligence in the next year'.[546]

Hector McNeil Plays Coalman
photo: Aberdeen Press and Journal

Later, MacDonald also took to the auctioneer's rostrum and used his time discussing an issue that had blown up as a result of comments from Robert Boothby, MP for Aberdeen and Kincardine East. Boothby had been part of a delegation which lobbied the Secretary of State for Scotland, Sir Godfrey Collins, on matters agricultural, and he now claimed that what MacDonald had said in a meeting at Kyle was untrue. MacDonald went on the offensive.

Unlike the other candidates, he said, whose promises would never be carried out, and who could therefore 'promise the moon', he had to weigh every word he said. The promises he had given could and would be implemented. Consequently, his opponents had spent the campaign trying to catch him out. Today, at last, they thought they had him. They claimed that in a meeting in Kyle, he said something contrary to government policy and which contradicted the words of the Secretary of State. These were the facts, said MacDonald: when asked about oats policy, he had said that the Secretary of State had received a deputation with a proposal for changes to the policy. He went on to say that the Secretary of State's view was that the proposal did not commend itself and he was examining alternative proposals. Mr Boothby was part of the delegation and he was now alleging that what MacDonald said was an incorrect summary of the meeting. MacDonald explained:

> Mr Boothby says that I am a liar. He does not use exactly that language. He says that my statement is not in accordance with the facts, which he says are these. The deputation met Sir Godfrey Collins and put their

proposal about oats before him. Sir Godfrey Collins replied that in principle he was opposed to subsidies, that he had given lengthy consideration to this problem, and that he had come to the conclusion that nothing could be done.

But, MacDonald said, immediately after the deputation an official statement was issued to the press, presumably approved by the leaders of the deputation, including Boothby. That statement read:

> Sir Godfrey Collins said that the objection to a scheme such as that proposed ... involving a direct Exchequer subsidy, had been found to be formidable, and that he was unable to see any prospect of a solution on those lines; but he fully sympathised with the position in which the oat growers found themselves, and would continue to have the situation examined to see whether any practicable scheme of assistance could be devised.

This was very different from the sentiments expressed by Boothby and was in accord with what MacDonald had said in the meeting in Kyle. MacDonald said, therefore, that he had nothing to apologise for.

It is perhaps a pity that Bob Boothby did not play a larger part in the by-election because he was one of the more interesting MPs of the time. Although he was a Unionist, the Liberals did not generally stand against him because they regarded him as one of their own.[547] He was first elected in 1924 and remained an MP until 1958, when he took a peerage, becoming Baron Boothby of Buchan and Rattray Head. He lived a colourful life, including having a lengthy affair with Lady Dorothy Macmillan, wife of Harold Macmillan. Boothby is reputed to

Bob Boothby MP
photo: Creative Commons

have fathered three children by the wives of other men.[548] Although he denied it, he was bisexual and played a key role in decriminalising homosexuality. A frequent visitor to Germany, he met Adolf Hitler in 1932. In his autobiography, he recalled that Hitler 'sprang to his feet, lifted his right arm, and shouted "Hitler!"...I responded by clicking my heels together, raising my right arm and shouting back "Boothby!"'[549]

As well as the market, MacDonald toured the Black Isle in the afternoon and evening, speaking to large crowds wherever he went. In the evening, he spoke in Avoch and Fortrose on the banks of the Moray Firth and concentrated on the record of the National Government. In Avoch, he said there was only one issue in the election, as had been the case in the general election: 'Are you in favour of the National Government?' If they were against, they had a choice of candidates. If they were for, they had no choice but to vote for the National Government candidate.

At this point he was heckled: 'You are a supporter of the National Government? But which party do you represent?' This alluded to the persistent comments by Randolph Churchill that he adopted National Labour when in London but National Government in Ross and Cromarty. MacDonald addressed the question:

> I am a supporter of the National Government in which Unionists, Liberals, and National Labour are combined and united together. I am associated with the National Labour group, which has cooperated with Liberals and Unionists for the last four years without a single division of opinion.

For this, he drew a round of applause but it is still a politician's answer, not directly answering the question. 'Associated with' is not the same as 'member of'.

At the Avoch meeting, he was assisted by Earl de la Warr, not without some difficulty, after some Socialist supporters chose to give the Earl a noisy hearing. They tried to do the same to MacDonald but he, a cannier campaigner, dealt with them more effectively. At one point the hecklers shouted 'Vote for McNeil!' To applause, MacDonald faced them and said that he was sure, had Mr McNeil been in attendance, he would ask his supporters to give a fair hearing to one of his opponents. 'I am quite certain the interrupters are winning me votes all the time', he added, and with this, the hecklers were silenced.[550]

In Fortrose, he talked about farming and imports and told the audience about an experience earlier. 'I met some farmers in Dingwall today who thought that the Dominions Secretary could not sit in the House of Commons', he said. Someone shouted from the audience, 'But they are an ignorant lot', raising laughter and ironic cheers. MacDonald explained that they claimed he was merely a representative of the Dominions and that he couldn't help Ross and Cromarty because he would have to look after the Dominions. 'This is absolutely untrue', he said, before adding:

> Some farmers call themselves Unionists, but I cannot understand why some of them were ever allowed into the Unionist party in the first place.

The audience laughed. 'If there is one thing which the Unionist Party places importance upon', he continued:

> it is in maintaining the strength of the British Empire. When I hear these farmers – who put up their own candidate, remember – talk about the Dominions as they do, I feel that if they had their way they would break up the British Empire within about twenty-five minutes.[551]

A prize should have been awarded to Allan Beaton, a Unionist politician from Edinburgh who was on the stump with MacDonald. With the county still in the grip of the blizzard, MacDonald was often late for meetings and today he was two hours late for his final stop. Beaton managed to fill in the time and, according to the *Edinburgh Evening News*, his 'fund of political anecdotes succeeded in amusing the meeting, and he had an ovation when he sat down'.[552]

Throughout the campaign, much of the press correspondence tended to focus on the imposition of MacDonald as the official candidate or on the conduct of Randolph Churchill. A letter from J T Cameron to *The Scotsman* took a different approach, focusing on the men's fathers. Ramsay MacDonald, he wrote, was Prime Minister for six years, his stint ending only recently. In that time, he allowed our defence forces to diminish 'almost below the safety limit'. At the same time, Russia, Japan, Germany and Italy have 'armed themselves to the teeth, and are prepared for instant war'. In 1914, 'we were saved because Winston Churchill had the fleet ready'. He concluded:

> It would be safer, now, to vote for the son of the man who had the fleet ready in 1914 rather than the son of the man who, as a pacific gesture and doubtless with the best intentions, has let down our fleet almost below the safety line.[553]

This was rather a partisan angle, perhaps, but it raised an issue which gained prominence during the campaign, and which was going to come to the fore of politics in the coming years leading, ultimately, to the appointment of Winston Churchill as Prime Minister.

From the end of the Great War to the first half of the 1930s, a policy of promoting disarmament had held sway, the horrors of the war rendering the population largely pacifist and the financial crash of 1929 making this a practical necessity in any case. J P B Dunbabin noted that, at the beginning of the 1930s, British politicians 'still hoped to achieve an agreed measure of international disarmament', and several international conferences were held.[554] However, a White Paper published in March 1935 referred to the 'vital necessity of putting our defences in order'. No actual increases in expenditure were proposed in the White Paper, though, which was one of the reasons Baldwin called an early election: in order to secure a mandate for rearmament – although, as we have previously discussed, the lack of debate on the subject during the campaign rendered this moot. It was an issue on which there was clear division within the government. Ramsay MacDonald, of course, was distinctly dovish, indeed resigning as Labour leader in 1914 because of his pacifist beliefs. Doubts remained for him. In a letter during the by-election campaign, he told Malcolm:

> Unless we are very careful we will just fall into the old militarist ruts, supported by the old militarist arguments and considerations every one of which has proved itself in history to be mistaken.[555]

However, talk of German rearmament was fuelling a growing fear among the British public of air warfare reaching our cities (a fear which would be greatly exacerbated by the brutal air bombings of Barcelona, Valencia, Guernica and many other cities during the Spanish Civil War). There was a feeling that aviation had, as Brett Holman explained:

> fundamentally changed war, making it faster and more destructive and – crucially – aimed principally at civilians rather than soldiers and sailors. Fears grew of a 'knock-out blow' and it was felt a British collapse might come 'mere days after the start of war'.[556]

The international situation was tense, not least because of the Abyssinian crisis, with the Conservative Party split on whether to appease Italy or oppose it. Some hawks were quite prepared to go to war with them, while others saw them as a bulwark against the threat of Hitler.[557] Brett Holman noted that because, under the provisions of the Treaty of Versailles, Germany was not permitted to rearm, a sense of complacency had set in. As a result, the readiness of Britain's military had declined worryingly, and plans were put in place to rearm the nation. In 1934, Baldwin pledged that British airpower would still be nearly 50 per cent stronger than Germany's in two years, despite the scale of Germany's rearmament. By May 1935, the pledge had increased to tripling British forces within two years.[558] But as we saw only two days before in a report in the *Dundee Courier*, news of Germany's massive advances in airpower was causing a panicked reassessment.

Since 1929, Britain's annual expenditure on defence as a percentage of GNP was either 2.7 or 2.8 per cent. As soon as Hitler came to power, Germany started rearming at a higher rate, 3.2 per cent of GNP in 1933/4, rising to 9.6 per cent in 1937/8 and 18.1 per cent in 1938/9, by which time British spending had risen to 8.9 per cent of GNP.[559] Whether we wanted it or not, an arms race had begun. This was an inevitability. As Simon Heffer noted in his history of Britain between the wars, from the mid-1930s the public's preoccupation started to move from financial security to national security.[560] This would change the tenor of the national debate completely, and what we can see in the by-election campaign is an early indicator that change was coming.

✡ ✡ ✡

Thursday, 6 February 1936

More Oats, Flying Stags and the Return of the Blackshirts

The day began with a letter in *The Scotsman* from D Ian Urquhart of Strathpeffer. In all the 'hurly-burly' of the present by-election, he wrote, an important point was being submerged beneath irrelevant side issues. He quoted the telegram sent to Stanley Baldwin by the local Unionist Association:

> Your action (in sending a telegram of support to Mr Malcolm MacDonald) challenges the whole democratic structure of the Unionist party.

Urquhart thought there could be no convincing answer to that charge because Churchill had been democratically adopted as a Unionist candidate by a majority vote. It may well be, he wrote, that it was in the national interest for MacDonald to be returned to Parliament but if a local Association was opposed by leaders in London:

> a shattering blow is dealt at popular representation as commonly conceived. The right of a constituency to make its own choice of a candidate freely, without fear or repudiation by national headquarters, is fundamental to the right working of our Parliamentary system. This is the reason why I will give my vote to the Unionist candidate.561

As the campaign began to wind down, the weather changed, a warm wind from the west bringing a rapid thaw. That was still too late to be of use to Malcolm MacDonald, who returned from the Black Isle in the early hours of the morning and rose at 6.30 am to be on the road for Opinan on the West Coast for a meeting at noon. He then motored back to Dingwall, a round trip of 220 miles, mostly on snow-covered roads. In the evening he addressed meetings at Hilton, Fearn and Portmahomack. It is hard to avoid the conclusion that the logisticians who devised the candidates' itineraries in the Ross and Cromarty by-election had only a casual acquaintance with the topography of the Highlands.

Meanwhile, Ishbel MacDonald was campaigning with Lady Wallace in Tain, Achterneed and Contin. Sheila MacDonald returned to the West

Coast to address meetings at Inverasdale and Gairloch and would remain in the West for the duration of the campaign. Katharine Elliot, wife of the Minister for Agriculture Walter Elliot was due to arrive to speak on Friday, further bolstering the number of women speakers for the National Government campaign.

Twelve Ross-shire women resident in London, all Macs, sent a telegram to MacDonald, urging 'all our friends to vote for Mr Malcolm MacDonald. We should feel honoured that one so distinguished and so modest represented our home county'.[562] The *Inverness Courier* reprinted the telegram and felt that MacDonald's stock was rising steadily, with some waverers who may have been inclined to give their support to the Unionist or independent Liberal candidates beginning to realise that in effect this would be a vote wasted. 'That the issue lies between Mr MacDonald and his Labour opponent, Mr McNeil, is now obvious to everyone in the constituency', it concluded.[563]

The *Press and Journal* noted that MacDonald was 'making friends in rather unexpected places'. It mentioned Avoch and Muir of Ord, in particular, both generally regarded as Socialist centres. 'Muir of Ord, however', it continued, 'has the remarkable reputation of being so impartial that it gives an unfavourable reception to all candidates in elections'. While MacDonald had performed creditably in Avoch, it said, he had not yet visited Muir Of Ord. Hector McNeil, perhaps unsurprisingly, did well there, while Randolph Churchill's experience was described, diplomatically, as 'lively' (see Friday, 30 January 1936).[564]

An interested observer of the campaign was the American Charles Aikin, who was staying with Lord Tarbat. 'One thing that impresses me', he said, 'is the calmness with which everybody discusses the political questions outside the meetings – but as soon as they get inside that calmness seems to disappear. American audiences are better behaved because they are anxious to hear the candidate'.[565]

Bob Boothby took to the pages of *The Scotsman* to reply to Malcolm MacDonald on the vexed question of oats. 'I wish Mr Malcolm MacDonald would do me the honour of reading my letter', he complained, 'It was not written without care.' If he did, he would see that Boothby had not accused him of being a liar (something MacDonald didn't exactly claim, because he qualified his words heavily) but said that he had mis-stated certain facts, which was 'quite a different thing'. He went on:

> He was not present at the oats deputation. I was. And the account I gave of what happened is strictly accurate. I stand by every word of it. The publication by the Scottish Office of a *communiqué* containing the usual formula about sympathy and consideration does not alter the facts, and the Government should not be allowed to ride off on that. I am not interested in the personalities of this election. What I am trying to do is to get from the Government a plain and unequivocal declaration of their agricultural policy.[566]

Boothby, remember, was a member of the governing party.

On a relatively quiet day, (albeit with one piece of good news when his loudspeaker van was dug out of a snowdrift on the Braemore to Dundonnell road),[567] Randolph Churchill attacked Malcolm MacDonald yet again in meetings in Ardgay and Tain. The *Inverness Courier* reacted gloomily:

> Throughout Ross-shire electors have long ago given up wondering why Mr Churchill should regard Mr MacDonald as being the candidate to be specially singled out for attack, and why he should practically ignore the Socialist and independent Liberal candidates, whose policies are so opposed to the Unionist principles which Mr Churchill professes.

The paper felt, however, that every attack resulted in an addition to the ever-growing ranks of MacDonald's supporters. So too did the pamphlets attacking Ramsay MacDonald written by Lady Houston and handed out at practically every meeting addressed by Malcolm. They were the cause of much amusement, the *Inverness Courier* noted.[568]

Churchill spoke also in Edderton and Invergordon, focusing on agriculture. A vote for any other candidate was a vote against agricultural protection, he warned, and a vote against the same fair treatment for Scottish agriculture that English agriculture was already receiving. Inevitably, he turned on MacDonald again:

> [T]he Government of which he is a member, by their trade agreements

> with the Argentines and the Danes, have made it quite impossible for us to get justice for the home producer, let alone put him first. The foreigner today is number one in determining British agricultural policy.[569]

In Ardgay, he told a crowded meeting that should he win:

> I shall judiciously increase my nuisance value, for this is the only way in which a Member of Parliament ever gets anything out of the Government.

He could have been elected to Parliament months before, he said, 'if I had chosen to be a Government lackey or lickspittle'. Since he lost as the government candidate in the election a few weeks before it is difficult to see much justification in this. Nonetheless, his enthusiastic reception led the *Daily Mail* to, once again, play up his chances of success. 'There are those who say', it declared, without offering a shred of evidence, 'that in some of these scattered communities the voters are for Mr Churchill to a man'.[570]

The *Mail* also featured heavily a report on Churchill's speech in Tain, in which he stated that Britain should without delay improve its air defences. 'We must not lose a single moment', Churchill said, 'in building the most efficient and modern types of aeroplanes so that the safety of our country can be assured'. He called the lead Britain had given to the Disarmament Conference 'foolish' and had involved the country in 'grievous peril'. The *Mail*'s report had a sub-heading titled, 'Mr Churchill and Need for Stronger Air Force'.[571] At this late stage in the campaign, defence and rearmament become a key election issue.

Churchill did have an alarming incident on the return journey from Wester Ross, on the road between Ullapool and Strathpeffer, when a stag emerged from woodland and jumped right over the bonnet of his vehicle.[572] This was a campaign which, for many different reasons, Randolph Churchill was unlikely to forget, but being hurdled by a Highland stag is possibly its defining metaphor.

Dr Thomas, the last campaigner still in the west of the constituency, tried but failed to emulate Malcolm MacDonald's crossing to Applecross, the sea being too rough. He went by road instead to Shieldaig. At Loch Maree, on a single-track road, he met Sheila MacDonald coming in the opposite direction. Owing to the narrowness of the road, Sheila had to reverse to the nearest passing place to allow them both to continue their journeys.[573] This National Government retreat would not be the defining metaphor of Dr Thomas's campaign.

Dr Thomas said he had found many Liberals in the West who had been misled into thinking MacDonald was standing as a Liberal and issued a challenge to MacDonald to declare openly that he was a Socialist supporter of the National Government (although he was too late because MacDonald had – sort of – done just that the evening before in Avoch). *The Scotsman* was having none of this, pointing to his provenance: 'a Welshman', it said, 'must credit the Highlanders with sufficient acumen to know the simple fact for themselves that he was brought into the constituency as an exponent of Samuelite Liberalism against the wishes of the county Liberal Association'.[574]

It was perhaps expedient that Dr Thomas was in the West, as he may not have been happy to see the outside of his committee rooms, which were above the entrance to the cinema. Directly beneath his windows was a panel showing the current pictures, and among them, in bold lettering was a film entitled 'Look Up and Laugh'.[575]

Hector McNeil spoke at Kildary and Nigg of his disappointment that opponents had attempted to attack him using 'underhand methods', referring to the *Vanguard* article. Whatever his faults, he said, his attitude to the Scottish Sabbath would compare favourably to that of anyone else in the campaign. Many of the features of Scottish life in which they took pride could be accounted for by the fact that Scotland had held on to its day of worship when other countries had let it go. He had consistently opposed every attempt to encroach on the Sabbath in his role as a councillor in Glasgow:

> As a Trades Unionist and a Christian, I think it essential that we should hold on as firmly as we can to our day of rest.[576]

As they had promised, without ever fully explaining why, four Blackshirts arrived in Dingwall during the day and held various meetings. 'Were it not for the sombre and depressing hue of their uniform', the *Inverness Courier* reflected, 'it might be said they gave a touch of gaiety to the campaign'.[577]

Blackshirts Arrive in Dingwall
photo: Aberdeen Press and Journal

✡ ✡ ✡

Friday, 7 February 1936

Doggerel, Some Odds, Some Oddities, Clement Attlee and the Importance (Or Not) of the 'Flapper Vote'

Prime Minister Stanley Baldwin, who Randolph Churchill was in no doubt would send a letter of support, instead chose the penultimate day of campaigning to send to the press a second letter of support for Malcolm MacDonald. Praising the achievements of the National Government over the past four years, he appealed to the electors of Ross and Cromarty to vote for MacDonald, warning that 'a vote given to any of your opponents is a vote against the system of national co-operation which has been, and still continues to be, productive of such good results'. He appealed to voters' sense of duty:

> I ask them to put national interests before all other considerations and return you to Parliament as a firm believer in National Government, so that you may be free to devote your energies and ability to your responsible task for which you have already shown yourself to be admirably well fitted.[578]

In its final edition before polling day, the *Inverness Courier* devoted a substantial amount of column inches to the by-election, including the letter from Baldwin printed in double-sized font. The paper felt sure that Baldwin's appeal would not fall on deaf ears because 'in spite of the bellowing of the Bulls of Bashan, the crowings of the young cockerel, the belated squealings of the Welsh Rabbit, and the facile promises of the eloquent apostle of a Socialist Utopia', the electors of Ross and Cromarty were neither easily defeated nor easily deluded.

Candidates McNeil and Thomas, it said, were out-and-out enemies of the National Government, while Churchill pretended that he was fighting for it, 'although all the time he is trying to stab it in the back'.

Their leader column, though, focused heavily on the international political scene, and the need to support the League of Nations. Churchill and the newspapers which backed him (the *Daily Mail* and the *Daily Express*) were the bitterest opponents of the League in this country, 'yet it is on the League that the peace of the world depends'. That was why, it said, the paper was so insistent that nothing should be done to weaken the National Government.[579]

To get its voters into the mood, the *Inverness Courier* printed a poem on the event from someone styling themselves 'AN 'UMBLE POET':

They come frae far, they come frae near,
This County tae contest;
Ae seat 'mangst four, and wha can say
With which we shall be blest?

Noo Malcolm's quite a likely chiel,
And talks o' taxin' oats.
Tae help the farmers in distress,
Wha'll help him wi' their votes!

And Randolph – sick a bonnie lad
Tae catch the ladies' e'e;
In fact tae him they've lost their hearts,
And say "I'll vote for thee"!

And Dr Thomas, what o' him?
I trust ye will na frown;
But gin ye want to run a play,
He'll mak' a first-class clown!

And last, and yet I do sae hope
The last will no be first,
We hae McNeil, wha wi' his zeal
Wad soon the County burst!

Just ae mair word intae yer lug,
Afore yer vote ye cast:
Pray put it on oor Premier's man,
Gin ye want trade tae last! [580]

A bookmaker in Aberdeen published odds for the candidates: MacDonald 2/1 on (i.e., 1/2); McNeil 2/1; Churchill 7/2; Thomas 25/1. This provoked William Webster, formerly Secretary of the Scottish Liberal Federation and now Dr Thomas's agent, into a righteous fury. He telegraphed a protest to the bookmaker, demanding he remove the odds and saying that in 40 years' experience of electioneering, he had never known a bookmaker advertise odds and invite bets on an election in this way. (He could perhaps be excused for not knowing that odds were previously published for this by-election on 16 January, because the independent Liberals hadn't managed to produce a candidate by then.) It was certainly liable to influence votes, he said, particularly if there was a small margin between the candidates. One can't help supposing, though, that the length of Dr Thomas's odds may have been a contributing factor to Mr Webster's annoyance. *The Scotsman* noted that betting on an election was an innovation in Ross and Cromarty, causing some shaking of heads 'in an area where bookmaking is not regarded with widespread favour'.[581]

Runners and Riders

Perhaps taking its lead from the betting odds, *The Scotsman* ran its eye over the runners and riders in what it called a 'unique election fight in the political history of the Highlands'. They began with Randolph Churchill:

> As a dust-raiser, Mr Churchill was in a class by himself. After a spectacular flight from Morocco, he galloped furiously into action, hitting out with the abandon of youth, which by its sheer impetuosity may have pleased his friends but which also repelled many others, and did not seriously perturb anybody in the opposition camps.

It concluded that 'as a serious political force his contribution to the fight appears to have suffered steady depreciation'.

Hector McNeil was treated more sympathetically. He was unlikely, they thought, to reach the peak figure of 6,710 which the Socialists polled in the 1929 general election; that election was the high-water mark for the Labour Party, and feeling then was also high against the Unionist government because of the Local Government (Scotland) Act 1929, which was very unpopular, particularly in the Highlands, after abolishing parish councils, district committees and some types of burgh government, replacing them with 33 County Councils, four City Councils and District and Burgh Councils.[582] McNeil had, though, fought a hard and capable campaign and was let down by the fact that there was no industrial centre in the constituency of the type on which Socialists could generally depend for a block vote. He would get support from farm workers, fishermen and small groups of industrial workers, like railwaymen. Nonetheless, this would be insufficient to make a dent in MacDonald's vote.

Dr Thomas had also battled courageously but his campaign was already compromised even before he joined the fray because of the 'unhappy episodes' during the independent Liberals' attempts to find a candidate.

Malcolm MacDonald's 'quiet courtesy, his modest bearing and his great skill on the platform' had greatly boosted his support during the campaign. While acknowledging the difficulties caused by the nature of MacDonald's nomination as the National Government candidate, the paper felt the strength of his performance on the stump had done much to 'dissipate the prejudice'. It seemed in no doubt who would win on election day.[583]

The *Press and Journal* also examined the efforts and prospects of the candidates. Malcolm MacDonald had a 'captivating manner' and impressed with the 'sense of responsibility one looks for in a Cabinet Minister'.

Churchill was a 'different type of man altogether'. He was the most handsome of the candidates, a fact which had the paper supposing he

MacDonald in Conon
photo: Aberdeen Press and Journal

would get 'the bulk of the flapper vote', which it considered 'an important point' these days but, it added sententiously, 'there is the serious-minded elector to be considered'. His prospects were not improved, it concluded, by reports that several leading Unionists had, in the past week or so, swung around in favour of MacDonald.

Hector McNeil's style was similar to MacDonald's, with both men proving quiet but convincing speakers. He had the advantage of knowing the constituency thoroughly and knew what he was talking about. Had he been one of the 'firebrand' types, the paper thought he would never have had a chance because 'agriculturists are not sympathetic to extremism in politics'. Rather, his approach was one of 'evolutionary socialism', the kind of policy that any Radical – and this was traditionally a Radical area – might support. He had campaigned quietly while 'others have captured the headlines' and he had made 'wonderfully good progress'.

Dr Thomas, they felt, was in the worst position of all. Late in the field, he had had little opportunity to meet the electors and, indeed, the eve of poll rally in the town hall the following night would be his first major meeting in Dingwall.[584]

Although no doubt weary, all four were as active as ever and the campaign, according to the *Dundee Courier*, was being 'conducted at whirlwind speed', with each of the candidates addressing half a dozen or so meetings a day.[585]

Malcolm MacDonald gave a direct hint about the government's new cattle policy. To provide greater help to cattle producers there needed to be a scheme of levies on imports, allied to deficiency payments for home producers. 'I am actively engaged with my colleagues in discussions with Dominion and Foreign governments with a view to getting that policy put into effect at the earliest possible moment', he said.

Randolph Churchill addressed six meetings, including the market in Tain. In Dingwall, he again turned to air defence. The *Daily Mail* once more chose this as a headline, noting that Churchill's declaration that Britain should be made 'supreme in the air' was cheered by his audience, 'showing how profoundly public opinion here, as all over the country, appreciates the urgency of decisive action to make Britain safe'.[586] With *The Times* turning towards appeasement, the *Daily Mail*'s increasingly bellicose tone indicated a rift in British debate.

After his meeting in Dingwall Churchill was carried shoulder high along the High Street, accompanied by a cheering (and some jeering) crowd of around 500 to his hotel, where he delivered a few words from the balcony. Many of the crowd, though, the *Press and Journal* noted, were children.[587]

Although Dr Thomas was still in the West, reports suggested he would return to Dingwall for the final day of campaigning.[588]

McNeil spoke during the day at Tain mart and in the evening at Fortrose, Invergordon, Achterneed and Cromarty. He was accompanied by National Labour leader, Clement Attlee.[589] Speaking of MacDonald, Attlee made a footballing analogy that might have worked better in McNeil's native Glasgow than in the Highlands: MacDonald, he understood, still professed Socialist opinions:

> He is rather like a man who used to play for Rangers but has been transferred to Celtic. He must play for the team which pays him, but his heart is with the team he has left.[590]

Saying that the country could not trust the promises of the government and that it appeared to have no real programme except rearmament, he continued:

> They profess, I believe, in collective security through the League [of

> Nations] but always talk in terms of national defence. The Labour Party is as determined as any other party to see that this country is made as safe as possible under existing conditions. When it professes a belief in collective security it means what it says, and it is prepared for this country to make its proper contribution. But the Government has never given us any indication of the amount or the character of that contribution. They have no coherent scheme of defence at all.[591]

Hindsight is a difficult thing. One can read speeches and think, yes I would be persuaded by that, at that time, in those circumstances. What no one in Ross and Cromarty, or anywhere else, could know was how profoundly the world would change in the next three and a half years.

✡ ✡ ✡

Saturday, 8 February 1936

A 'Veritable Orgy of Oratory', More 'Flappers' and 'The Mask of Solidarity' is Torn Aside

On his way to the cattle market in Tain, Randolph Churchill took time to appraise the prospects of himself and his fellow candidates for publication in his regular column in the next morning's *Sunday Dispatch*. Dr Thomas, he felt, had made considerable progress despite the farcical events that preceded his adoption. Those who expected him to lose his deposit underestimated the strong and inherent Liberal streak in the county. Churchill was less certain about Hector McNeil's prospects but predicted he would gain between 4,000 and 6,000 votes. Malcolm MacDonald, he conceded was a 'strong candidate', despite the resentment at the way he had been imposed on the constituency. While he had the support of the party hierarchy, it was noticeable that 'few Unionists of mark or merit have appeared on his platforms'. This is untrue, but it allowed Churchill to claim, 'the political machine is increasing its power'. Finally, he turned to his prospects. He had not been able to rely on the party for support and could call only on local Unionist supporters and leading agriculturists. All the same, he had transformed what appeared at the outset to be a 'forlorn hope' into a serious and mounting challenge which had 'alarmed and disheartened the Government organisers'. He claimed that Central Office predicted he would lose his deposit and declared they would have a 'rude awakening'. Finally, he returned to disarmament, which both the Socialist and Liberal candidates supported, while MacDonald seemed 'painfully neglectful' on the matter. He ended by once again calling for the reconstruction of the Air Force.[592]

That Churchill should end his article on disarmament is instructive. He knew he would lose in the election, and he still resented the way MacDonald's candidature had been manufactured but his outrage at the carpetbagging was greatly overplayed. His real interest was international, and he believed the government was being negligent in its moves to rearmament. This, and not the MacDonalds, was the key to Churchill's decision to fight in Ross and Cromarty.

Now that the campaign was drawing to a conclusion, the papers were taking stock. The *Press and Journal* thought that 'Few elections have been more remarkable than this. Practically every day there has been some new sensation'.[593] *The Scotsman* felt it good that any Parliamentary constituency should be shaken out of lethargy and, in Ross and Cromarty during the many years that Sir Ian Macpherson was its Member, his 'dominion was so secure that there was little cause for excitement at election times'. In this election, however, there had been 'too much excitement' or, at the very least, too much ill feeling. It talked of families being divided by the personalities, and friends of long-standing no longer speaking. The situation was, it thought, a 'deplorable exhibition of factions in politics'.[594]

After the weeks of snow and blizzards, and the worst winter since 1895,[595] the weather for the final day of campaigning (there would be none on the Sabbath, of course) was ideal, with crisp sunshine and temperatures through the day normal for February. The day was described as 'exceptional', and the 'excitement on the streets was extraordinary'. *The Scotsman*'s correspondent, seeing the 'douce folk of the town going to church to worship' the following morning could scarcely believe that the political temperature had been so high only a few hours before.[596]

What was a 'veritable orgy of oratory' began at 2.30 pm in the town hall, when Randolph Churchill gave an address, and the other candidates followed in timed slots, with further speakers filling the remainder of the afternoon. Following that, Malcolm MacDonald had arranged with Donald Davidson, the cinema manager, to hire the picture house for the final addresses during the evening.[597]

Churchill's meeting in the town hall on Saturday afternoon went well, although the *Press and Journal* was far from impressed that women were in the majority. 'Although some observers might point out rather scornfully that many of them were "flappers"', the paper said, 'still a flapper's vote, in itself, is just as valuable as her father's'.[598] Ironically, Churchill himself might have agreed with this antediluvian analysis. In an interview with Clive Irving, editor of the *Sunday Times*, printed as an appendix to his autobiography *Twenty-One Years*, Irving asked him if women had been bad for politics. 'Certainly', Churchill replied. 'But obviously the women's vote is here to stay. It's always struck me as a great mistake on their part. The influence of women is only successful when it's indirect.' Then it can be quite influential, mused Irving. 'So long as it's exercised in country houses, at the dining-room table, in the boudoir and the bedroom, it can often be very beneficial', Churchill confirmed.[599] It may be that he had his wife, Pamela, in mind when he wrote those words. A new biography of Pamela Churchill Harriman, published in 2024, details her extraordinary life, which included effectively being 'pimped out' by Lord Beaverbrook and her father-in-law, Winston Churchill, as part of the war effort, acting as an intermediary between the British Government and the Americans and having (simultaneous) affairs with the Head of US Bomber Command and the British Chief of Air Staff.[600]

Speaking to his town hall audience, both distaff and spear sides, Churchill declared, 'You have a tremendous opportunity to strike a blow in this election'. They had a three-fold duty to discharge:

> [F]irst, to vindicate the principle of representative government; secondly, to sustain the interest of Scottish agriculture; and thirdly to enter an emphatic plea for stronger national developments. All these three great causes can be upheld without in any way doing violence to the concept of national government. My candidature is by no means hostile to the principle of cooperation between all men and women of goodwill in resisting the menace of Socialism.

All of this sounded reasoned and reasonable, but in his next statement he revealed, perhaps, a fourth duty that he thought the electorate might help him with:

> Indeed I would like to see the present administration strengthened by the inclusion in it of more statesmen with patriotic records and established national positions.

People like Winston Churchill, perhaps. He finished with a bit of fine oratorical rabble-rousing:

> I stand for a greater Britain, a Britain whose internal economy is based upon the sure foundations of a prosperous agriculture, a Britain strong at sea and predominant in the air, a Britain which will reassert its will to live and its right to rule, a Britain pledged to treasure within imperishable walls the historic happiness of British homes, a Britain reaching out strong hands across the seas to unite with the Dominions and Colonies of the British Empire – that stupendous achievement of our race which has brought liberty and justice to one quarter of the whole world, which our ancestors fought and died to build, and which it is the sacred trust of our generation to guard and strengthen among the welter of this day and age, as the one impregnable buttress of peace and civilisation.[601]

Any longer and he might have pondered, as in the Tony Hancock episode, 'Twelve Angry Men', of Magna Carta, whether she died in vain. After his speech, he went out into the constituency again and did not return to Dingwall until after midnight, which was most unfortunate (or perhaps intentional) because it meant he missed the clamour that built up around his nemesis, Malcolm MacDonald.

Immediately following Churchill on the town hall stage was Hector McNeil, rounding off his impressive campaign. The Socialists held 150 meetings with an estimated combined attendance of 15,000. Allowing for those who attended more than once, they reckoned they had contacted 11,000 of the 27,000 eligible voters in the constituency, a record reach for the party.[602] His audience, the *Press and Journal* noted, was essentially working class, with men far outnumbering women. His final campaign speech was probably his best, the *Press and Journal* reporting that this 'quiet, rather studious man' was transformed into someone 'giving his message and making his appeal to the humanity of his audience with the burning zeal of the evangelist'.[603]

The fatuity of the independent Liberal campaign can be summed up by their decision to devote much of the final day of campaigning to conferring with counsel over whether to take legal action against the Aberdeen bookmaker whose betting odds, they believed, could turn many votes from Dr Thomas. Newspapers who printed the odds, too, could be included in any writ raised. 'These odds are a travesty of the true position', William Webster said, suggesting that the bookmaker must have been seriously misled by his local adviser. 'The question is a simple one', he continued:

> Has the publication of the odds affected votes? Dr Thomas has not the slightest doubt that it has, and if so it is a clear breach of the election rules.[604]

Dr Thomas might have been better served by his supporters speaking up for his candidacy, not pursuing a trivial vendetta.

A lull before the allotted time for the independent Liberals in the town hall was taken by some speakers for the National Government, including Katharine Elliot. They were well received but, once the independent Liberals took their turn, affairs became more listless. The speakers before Dr Thomas were uninspiring and did little to rouse a half-empty hall. 'So indifferent did they seem to be', thought *The Scotsman*, 'that nobody even bothered to interrupt'. Even Dr Thomas, an accomplished and able speaker, found that 'his Welsh eloquence failed to dissipate the atmosphere of apathy'.[605]

It was Malcolm MacDonald, however, who was the central character in this remarkable day. He had been speaking in Easter Ross, Mid Ross and the Black Isle during the day and now returned to finish with a rally in the Picture House. The town hall emptied before the last of the speakers as people headed for the cinema. As soon as the doors opened the crowds swarmed in and within minutes it was full. Up to 500 people were left outside, where loudspeakers had been set up to relay the speeches. The night had turned cold, cloudless skies ensuring what scant heat had been generated during the day had long dissipated, and the speeches lasted an hour and a half but the enthusiasm of the listeners – inside and outside – did not wane. When finally the main act, Malcolm MacDonald, appeared on stage he was greeted rapturously. Socialists in the cinema booed and called for Hector McNeil but MacDonald faced them down and talked of his former allegiance to their party.[606]

> The most able, the most sincere and the most formidable of my opponents is the Labour candidate. There are people who accuse me of disloyalty for having separated from the Labour Party.... I did not join the Labour Party in order to serve the Labour Party: I joined the Labour Party in order to serve the people of this country.
>
> And when in the hour of crisis I found that the leaders of that Labour Party were not prepared to put through the policy which, however unpopular, was in the best interests of the people, I decided to break with that party.[607]

MacDonald was greeted with a huge round of applause and cheering, albeit with some boos thrown in. It was an adroit piece of oratory. It brought the audience back to Baldwin's central issue of acting in the national interest and placing himself as the man to help them do that. He was cheered as he sat down and when he emerged from the cinema some minutes later he was seized by his admirers and hoisted, again, onto the shoulders of his admirers (four-two to MacDonald). This time, wisely, he removed his spectacles. 'The street was literally seething', wrote *The Scotsman* (pedant alert: it wasn't) as 'every man, woman and child in the town seemed to have joined the excited procession'. MacDonald was carried down the street, his supporters slipping and sliding ominously as they gripped him to their shoulders. An electric torch had been mounted on a long pole and its dancing light 'gave a carnival touch' to proceedings. Although there were Socialists and Unionists among the crowd, shouting for their men, they remained good-humoured. There were perhaps a couple of thousand people in the centre of town and the police had to force a way through for MacDonald and his bearers. 'The mask of stolidity', wrote the *Press and Journal*, 'with which tradition clothes the

Highlander was torn aside to reveal an enthusiast concerned only with furthering the cause of his champion'. *The Scotsman*, too, was complimentary: the method of his adoption had been a mistake, but he had proved himself 'an admirable candidate'.[608]

Finally, MacDonald reached the National Hotel and he jumped onto the National Government cinema van. He tried to thank his supporters but such was the noise from the crowd that, even with a loudspeaker, he couldn't make himself heard. Everyone cheered. Odd shouts of 'Good old Hector' rang out, even the occasional 'We want Churchill'. There was no approbation for Dr Thomas. MacDonald went into the hotel but the crowds remained and he appeared on the balcony a couple of times. On one occasion, Dr Thomas appeared on the balcony too, to great acclaim, but the *Press and Journal* wondered whether, in the darkness of the evening, anyone realised it was him. Hector McNeil, newly arrived back from electioneering in the district, appeared at his first-floor window and took the cheers of his supporters. He reminded them they were now into the Sabbath and urged them to make their way home. Gradually, the crowds began to disperse and in the early hours of the Sabbath, the centre of Dingwall was once again a demure and respectable place.[609]

Into this calm, Randolph Churchill arrived at some time after midnight, quiet and alone, the putative man of the moment having undeniably and completely managed to miss the moment.

✲ ✲ ✲

Monday, 10 February 1936

By Land, By Sea, On Horseback or Foot, By Car and Cart, the People Came to Vote

Ross and Cromarty was the fourth largest constituency in the United Kingdom but had a tiny electorate of 27,748, broken down as follows:

Easter Ross	9,142
Mid Ross	6,040
Black Isle	6,140
Wester Ross	6,426

Dingwall, with 1,264 voters in the landward area and 1,878 in the burgh, was the most populous town. The *Inverness Courier* reckoned that perhaps 2,000 of those on the register could be discounted due to deaths, absent voters and removals, while old age and the long distances to be travelled to some polling stations would prevent many from voting. In the circumstances, it thought a turnout of over 60 per cent would be extraordinary.[610]

Covering the constituency were 38 polling stations. Of these, 22 were in the relatively compact area in the East comprising Easter Ross, Mid Ross and the Black Isle. The West Coast had fourteen stations, covering many miles of mountainous countryside. There was a huge expanse in the middle of the constituency served by a single polling station at Loch Luichart and its voters would have to travel considerable distances to reach it. Voters in Letterewe would have to cross Loch Maree to poll at Torridon, a distance of 20 miles. In Strathconon, some residents would have to travel 22 miles to vote. The most northerly station was Achiltibuie. The campaign teams had organised fleets of cars to help convey voters to the booths – Malcolm MacDonald had 250 vehicles available, Randolph Churchill around 150 and McNeil and Thomas around 50 each. It was interesting, said the *Press and Journal*, to stand on a normally quiet country road and watch the constant stream of cars flash past. Remember, this was a time when there was one car for every 36 people in Scotland, and the ratio would be even higher in this rural area.[611] Even so, in some quarters offers of transport were declined, with the explanation that there were no made roads in the vicinity, only footpaths. 'Most everyone has a boat to get across the loch', one resident explained. Voters descended on the polling station from mountainside crofts and remote hamlets, on foot, in farm carts over unmade roads, by boat, or on horseback.

The polls opened at 7.30 am and closed at 9 pm when all the ballot boxes had to be transported to Dingwall for the count. In the case of the boxes from Applecross, this required a boat trip to Kyle and from there the train to Dingwall. Consequently, it was anticipated that the count would not be complete until around 7 pm the following evening.

Polling in many places was said to be 50 per cent heavier than in the general election. At Aultbea a crowd was waiting at 7 am for the doors to open. Several farmers voted early before travelling to Perth for the bull sales. Three women travelled from Aberdeen to their hometown Dingwall to cast their vote for Mr Churchill (flappers, no doubt). One man travelled from Garbat to vote in Dingwall, a trip of 50 miles. A group of locals hired a boat to cross Loch Broom to Ullapool, rather than taking the tortuous road. The loch was rough and the locals cautioned against older people taking the trip. Undeterred, John Munro, aged 81, was the first to board. Conditions deteriorated and the voters were drenched by the time they had made the crossing. At Ullapool, the water was so rough they could not make the pier and had to head instead for a sheltered inlet, where they were ferried to shore by rowing boat. John Munro met Hector McNeil and the two men engaged in a lengthy conversation.

The papers reported a tragedy that occurred during the election day, Mr Alexander Chisholm of Letterfearn collapsing and dying outside a friend's cottage shortly after he had been to vote.

Larger stations at Cromarty, Fortrose and Muir of Ord were busy early, but the biggest centres were busiest in the evening. The more remote stations did most of their business in the afternoon, giving the voters time to travel from home and back. Lady Wallace, canvassing on behalf of MacDonald came across a woman busy at her washtub. On hearing the woman was a MacDonald supporter, she urged her to vote. 'I cannot go to vote like this', the woman said. 'I must be in my Sunday best.' And later, so adorned, she cast her vote.

Several children whose names appeared on the voters' roll were taken to the polling stations to exercise their right to vote. One four-year-old was taken to Tain, where the presiding officer, uncertain how to proceed, refused to accept the vote until he had received instructions from the returning officer. Sheriff Principal Mackintosh decided the vote could not be accepted.

Baby Voter
photo: *Aberdeen Press and Journal*

Although there was less excitement than on Saturday, there was plenty of bustle. Everywhere, campaign workers exhorted people to get out and vote for their candidate. Not everyone was enamoured of the amount and style of this electioneering. Alexander Cameron, of Dingwall, writing in *The Scotsman*, concluded:

> It is clear that if this form of mass pressure becomes habitual, this country will soon become Nazified and drilled into an attitude of submission to the whip of a dictator.[612]

Rosettes in party colours were worn by many voters, particularly in the larger towns. It was, though, hard to distinguish between Churchill's and MacDonald's, both red, white and blue, except for those MacDonald supporters who pimped theirs up with a piece of MacDonald tartan. Churchill's rosette was the size of a dinner plate. MacDonald's car was beribboned in red, white and blue and a horseshoe decorated with the MacDonald tartan and some lucky white heather – a gift from a supporter – was fixed to the front. Hector McNeil's car was even more striking, with an imposing set of deer's antlers – also a gift – attached to the radiator. Churchill's gift from an admirer was less lavish – a threepenny bit found in the street and given to him as a lucky charm. Each of the candidates had their campaign slogan emblazoned on placards and shouted by supporters:

> A Highlander for a Highland Seat
> Vote for Churchill and Keep Two Socialists Out
> Another for Hector
> Liberals Vote Liberal

Some, it must be said, were more inventive than others.

One More Push

On what would prove to be the sunniest day of the campaign (not that this was saying much) the candidates decamped for a heavy day of campaigning. Hector McNeil was up and about first, heading west at 6 am. In the afternoon he turned his attention to Easter Ross and the Black

Isle. MacDonald departed Dingwall at 7.30 am, accompanied by his sister Sheila, and headed for Portmahomack, with the intention of visiting every polling station on the eastern seaboard. He reached as far as Kinlochluichart and covered the entire Black Isle, finishing at Cromarty at 8.30 in the evening. During the day he stopped to visit Maurice Morrison, his chauffeur, who had suffered a broken arm earlier in the campaign, a story seemingly so mundane in this rich drama it hadn't previously warranted a single mention in any newspaper. Dr Thomas and his wife headed for the Black Isle and Easter Ross shortly before 9 am and Churchill left for a grand tour of the polling stations early.

It must be a strange experience for any election candidate, once the polls close, particularly when, as in this case, the votes won't be counted until the next day and it would be almost 24 hours before the result was known. One imagines they would have retreated to their respective hotels, presumably exhausted, having run on adrenalin for four weeks. The streets of Dingwall would have been quiet, normality enveloping the steady capital of Ross-shire once more, the hubbub over.

All they could do now was wait.

* * *

Tuesday, 11 February 1936

A Triumph of No Ordinary Kind

The count took place in Dingwall's town hall, beginning around two o'clock when the final ballot box had arrived from Applecross. By the time the candidates arrived, there were perhaps a thousand people outside. Some young men had brought with them fireworks and the wait was punctuated by loud explosions. By 9 pm, when the count had concluded, the crowd had swelled to over 2,000. Led by the bewigged returning officer, Professor James Mackintosh KC, Sheriff of Ross and Cromarty and Sutherland, the candidates made their way to the balcony of the town hall, Malcolm MacDonald accompanied by his sister, Sheila, and Sir William Martineau, and Dr Thomas by his wife. Their appearance excited the crowd even further and it was some minutes before Professor Mackintosh could speak. When he announced Malcolm MacDonald's name first, the crowd assumed he had won and the cheers started up again.[613]

With difficulty, he read out the votes for each candidate:

Malcolm MacDonald, National Government	8,949
Hector McNeil, Socialist	5,967
Randolph Churchill, Unionist	2,427
Dr W S Russell Thomas, Liberal	738
National Government majority	2,982

Result
photo: The Scotsman

Dr Thomas forfeited his deposit. Randolph Churchill came within 167 votes of losing his. MacDonald was only 183 votes short of an absolute majority. The total number of votes cast was 18,081, far higher than the 14,094 at the general election the previous year. Turnout was 66 per cent, which was considered exceptional.[614] In Applecross, turnout from the 250 electors was 85 per cent.[615] This was the village visited by Malcolm MacDonald, the first politician to do so in 25 years, and it is reasonable to surmise that the majority of those votes were in his favour.

The bedlam in the crowd continued as, one by one, the speakers acknowledged the result. Fireworks were let off and each candidate was cheered wildly. A bag of flour was thrown but it struck the veranda.

'You can't shoot as well here as they can in Ullapool', said MacDonald, referring to his snowball injury.

'It has been a grand battle', he said, 'under the most desperate conditions that the Highlands could produce, and I should like to thank my opponents Mr McNeil and Dr Thomas for their fair fight'. It is unlikely that Randolph Churchill summoned the good grace to look chagrined by his omission. MacDonald continued:

> Those of us who loyally support the Government have faced opposition from sections of all the three old parties. A few years ago a candidate fighting against such a combination would have forfeited his deposit. The fact that today I have beaten the combination is eloquent testimony to the change which has taken place in our politics, and of the strength of the people's support for the National Government. We have sent a message of hearty encouragement to the leaders of the Government, whose courageous and patriotic cooperation since 1931 has achieved so much for our country.[616]

Hector McNeil, who came a creditable second, spoke next and somewhat lost the goodwill of the audience by the end of his speech:

> Labour's is the only vote at this time that can clearly be said to have increased. The diminished National majority in Ross and Cromarty typifies the feeling throughout the whole country that the Government has lost its grip, internationally and nationally. We must have a peace policy, and we must have justice for the North.
>
> ...
>
> Unless something is done to relieve conditions in Ross and Cromarty immediately, I shall never forgive Malcolm MacDonald in my political life. The poverty and distress of the county has stunned me.[617]

This caused a sustained outbreak of booing from the crowd and shouts of 'Where? Where?'[618] McNeil's distress at the living conditions, though, was heartfelt. At an event in Skye a couple of weeks later he talked of the election campaign, and again discussed the 'appalling' condition of some of the housing, calling it 'worse than any slums found in Glasgow'. Again, his view was not wholly positively received.[619]

Churchill said he hoped the other candidates had enjoyed the election as much as he had, and had profited as much by all their experiences as him. He accused Hector McNeil of being 'a little arrogant' with his boast of being the only party which had increased his vote, suggesting that the last time the Unionists had stood in the constituency, in 1911, they had polled only 1,100 votes so he had more than doubled it.[620] The *Inverness Courier* called that 'characteristically misleading', pointing out that the electorate was now three-and-a-half times the size it had been in 1911, so Churchill had reduced the Unionist vote by nearly one-half.[621]

Of the campaign, Churchill said:

> This result shows the difficult task in these days of challenging the will of the Executive. None the less, the fight we have fought for the integrity of representative government and for the protection of Scottish agriculture has been well worth while.
>
> We have succeeded in advertising some of the outstanding grievances of the Highlands, and we have shown that the cause of Unionism is by no means dead in this part of the world.[622]

Dr Thomas was rueful, aware that he had been trounced but convinced he was right to stand. He said:

> The result is disappointing but the fight has been worth while. We have had to contend with enormous odds, and the usual influences operated during the last few days of the campaign to turn Liberal votes from the Liberal candidate. Many votes were culled for the "National" candidate to keep the Socialist out, and vice versa. Every Liberal candidate in these days has this obstacle to overcome, and it is often insuperable.
>
> But the campaign in Ross-shire has shown that there is a solid nucleus of Liberals who will have no truck with either Tories or Socialists, and it was worth fighting to consolidate this body of honest opinion. When the 'National' ramp comes to an end and we get back to clean politics this body of Liberal opinion will secure effective representation in Parliament.[623]

Speeches over, the candidates emerged from the town hall and MacDonald, McNeil and Churchill were each carried shoulder high by their supporters (five-three to MacDonald, game over). Again, the police had to clear a passage for them and when Malcolm MacDonald reached the National Hotel he assumed his position, once more, on the hotel balcony. He tried to make a speech but the noise of cheering was deafening. Two floodlights lit up the balcony and the street in front and, according to the *Press and Journal*, 'the crowd presented what was a sea of upturned faces' (a pedant returns: no it didn't). It was several minutes before MacDonald could speak and, even cupping his hands to his mouth he found it difficult to make himself heard. 'Thank you for a wonderful victory', he shouted, and every word was punctuated by cheers. By acclaim, Sheila MacDonald also spoke. A bag of shortening was thrown at them, and a few tomatoes, but the mood remained cheerful.[624]

A contemporaneous account of the excitement and chaos of the evening was presented in a letter to MacDonald from Alex J Stewart of Strathconon congratulating him on his success. The younger members of Stewart's family, he wrote, had waited for two hours at the town hall for the results and were overjoyed when they saw MacDonald appear with the Sheriff. He went on:

> They afterwards tried their best to get in touch with you to congratulate you, but found it impossible to get near you with the mixed crowd and the Authorities who were keeping them in subjection. They followed up to the Hotel, but found it nothing easier there, so they had to leave for home, very happy but also disappointed at not having the pleasure and privilege of shaking hands with their Member of Parliament.[625]

As had happened on Saturday evening, the crowd seemed reluctant to disperse but the triumphant National Government campaigners retreated to the hotel to launch their victory party. Malcolm MacDonald invited Hector McNeil to join them and, when he arrived, MacDonald proposed his health and thanked him for the clean fight. 'I predict a brilliant career for Mr McNeil', he said.[626] In turn, McNeil thanked MacDonald for a 'very fair and fine fight'.[627]

Afterwards, they encountered Randolph Churchill alone in the hotel lounge. They invited him to join them and he did. At some stage in the proceedings, presumably after a few celebratory whiskies had been downed, Malcolm walked the length of the room on his hands. The watching Randolph Churchill observed: 'I would rather be able to do that than win Ross and Cromarty.'[628]

The papers took stock of the outcome. For *The Scotsman*, the majority – as it had been in the Scottish Universities by-election – was 'an agreeable surprise'. Both results testified to the hold the National Government could still claim on the loyalty and respect of the electorate. Far too much had been made during the campaign of the idea that MacDonald had been foisted on the electorate, although they did agree there was an issue at stake here:

Sheila and Malcolm
photo: *Evening Standard*

> It is not desirable that a government show too plainly their anxiety to have a particular candidate adopted. The implication is that they are making a convenience of the constituency, and that is naturally resented by independent-minded electors.[629]

Suggesting he would take his seat on Monday, the *Press and Journal* agreed MacDonald's success was much more impressive than had been expected.[630]

The *Dundee Courier* reported that in government circles, MacDonald's victory by so large a majority was regarded as a real triumph.[631] It was, too, a 'great personal triumph' for MacDonald, and also a 'resounding rebuff' for the 'two factionist candidates [Churchill and Thomas] who entered the contest for the single purpose, not of winning it, but of encompassing Mr MacDonald's defeat'. For the candidates, the entertainment was over, and at two at least of them would 'fade out of the scene with a strong feeling that the end of the play was extremely disagreeable'.[632]

For the *Inverness Courier*, it was a 'triumph of no ordinary kind'. It revelled in the 'completeness of the rout of the two candidates which a combination of petty-mindedness and personal spite had foisted on the constituency'. In contrast, it said, both MacDonald and McNeil won the regard of the electors for the fair and courteous manner in which they conducted their respective campaigns.[633]

The papers agreed that Hector McNeil had done well. He had put up a good fight and would be heard of again, thought *The Scotsman*.[634] The *Dundee Courier*, although agreeing McNeil had campaigned well, thought McNeil's showing reflected in part the 'generalised discontent' which abounded in Ross and Cromarty as it did everywhere else, and which had resulted in the return of a Socialist candidate in the Western Isles in the general election. It criticised the '2,427 hard-baked Conservative Party men who permitted themselves to be made tools in the Churchill anti-MacDonald vendetta and are now sharing Mr Churchill's chagrin in a fiasco. For that is what a candidature which just avoids a forfeited deposit by a narrow margin amounts to'. It had harsh words for the independent Liberals, too, accusing them of 'almost limitless self-deception'.[635]

One Liberal, though, John Hogg, who had spoken in support of Dr Thomas, was effusive about the people of Ross and Cromarty:

> [They had been] badgered by much diversity of political opinion yet, however opposed to a speaker's policy, [they] have set a magnificent example to the people of Britain, and have shown how chivalry can be preserved in elections.[636]

As news of the triumph spread, congratulations were given to the winning candidate. Stanley Baldwin, apparently, 'permitted himself a broad smile',[637] and sent a telegram: 'Warmest congratulations on your magnificent victory'.[638] Ramsay MacDonald also telegrammed, telling his son:

> All friends here rejoicing. Heartiest congratulations on fine, upright fight and big majority. – Daddie, House of Commons.[639]

Letters began to come in. The artist, William Rothenstein, reflected on the relief and happiness the result would give Malcolm's father.[640] F Lewis Donaldson, a pacifist Anglican priest (and later Archdeacon of Westminster) admitted to a 'conflict of feelings' regarding Labour's defeat but was nonetheless relieved by the result.[641] (Canon Donaldson must have sent a similar letter to Ramsay MacDonald because in MacDonald's archives there is a tart reply: 'Labour was not defeated in Ross and Cromarty. Labour was victorious; and a queer mixture which had neither principle not political policy, now known as Opposition Labour, was defeated.')[642] Liberal politician Norman Crump, writing from Switzerland, said that he and two others had listened in specially for the result.[643] Anthony Eden called the result a 'great personal triumph'.[644] Fellow Conservative MP, James Despencer-Robertson, said, 'Not the least joyful thing about it is the shocking show put up by Randolph and the Ind Lib!'[645] Duff Cooper, soon to be Secretary of State for War, thought MacDonald would now have a safe seat for life, but he gathered 'it is not quite such a convenient constituency for getting about on St George's Westminster'.[646] A postcard signed 'One of the Clan MacLean' (but addressed from Weymouth) proclaimed: 'You have now wiped out the sting of Culloden and kept the sassenach out of Ross-shire'.[647] Perhaps the oddest letter came from Arthur L Bateman, a former Conservative MP and a controversialist of some renown (at the 1935 election he had refused to stand again in his constituency because his constituents had shown him 'no gratitude').[648] He wrote:

> Congratulations, you are lucky, but (*sic*) you must be aware comments are of the most ferocious and far from felicitous from the masses of the people from the whole of the country.
>
> We all live not unmindful of the facts that retribution will surely overtake all those people that are selfish and unmindful of others (*sic*) wants.
>
> Yours sincerely.
>
> Arthur L Bateman
> 28 years Member of the Tory party and Ex Everything in Local-Central and Imperial Houses.
>
> P/S The same sentiments are conveyed to toue (*sic*) father.[649]

Members of Parliament must be well-used to receiving 'green ink' letters from constituents, but not so often from fellow MPs.

Winston Churchill was less effusive about the outcome. When the result was telephoned to his home in Westerham, Kent, his secretary said that Mr Churchill had no comment to make.[650]

Oliver Baldwin, however, was caustic. In his column in the *Sunday Dispatch* (which he alternated with Randolph Churchill), he declared that MacDonald had:

> fought and won, but he has done it on the right flank, the left flank and in the centre at the same time.
>
> As a Conservative – Liberal – Socialist he has done his utmost to prevent the nation from losing his invaluable aid in the ruling of his country, and Ross and Cromarty have appreciated it.
>
> Perhaps they care less for consistency of political belief up there than they do in Bassetlaw [where MacDonald lost in the general election], and yet for years they have been true to Liberalism. They have now voted for MacDonaldism, which is a creed I hope will not exist longer than is absolutely necessary even for the proper safeguard of capitalism.[651]

The result, though, meant that Randolph Churchill had endured another chastening defeat, his third at the hands of the electors in quick succession. Those votes he did receive, claimed *The Scotsman*, were not in support of him but represented a 'revolt of farmers against the treatment meted out to Scottish agriculture'.[652]

And so the circus came to an end. For all the seriousness of life's affairs, they eventually come to naught. The big tent was dismantled, the actors dispersed, life recommenced. Ross and Cromarty continued as before: quiet, steady, honest and decent.

✡ ✡ ✡

Postscript

Predictions

Returning to our anonymous pundit earlier in the campaign who predicted the outcome, he did reasonably well:

	Prediction	Actual
Churchill	1,800-2,000	2,427
McNeil	6,000	5,967
Turnout	15,000-16,000	18,081

Churchill did far better than predicted, albeit with a much larger turnout than expected. McNeil's vote was uncannily close. The extremely large turnout could probably not have been predicted. All in all, the pundit did rather well, probably better than the poor, berated Aberdeen bookmakers.

Expenses

The election expenses of each of the candidates were declared a month or so after the result. Malcolm MacDonald spent £849 14s 3d and Hector McNeil £567 5s 7d.[653] Somehow, Russell Thomas, despite being in the campaign for only a short period, spent £699 4s 9d, while Randolph Churchill, who campaigned virtually alone throughout, spent the highest of anyone, with £968 3s 9d.[654] This equates to a scarcely believable £57,306 in today's money.[655] Unsurprisingly, in March, Randolph wrote to Lady Houston requesting a further £300 to cover his final expenses. She paid, but after this, she gave Randolph Churchill no more support.[656] *Perhaps, he had a 'cloven hoof' after all.*

The *Press and Journal* worked out how much each vote cost the candidates:

MacDonald:	1s 10d per vote
McNeil:	1s 10d
Churchill:	7s 11d
Thomas:	18s 3d[657]

Nomenclature

As it turns out, Randolph Churchill was right to be cynical about the MacDonalds calling themselves 'National Government' candidates rather than National Labour. The *Edinburgh Evening News* reported on 20 February 1936, fewer than two weeks after the election, that Government Whips had now decided they would be classed as National Labour, raising the strength of that group from eight to ten. The paper mused that this meant National Labour had gained the Scottish Universities seat from the Conservatives and Ross and Cromarty from the Liberal Nationals. 'Read in that way, the decision has an odd look', it concluded.[658]

And with that, the 1936 Ross and Cromarty by-election was over.

✡ ✡ ✡

What Happened Next

During the campaign, the antics of the candidates, in particular Randolph Churchill and the increasingly frantic independent Liberals, took most of the column inches in the press. It is interesting, from the distance of nearly 90 years, to reflect on the Ross and Cromarty by-election, because we can see now that it revealed many of the cracks in the seemingly impregnable National Government which developed into fissures in the years following. *Politics would never quite be the same again.*

Naked Politics

At the beginning of the campaign, the focus was on carpetbagging and political jobbery, men who had only weeks before been cast aside by the electorate being eased (greased?) back into office. Those who objected to the 'foisting' of candidates on them had genuine grievances. People like Sir William Martineau held their noses and acted in 'the national interest'. Perhaps they shouldn't have. What happened in the Scottish Universities and Ross and Cromarty was a stitch-up, and *The Scotsman* was right to suggest the government were making a 'convenience of the constituency'. In 2025, this is established practice; parties imposing candidates, removing candidates, enforcing Central Office will on constituency parties with impunity.

Over time, the focus of the campaign shifted. Local concerns, principally the state of the farming and fishing industries, naturally came to the fore. The solutions were largely based on intervention, subsidy and protection. As a result, the traditional Liberals were seen as out-of-date, their free trade imprecations seemingly from another age. They would not be a major political force again until the early years of the twenty-first century. Perhaps, they will never regain the prominence they enjoyed in the nineteenth century.

A 'New Deal'

After the tumult, Ross and Cromarty returned to normal but the issues that affected the area remained as before. The problems identified by Dr Thomas and Hector McNeil were hidden in full sight. In towns and cities, poverty and poor housing were concentrated and therefore visible. The scattered nature of rural areas, however, meant that, as Richard Findlay has elucidated, 'deep-seated poverty' was hidden.[659] The region's dependence on agriculture, too, was problematic. As Catriona MacDonald explains:

> Making money from Scottish agriculture has always been a challenging prospect. More than any other industry, farming must work with the landscape – whatever its limitations – and Mother Nature still has success in her gift.[660]
>
> ...
>
> The main features that have distinguished the Highlands throughout their history – ostensibly the area's topography and climate and the culture of its dispersed population – remained the determining features of Highland progress in the twentieth century.[661]

Poverty, topography, climate and culture all played their part in the 1936 Ross and Cromarty by-election and would continue to affect the lives of its people. Change was coming, if slowly. There was much talk at the time of a 'New Deal' for the Highlands, promoted by the publication of Dr Lachlan Grant's pamphlet, *A New Deal for the Highlands*, inspired by Roosevelt's Tennessee Valley Authority[662] (which, although ultimately successful in improving economic and agricultural conditions, did so at enormous social, environmental and archaeological cost, and may not be a model to be adopted in its entirety). Lachlan Grant was the founder and President of the Highland Development League, established in 1936 to further the demand for immediate and comprehensive reconstruction of the Highlands and Islands. He was also, of course, one of the many names suggested as an independent Liberal candidate in the early days of the campaign.

In 1936, the New Deal proposals were still at an early stage. The *Press and Journal* thought them 'mostly too vague to be useful' and called for cut-and-dried proposals. It explained:

> Previous movements for regeneration fell short of expectations because of sentimentality, a glowing vision of a contented and prosperous peasantry, and a few hasty fads about this, that and the other remedy for poverty and depopulation, have filled the minds of the reformers. What is needed is sheer, hard thinking combined with open mindedness, resource and unremitting application.[663]

Dr Lachlan Grant campaigned on medicine and health provision as well as the economic revival of the Highlands. As it turned out, he left a greater legacy in the Highlands than any of the by-election candidates, including the winner, Malcolm MacDonald, and it is fascinating to imagine what more he could have achieved if he had made it to Parliament. He continued to press for the region's interests until his death in 1945. He was a true champion.

Proposals to revive the Highlands continued through the 1930s. The Highland Development League called for 'an administrative or central board for the Highlands'.[664] Organisations such as the Scottish National Development Council and the Scottish Economic Committee worked to address the economic and environmental issues. The Hilleary report in 1939 called for a fundamental shift through the development of new industries.[665] In response, the government proposed developments based on: Roads and Piers; Land Improvement; Marketing; Veterinary Services; Fishing; Agricultural Training; Freights; Handcrafts; and Forestry.[666]

The war, of course, intervened, followed by years of national regeneration. Labour, nevertheless, brought in the Highland Development Bill in 1964, leading to the creation of the Highlands and Islands

Development Board on 1 November 1965.[667] In 1991, it was replaced by Highlands and Islands Enterprise, with a remit to build sustainable economic growth in all parts of the region. Its current priorities are:

> The reversal of population decline.
> Support for growth and a green recovery.
> Successful, resilient enterprises.
> Strong, capable and resourceful communities.[668]

The 1930s was a period when Highlanders stopped looking to the past, seeking restitution of rights and properties lost during the Clearances, and started to look forward to a new, more prosperous region. There is still much to be done but the initiatives and ideals explored during the by-election paved the way to a better future.

Rearmament and Appeasement

By the end of the campaign, the debate was broadening out even further and international relations came to the fore. Hector McNeil chose his loser's speech to comment, not only on the poverty he had found in the county but on the need for peace. Randolph Churchill referred to the need for rearmament throughout his campaign. Indeed, he was only truly energised when talking about either international affairs or Malcolm MacDonald. Clement Attlee, in his speech supporting McNeil, chose rearmament to attack the record of the National Government. This, then, was the new faultline in British politics. Disarm or rearm? If rearm, how much? Baldwin remained ambivalent on the matter throughout his tenure as Prime Minister. In a Parliamentary debate a few months after the by-election, in November 1936, Winston Churchill declared himself 'baffled' by the apparent contradictions in Baldwin's pronouncements on the subject, sometimes saying there would be no great move to rearm, other times talking about the need for rearmament. The weariness inherent in Baldwin's reply speaks of the fear and tension which was overcoming the country:

> a democracy is always two years behind the dictator. I believe that to be true. It has been true in this case. I put before the whole House my own views with an appalling frankness. From 1933, I and my friends were all

very worried about what was happening in Europe.[669]

In 1933, the National Government lost the Fulham by-election by around 7,000 votes. This would come to be known as the 'Peace By-election' because pacifism was considered the major factor in the government's surprise defeat. It seriously affected Baldwin. He went on:

> That was the feeling in the country in 1933. My position as the leader of a great party was not altogether a comfortable one. I asked myself what chance was there—when that feeling that was given expression to in Fulham was common throughout the country—what chance was there within the next year or two of that feeling being so changed that the country would give a mandate for rearmament? Supposing I had gone to the country and said that Germany was rearming and that we must rearm, does anybody think that this pacific democracy would have rallied to that cry at that moment? I cannot think of anything that would have made the loss of the election from my point of view more certain.

Although Baldwin was still highly respected – up to and beyond his resignation as Prime Minister – this passage marked the beginning of his fall from grace. His stock steadily decreased over the years, only beginning to recover in recent years. Was he putting party before country? Were political concerns taking precedence over national security? He resigned as Prime Minister in May 1937 and was replaced by Neville Chamberlain. Chamberlain's policy of appeasement would complete the process of splitting the country.

One of the principal reasons for Randolph Churchill's serial attempts to enter Parliament was to upset the National Government and force a way for the return of his father to frontline politics. Appeasement was the issue which brought this to fruition. In October 1940, Chamberlain resigned and was replaced as Prime Minister by Winston Churchill. Randolph had got his way.

Ramsay MacDonald

The death of King George V affected Ramsay MacDonald greatly, damaging his already poor health. In 1937, he went on a cruise with daughter, Sheila, and died on board on 7 November at the age of 71.[670]

Malcolm MacDonald

Malcolm MacDonald probably wasn't a natural politician. Indeed, even before his defeat in the 1935 general election, he had talked of abandoning the career. While he might have been expected to use that loss to make the break, he was persuaded to stand again in Ross and Cromarty, and Clyde Sanger speculates this may be because his relatively new position of Dominions Secretary was one that he found very enjoyable. It would seem to lead naturally to his future career as an ambassador.[671]

In 1940, in Winston Churchill's government, MacDonald was appointed Minister of Health. This role included oversight of areas such as food rationing policy, hospitals, and air-raid shelters during the Blitz. In 1941, he became British High Commissioner in Canada – a career change – and subsequently held diplomatic posts in Malaya, Singapore and British Borneo. He was Commissioner-General for the UK in South East Asia from 1948 until 1955. He then became High Commissioner in India and in 1963 became Governor and Commander-in-Chief of Kenya in the period leading to independence.[672]

On his retirement in 1969, he took up several voluntary and public roles. He died on 11 January 1981. His papers are archived at Durham University, whose website describes him thus:

> Malcolm MacDonald's particular gift was the achievement of cordial relationships with people of varied backgrounds and viewpoints; much of his work as a diplomat and an administrator was based on personal contact, rather than formal meetings and documents.[673]

Of all the candidates in the by-election, Malcolm MacDonald is the most difficult to understand. He seemed above the fray, somehow, while the characters of his opponents became very clear over time. Perhaps he was feeling his way into his career: politics, as typified by the shameless manoeuvring of Randolph Churchill or the naiveté of Dr Thomas, was not his *forté*. Many newspaper reports during the campaign talked of how well he came across, his affable nature and his willingness to listen. That seems to be what served him so well when he finally found his true vocation as a diplomat.

Randolph Churchill

Enoch Powell's second-most famous quote claims 'all political lives, unless they are cut off in midstream at a happy juncture, end in failure, because that is the nature of politics and of human affairs'.[674] Randolph Churchill's began in failure too, with a third successive election defeat. He eventually achieved his long-held ambition to become an MP, in the Preston by-election in 1940, but he was unopposed. He stood for Parliament again in 1945, 1950 and 1951 and lost on each occasion, so ended his career without ever winning an election.

During the war, he was an intelligence officer in the Middle East and Yugoslavia. He remained a journalist and, later in life, took on the task of biographer for his father, Winston Churchill. Ill health – brought on largely by alcoholism and a louche lifestyle – dogged him in his later years and by the time of his death in 1968 he had completed only two of the projected five volumes of his father's biography. He died on the day of Robert Kennedy's assassination, bumping him off the front pages of the newspapers, so even in death Randolph Churchill was mired in disappointment.[675]

Hector McNeil

Malcolm MacDonald was right about Hector McNeil having a bright future. Like Churchill, he was elected to Parliament unopposed in 1941, for the constituency of Greenock. In 1946, in the early years of Attlee's Labour government, he was appointed junior minister in the Foreign Office and promoted a year later to Minister of State. In 1950, he was made Secretary of State for Scotland (ironically replacing Arthur Woodburn, his election agent in the by-election) but lost his position when Winston Churchill won the 1951 general election.

On 11 October 1955, he suffered a stroke on a transatlantic crossing on the *Queen Mary* and died of a brain haemorrhage at the tragically young age of 48.[676]

Dr Russell Thomas

In June 1936, Dr Thomas joined the Liberal National Party. He did not turn his back easily on old loyalties, he said, but,

> the tendency of the Liberal Opposition to flirt with the parties of the extreme Left is, to my mind, antagonistic to what is best in Liberalism, and can only end in disaster and complete obliteration.

He also believed their 'blind devotion' to collective security hindered rearmament and showed a 'lack of realism I can no longer support'.[677]

He was the National Liberal candidate in the 1940 Southampton by-election and was returned unopposed. Remarkably, then, from 1941 to 1945 all four candidates in the Ross and Cromarty by-election were Members of Parliament. In the 1945 general election, he finished fourth. He lost in Middlesbrough East in the 1950 general election and came third in Brecon and Radnor in 1955.[678] Like Randolph Churchill, he never won a popular vote.

The Last Word

The last word on the Ross and Cromarty by-election should go to the anonymous man who said of MacDonald, Churchill, McNeil and Thomas:

> Dingwall has given them all a very warm welcome because the people know they will soon be away and they will maybe not see them again in this world – and certainly not in the next.[679]

✡ ✡ ✡

Bibliography

Newspapers

Aberdeen Press and Journal
Belfast Telegraph
Birmingham Gazet
Daily Express
Daily Herald
Daily Mirror
Daily Record
Daily Record and Mail
Daily Telegraph
Derby Daily Telegraph
Dundee Courier
Edinburgh Evening News
Evening Standard
Evening Telegraph
Glasgow Herald
Gloucestershire Echo
Hartlepool Northern Daily Mail
Inverness Courier
Leicester Evening Mail
Leicester Mercury
Liverpool Echo
Manchester Guardian
News Chronicle
Nottingham Journal
Oban Times
Reynolds's Illustrated News
Shields Daily News
Staffordshire Sentinel
Sunday Dispatch
Sunday Pictorial
Sunday Post
Sunday Times
Sunderland Daily Echo
The Independent
The Observer
The Scotsman
The Times
Toronto Star
Yorkshire Evening Post

Monographs

Boothby, Robert, *Boothby. Recollections of a Rebel* (London: Hutchinson, 1978)

Brown, Alice, McCrone, David and Paterson, Lindsay, *Politics and Society in Scotland* (Basingstoke: Macmillan, 1996)

Churchill, Randolph S, *Twenty-One Years* (London: Weidenfeld and Nicholson, 1964)

Churchill, Winston S, *His Father's Son: The Life of Randolph Churchill* (London: Phoenix, 1996)

Crompton, Teresa, *Adventuress: The Life and Loves of Lucy, Lady Houston* (Cheltenham: The History Press, 2020)

Devine, T M, *The Scottish Nation 1700-2000* (London: Penguin, 1999)

Doan, Laura, *Fashioning Sapphism: The Origins of a Modern English Lesbian Culture* (New York: Columbia University Press, 2001)

Emerson, Ralph Waldo, *Essays* (New York: Charles E Merrill, 1907)

Findlay, Richard J, *Modern Scotland 1914-2000* (London: Profile Books, 2004)

Fraser, W Hamish, *Scottish Popular Politics: From Radicalism to Labour* (Edinburgh: Polygon, 2000)

Gardiner, Juliet, *The Thirties: An Intimate History* (London: Harper Press, 2011)

Gilbert, Martin, *Churchill: A Life* (London: Heinemann, 1991)

Gilbert Martin (ed), *Companion Volume 5. Part 2: The Wilderness Years 1929-1935* (London: Heinemann, 1981)

Harvie, Christopher, *No Gods and Precious Few Heroes: Scotland 1900-2015* (Edinburgh: Edinburgh University Press, 2016)

Harvie, Christopher, *Travelling Scot: Essays on the History, Politics and Future of the Scots* (Glendaruel: Argyll Publishing, 1999)

Heffer, Simon, *Sing As We Go: Britain Between the Wars* (NL: Penguin, 2024)

Hutchison, I G C, *Scottish Politics in the Twentieth Century* (Basingstoke: Palgrave, 2001)

Linklater, Eric, *Magnus Merriman* (Edinburgh: Canongate Classics, 1990)

MacDonald, Catriona M M, *Whaur Extremes meet: Scotland's Twentieth Century* (Edinburgh: John Donald, 2009)

McHenry, Dean E. *The Labour Party in Transition 1931-1938* (London: George Routledge and Sons, 1938)

Marquand, David. *Ramsay MacDonald* (London: Jonathan Cape, 1977)

Middlemass, Robert Keith, *The Clydesiders: A Left Wing Struggle For Parliamentary Power* (London: Hutchinson & Co, 1965)

Morgan, Kenneth O, *Labour People: Leaders and Lieutenants: Hardie to Kinnock* (Oxford: Oxford University Press, 1987)

Parris, Matthew and Maguire, Kevin, *Great Parliamentary Scandals: Five Centuries of Calumny, Smear and Innuendo* (London: Robson Books, 2004)

Sanger, Clive. *Malcolm MacDonald: Bringing an End to Empire* (Liverpool: Liverpool University Press, 1995)

Papers

Ball, Stuart, 'The Conservative Party and the Formation of the National Government: August 1931', *The Historical Journal*, 29:1 (1986)

Cameron, Ewan A, '"Rival foundlings" the Ross and Cromarty By-Election, 10 February 1936', *Historical Research*, 81:213 (August 2008)

Cameron, Ewan, 'The Political Histories of Modern Scotland', *Scottish Affairs*, 85:1 (2013)

Cullen, Stephen M, 'The Fasces and the Saltire: The Failure of the British Union of Fascists in Scotland 1932-1940', *Scottish Historical Review*, 88:2:224 (October 2008)

Dunbabin, J P D, 'British Rearmament in the 1930s: A Chronology and Review', *The Historical Journal*, vol. 18:3 (1975)

Holman, Brett, 'The Air Panic of 1935: British Press Opinion between Disarmament and Rearmament', *Journal of Contemporary History*, 46:2 (2011)

Moore, Joseph G, 'Did Clinton Lie?', *Analysis*, 60:3 (July 2000)

Mowat, Charles L, 'The Fall of the Labour Government in Great Britain, August 1931', *Huntington Library Quarterly*, 7:4 (August 1944)

Muir, Willa, 'Women in Scotland' in Deane, Patrick (ed), *History in Our Hands: A Critical Anthology of Writings on Literature, Culture and Politics from the 1930s* (London: Leicester University Press, 1998)

Robertson, James C, 'The British General Election of 1935', *Journal of Contemporary History*, 9:1 (1974)

Tanner, Duncan, 'Ideological Debate in Edwardian Labour Politics: Radicalism, Revisionism and Socialism' in Biagini, Eugenio and Reid, Alastair (eds), *Currents of Radicalism: Popular Radicalism, Organised Labour and Party Politics in Britain, 1850-1914* (Cambridge: Cambridge University Press, 1991), pp271-293.

Thane, Pat, 'Labour and local politics: radicalism, democracy and social reform, 1880-1914' in Biagini, Eugenio and Reid, Alastair (eds), *Currents of Radicalism: Popular Radicalism, Organised Labour and Party Politics in Britain, 1850-1914* (Cambridge: Cambridge University Press, 1991), pp244-270

Watson, Francis, 'The Death of George V', *History Today*, 36:12 (December 1986)

Theses and Dissertations

Whatley, Patricia E, 'The Development of Medical Services in the Highlands and Islands of Scotland, 1843-1936', unpublished PhD thesis, University of Dundee (2013)

Williams, Alan, 'The Highlands and Islands Development Board 1965-70: Policy-making in an administrative setting', unpublished MLitt dissertation, University of Glasgow (1973)

Websites

1650 Psalter: 1650psalter.com/introduction/

Amersham Museum: amershammuseum.org

Bank of England: bankofengland.co.uk

Basque Children: basquechildren.org

British Library: blogs.bl.uk/untoldlives/

Conservative Manifestos: conservativemanifesto.com

Cooperative Individualism: cooperative-individualism.org

Encyclopaedia Britannica: britannica.com

Find *A Grave*: findagrave.com

Highlands and Islands Enterprise: hie.co.uk

Malcolm MacDonald Papers: reed.dur.ac.uk/xtf/view?docId=ark/32150_s13197xm06v.xml

North Coast 500: northcoast500.com

Oxford Reference: oxfordreference.com

Time: time.com

UK Government: gov.uk

UK Parliament: hansard.parliament.uk

University of Edinburgh School of History, Classics and Archaeology: hca.ed.ac.uk/

Wikipedia: wikipedia.org

✲ ✲ ✲

Endnotes

1 Ball, Stuart, 'The Conservative Party and the Formation of the National Government: August 1931', *The Historical Journal*, 29:1 (1986), p163.

2 '1935 Conservative Party General Election Manifesto', *Conservative Party Manifestos*. http://www.conservativemanifesto.com/1935/1935-conservative-manifesto.shtml. Accessed 16 August 2024.

3 Cameron, Ewan A, '"Rival foundlings": the Ross and Cromarty By-Election, 10 February 1936', *Historical Research*, 81:213 (August 2008), p514.

4 Marquand, David, *Ramsay MacDonald* (London: Jonathan Cape, 1977), p782.

5 'Ross and Cromarty', *Edinburgh Evening News*, 1 January 1936, p6.

6 'Peace With Dishonour', *Inverness Courier*, 17 December 1936, p5.

7 'Edinburgh Inverness-shire Dinner', *Inverness Courier*, 17 December 1936, pp5-6.

8 'Death of Highland Chief', *Inverness Courier*, 17 December 1936, p6.

9 'Inverness Town Council: Three Important Appointments', *Inverness Courier*, 17 December 1936, p5.

10 'Sir Ian Macpherson MP Suffering from Ill-Health', *Inverness Courier*, 17 December 1936, p5.

11 'Sir Ian Macpherson', *The Scotsman*, 17 December 1935, p8.

12 'Resignation of Sir Ian Macpherson', *Inverness Courier*, 24 December 1935, p5.

13 'The Member for the Highlands', *Inverness Courier*, 24 December 1935, p4.

14 'Ross MP To Retire: Sir Ian Macpherson's Health', *Aberdeen Press and Journal*, 24 December 1935, p7.

15 'Scottish MP To Resign', *Dundee Courier*, 24 December 1935, p6.

16 'Sir I Macpherson: MP for Ross and Cromarty to Retire', *The Scotsman*, 24 December 1935, p9.

17 'Our London Letter: May Carry On', *Daily Record and Mail*, 24 December 1935, p10.

18 'MP Gives Up His Seat: MacDonald Jnr May Step In', *News Chronicle*, 24 December 1935, p1.

19 'The Return of the MacDonalds', *Yorkshire Evening Post*, 24 December 1935, p10.

20 'Scottish MP Resigns', *Birmingham Gazette*, 24 December 1935, p1.

21 'Sir Ian Macpherson MP To Resign', *Daily Mail*, 24 December 1935, p9.

22 'One-Time Chief Secretary', *Belfast Telegraph*, 24 December 1935, p1.

23 'Liberal MP Resigns His Seat', *Nottingham Journal*, 24 December 1935, p7.

24 'Ross and Cromarty Vacancy: Mr M MacDonald to be Approached', *Aberdeen Press and Journal*, 26 December 1935, p7.

25 'The London Letter: Ross-shire Vacancy Speculation', *Aberdeen Press and Journal*, 26 December 1935, p6.

26 Cameron, 'Rival foundlings', p510.

27 'Ross and Cromarty Vacancy: Mr M MacDonald to be Approached', p7.

28 'Labour to Fight By-Election', *Daily Herald*, 26 December 1935, p9.

29 'Sir Samuel Hoare Gives His Eagerly-Awaited Explanation', *Aberdeen Press and Journal*, 20 December 1935, p5.

30 UK Parliament. *Hansard*, 307:19 (December 1935).

31 Heffer, Simon. *Sing As We Go: Britain Between the Wars* (NL: Penguin, 2024), pp604-613; Brendon, Piers. *The Dark Valley: A Panorama of the 1930s* (London: Jonathan Cape, 2000), pp360-364.

32 'His Majesty "In Excellent Health"', *Aberdeen Press and Journal*, 27 January 1935, p7.

33 'Surprise in Ross Bye-Election', *Dundee Courier*, 21 January 1936, p12.

34 Sanger, Clive, *Malcolm MacDonald: Bringing an End to Empire* (Liverpool: Liverpool University Press, 1995), p102.

35 Thane, Pat, 'Labour and local politics: radicalism, democracy and social reform, 1880-1914' in Biagini, Eugenio and Reid, Alastair (eds), *Currents of Radicalism: Popular Radicalism, Organised Labour and Party Politics in Britain, 1850-1914* (Cambridge: Cambridge University Press, 1991), p261-263.

36 Fraser, W Hamish, *Scottish Popular Politics: From Radicalism to Labour* (Edinburgh: Polygon, 2000), p148.

37 Tanner, Duncan, 'Ideological Debate in Edwardian Labour Politics: Radicalism, Revisionism and Socialism' in Biagini and Reid (eds), *Currents of Radicalism: Popular Radicalism, Organised Labour and Party Politics in Britain, 1850-1914*, p279.

38 McHenry, Dean E, *The Labour Party in Transition 1931-1938* (London: George Routledge and Sons, 1938), p254.

39 'Surprise in Ross Bye-Election', *Dundee Courier*, 21 January 1936, p12.

40 'Liberals Call at the Hillocks', *Dundee Courier*, 27 December 1935, p5.

41 'MacDonaldites v Simonites', *Daily Herald*, 27 December 1935, p9.

42 'Mr M MacDonald: Likely Candidate for Ross and Cromarty', *Edinburgh Evening News*, 27 December 1935, p2.

43 'Safe Seat Mission to Malcolm', *News Chronicle*, 27 December 1935, p2.

44 'London News: Ross and Cromarty', *The Scotsman*, 28 December 1935, p10.

45 Devine, T M, *The Scottish Nation 1700-2000* (London: Penguin, 1999), p300.

46 Hutchison, I G C, *Scottish Politics in the Twentieth Century* (Basingstoke: Palgrave, 2001), p38.

47 Hutchison, *Scottish Politics in the Twentieth Century*, p40.

48 'Mr Ramsay MacDonald Chosen by Unionists', *The Scotsman*, 28 December 1935, p11.

49 'News Phoned to Hillocks', *Aberdeen Press and Journal*, 28 December 1935, p7.

50 Sanger, Clive, *Malcolm MacDonald*, p99.

51 'Mr MacDonald on University Votes', *News Chronicle*. 31 December 1935, p2.

52 Mowat, Charles L, 'The Fall of the Labour Government in Great Britain, August 1931', *Huntington Library Quarterly*, 7:4 (August 1944), pp382-383.

53 Mowat, 'The Fall of the Labour Government', pp374-375.

54 Morgan, Kenneth O. *Labour People: Leaders and Lieutenants: Hardie to Kinnock* (Oxford: Oxford University Press, 1987), pp48-49.

55 Ball, 'Conservative Party and the Formation of the National Government', p168.

56 Gardiner, Juliet, *The Thirties: An Intimate History* (London: Harper Press, 2011), p117.

57 UK Parliament. https://webtest.parliament.uk/uk-general-elections/elections/14124. Accessed 12 September 2024.

58 'Prospect of a Liberal Candidate', *Edinburgh Evening News*, 27 December 1935, p9.

59 'Ross and Cromarty: Unionist Opposition to Mr Malcolm MacDonald', *The Scotsman*, 30 December 1935, p9.

60 'Hubbub Over Seats for the MacDonalds', *Sunday Post*, 29 December 1935, p1.

61 'The Defeated MacDonalds', *Reynolds's Illustrated News*, 29 December 1935, p4.

62 'The Defeated MacDonalds', p4.

63 'Liberals and Mr Malcolm MacDonald', *Edinburgh Evening News*, 28 December 1935, p10.

64 'Invitation to Oppose Mr M MacDonald', *Daily Mail*, 30 December 1935, p12.

65 'London Letter: Ross and Cromarty', *Dundee Courier*, 30 December 1935, p5.

66 'Sir Herbert Samuel Not to Stand', *Evening Telegraph*, 28 December 1935, p4.

67 'By-Election in Ross-shire: Party Meetings in Dingwall Today', *Inverness Courier*, 31 December 1935, p5.

68 'By-Election Splits in Ross-Shire', *Daily Record*, 30 December 1935, p36.

69 'Ross and Cromarty: Unionist Opposition to Mr Malcolm MacDonald', *The Scotsman*. 30 December 1935, p9.

70 Crompton, Teresa. *Adventuress: The Life and Loves of Lucy, Lady Houston* (Cheltenham: The History Press, 2020), p273.

71 'Our London Letter', *Daily Record*, 30 December 1935, p16.

72 Harvie, Christopher, *No Gods and Precious Few Heroes: Scotland 1900-2015* (Edinburgh: Edinburgh University Press, 2016), p93.

73 Heffer, *Sing As We Go*, p430.

74 Churchill, Winston S, *His Father's Son: The Life of Randolph Churchill* (London: Phoenix, 1996,) p101.

75 Churchill, *His Father's Son*, pp114-115.

76 Crompton, *Adventuress*, pp195-196.

77 Crompton, *Adventuress*, p244.

78 'After the Mad-Hatter Election: By "Listener"', *Liverpool Echo*, 11 February 1935, p3.

79 Gilbert, Martin, *Churchill: A Life* (London: Heinemann, 1991), p548.

80 Churchill, *His Father's Son*, p36.

81 Churchill, *His Father's Son*, pp74-75.

82 Churchill, *His Father's Son*, pp104-117.

83 'Keeping the National Government', *Dundee Courier*, 30 December 1935, p6.

84 Churchill, *His Father's Son*, p125.

85 'New Crisis Faces The Premier', *Sunday Dispatch*, 29 December 1935, p12.

86 Sanger, Clive. *Malcolm MacDonald*, pp100-101.

87 Harvie, Christopher, *Travelling Scot: Essays on the History, Politics and Future of the Scots* (Glendaruel: Argyll Publishing, 1999), p88.

88 'Fakes', *Daily Herald*, 31 January 1936, p8.

89 Heffer, *Sing As We* Go, p436.

90 'Doubts About Adoption of Mr Malcolm MacDonald', *The Scotsman*, 31 December 1935, p9.

91 'Ross and Cromarty: Unionist Opposition to Mr Malcolm MacDonald', p9.

92 'Doubts About Adoption of Mr Malcolm MacDonald', p9.

93 'Dingwall To Decide Today', *Daily Record*, 31 January 1935, p3.

94 'Ross Situation Still More Involved', *Aberdeen Press and Journal*, 31 December 1935, p7.

95 Heffer, *Sing As We Go*, p483.

96 Heffer, *Sing As We Go*, pp434-435.

97 'Ross Situation Still More Involved', p7.

98 'Rush to Oppose MacDonalds', *News Chronicle*, 31 December 1935, p2.

99 'By-Election in Ross-shire: Party Meetings in Dingwall Today', *Inverness Courier*, 31 December 1935, p5.

100 'Dingwall To Decide Today'

101 Churchill, Randolph S, *Twenty-One Years* (London: Weidenfeld and Nicholson, 1964), p11.

102 Churchill, *His Father's Son*, pp35-52.

103 Churchill, *His Father's Son*, p66.

104 Churchill, *His Father's Son*, p55.

105 Churchill, *His Father's Son*, pp74-80.

106 Churchill, *His Father's Son*, p86.

107 '"Turncoat? Nonsense" Says MacDonald', *The Toronto Star*, 11 February 1936, p16.

108 Churchill, *His Father's Son*, pp52-53.

109 'Scots By-Elections: More Opposition to Ex-Premier?', *Edinburgh Evening News*, 30 December 1935, p2.

110 'Ross and Cromarty: Leader Column' *Inverness Courier*, 31 December 1935, p4.

111 'By-Election in Ross-shire', p5.

112 'Ross-Shire By-election Differences', *Aberdeen Press and Journal*, 1 January 1936, p9.

113 'Ross-Shire By-election Differences', p9.

114 'The New Year: Ross and Cromarty', *Edinburgh Evening News*, 1 January 1936, p6.

115 'Thinking It Over: Mr M. MacDonald and Ross-shire', *Edinburgh Evening News*, 1 January 1936, p5.

116 'Tory Rebels Must Toe Line', *Daily Mirror*, 2 January 1936, p4.

117 'Ross-shire Socialist Election Move', *Aberdeen Press and Journal*, 2 January 1936, p7.

118 'Ross-shire Socialist Election Move', p7.

119 'Ross-shire Socialist Election Move', p7.

120 'Independent Liberal Enters Field', *Aberdeen Press and Journal*, 3 January 1936, p7.

121 'Independent Liberal Enters Field', p7.

122 '"Pocket Seat" for Mr MacDonald', *Daily Mirror*, 3 January 1936, p2.

123 'Independent Liberal Enters Field', p7.

124 'Independent Liberal Enters Field', p7.

125 'Independent Liberal Enters Field', p7.

126 'Independent Liberal Enters Field', p7.

127 'Bound For Lossiemouth', *Dundee Courier*, 4 January 1936, p4.

128 'The By-election: Ross-shire and Mr M MacDonald', *Edinburgh Evening News*, 3 January 1936, p9.

129 'The Unionist Opposition', *Daily Telegraph*, 4 January 1936, p11.

130 MacDonald, Malcolm. 'Letter, 4 January 1936'. *Malcolm MacDonald Papers*, 3/4/27.

131 'The Unionist Opposition', p11.

132 'Sister to Help Mr MacDonald', *Dundee Courier*, 6 January 1936, p7.

133 'Sister to Help Mr MacDonald', p7.

134 'The By-Elections: Mr Hector McNeil'. *The Scotsman*, 4 January 1936, p11.

135 'Ross Liberals Reject Churchill Offer'. *Evening Standard*, 13 January 1936, p2.

136 'Ross Liberals Reject Churchill Offer,' p2

137 'The By-Election: Ross-shire and Mr M MacDonald', p9.

138 'The By-Elections: Mr Hector McNeil', p11.

139 Cameron, Annie. Letter, 12 February 1936, *Malcolm MacDonald Papers*. 3/7/26.

140 Cameron. 'Rival foundlings', p512.

141 Cameron. 'Rival foundlings', p516.

142 Cameron. 'Rival foundlings', p529.

143 'Bound For Lossiemouth', p4.

144 'The Scottish Highlands: Aims of the "New Deal" Movement', *Glasgow Herald*, 18 January 1936, p10.

145 'The By-Elections: Mr Hector McNeil', p7.

146 'Rejected Again: Tories Turn Down Mr M MacDonald', *Edinburgh Evening News*, 4 January 1936, p11.

147 'Ultimatum by Ross Unionists', *Aberdeen Press and Journal*, 6 January 1935, p7.

148 'Ultimatum by Ross Unionists', p7.

149 'Rejected Again: Tories Turn Down Mr M MacDonald', p11.

150 'Rejected Again: Tories Turn Down Mr M MacDonald', p11.

151 'Rejected Again: Tories Turn Down Mr M MacDonald', p11.

152 'Rejected Again: Tories Turn Down Mr M MacDonald', p11.

153 'Rejected Again: Tories Turn Down Mr M MacDonald', p11.

154 'Ross and Cromarty By-Election: The Moral for Liberals'. *Manchester Guardian*, 4 January 1936, p7.

155 Hutchison. *Scottish Politics in the Twentieth Century* p47; '1936 Greenock By-Election', https://en.wikipedia.org/wiki/1936_Greenock_by-election. Accessed 30 August 2024.

156 'Mr M MacDonald. To Fight Ross-Shire By-Election: As Government Candidate', *Edinburgh Evening News*, 4 January 1936, p8.

157 'Ross Invitation to Mr R Churchill: Unionists' Unanimous Decision: Sir Robert Brooke Resigns Office', *Aberdeen Press and Journal*, 7 January 1936, p7.

158 MacDonald, Malcolm. 'Draft Press Release', *Malcolm MacDonald Papers*, 3/4/28.

159 MacDonald, Malcolm. Letter, *Malcolm MacDonald Papers*, 3/4/27.

160 MacDonald, Malcolm. Letter, *Malcolm MacDonald Papers*, 3/4/29.

161 'Ultimatum by Ross Unionists', p7.

162 Hutchison. *Scottish Politics in the Twentieth Century*, p32.

163 'The Ross-shire Election', *Dundee Courier*, 6 January 1936, p6.

164 'The Ross-shire Election', p6.

165 'Supreme Court Blow to Mr Roosevelt', *Daily Telegraph*, 7 January 1936, p13.

166 'Points of View: Ross and Cromarty By-Election', *The Scotsman*, 6 January 1936, p11.

167 Baldwin, Oliver. 'A Job for the Post Office', *Sunday Dispatch*, 5 January 1936, p12.

168 This is extremely unfair on Walter Elliot, who was one of the most eminent Scottish politicians of the prewar and immediate postwar period. As Minister of Agriculture (1932-1936) he introduced a number of innovations, including the foundation of marketing boards and subsidies. As Secretary of State for Scotland (1936-38) he oversaw the historic move of the Scottish Office from London to Edinburgh. As Minister of Health (1938-40) he led much of the preparation against German bombing campaigns. See Harvie, Christopher, 'Walter Elliot: the White Marxist' in Harvie, *Travelling Scot*, pp122-131.

169 'Ross Invitation to Mr R Churchill: Unionists' Unanimous Decision', p7.

170 'Sheila in New Battle of Clans', *Daily Mirror*', 6 January 1936, p2.

171 'Sheila in New Battle of Clans', p2.

172 'Ross-shire Unionists' New Move: Mr Randolph Churchill Invited to Attend Association Meeting', *The Scotsman*, 7 January 1936, p9.

173 Churchill. *His Father's Son*, p114-115.

174 Crompton, *Adventuress*, p279.

175 Crompton, *Adventuress*, pp148-149.

176 Crompton, *Adventuress*, p193.

177 Crompton, *Adventuress*, p248.

178 Crompton, *Adventuress*, p264.

179 Crompton, *Adventuress*, p177-178.

180 'People', *Time Magazine*, 10 January 1938.

181 'Ross Invitation to Mr R Churchill: Unionists' Unanimous Decision', p7.

182 'The Bulls of Bashan', *Inverness Courier*, 7 January 1936, p4.

183 The Scottish Psalter was compiled in the 17th century by Puritans. It is set to metre and rhyme to aid singing and its language is "simple", in that it is easy to use (but not, in modern parlance, dumbed-down). There is a common metre of four lines per stanza, the first and third lines with eight syllables and the second and fourth lines with six. This is thought easy to remember and intone.
The Scottish Psalter is considered to be as accurate as possible to the original Hebrew, following extensive revision.

184 Bashan is now known as the Golan Heights.

185 'Ross-shire Unionists' New Move: Mr Randolph Churchill Invited to Attend Association Meeting', p9.

186 Findlay, Richard J, *Modern Scotland 1914-2000* (London: Profile Books, 2004), p111-112.

187 Findlay, *Modern Scotland* p112; Harvie, Christopher. *No Gods*, p105.

188 Cameron. 'Rival Foundlings', p518.

189 'Mr R Churchill's Decision: To Attend Ross Unionist Association Meeting', *The Scotsman*, 8 January 1936, p11.

190 'MacDonald Gains Ground in Ross Bye-Election', *Dundee Courier*, 8 January 1936, p6.

191 'Mr R Churchill for Dingwall: Flying in Stages From Morocco', *Aberdeen Press and Journal*, 8 January 1936, p7.

192 'Mr R Churchill for Dingwall', p7.

193 'Mr R Churchill's Decision: To Attend Ross Unionist Association Meeting', p11.

194 'Mr R Churchill's Decision: To Attend Ross Unionist Association Meeting', p11.

195 'Mr R Churchill's Decision: To Attend Ross Unionist Association Meeting', p11.

196 Churchill, *His Father's Son*, p126-127.

197 'Mr R Churchill's Decision: To Attend Ross Unionist Association Meeting', p11.

198 'Mr R Churchill's Decision: To Attend Ross Unionist Association Meeting', p11.

199 Mr R Churchill for Dingwall', p7.

200 'MacDonald Gains Ground in Ross Bye-Election', p6.

201 'Mr R Churchill for Dingwall', p7.

202 'MacDonald Gains Ground in Ross Bye-Election', p6.

203 'Independent Liberal Candidate: Mr Basil Murray Likely', *Edinburgh Evening News*, 8 January 1936, p9.

204 Doan, Laura, *Fashioning Sapphism: The Origins of a Modern English Lesbian Culture* (New York: Columbia University Press, 2001), pp56–60

205 'Leader', *Daily Express*, 9 January 1936, p4.

206 Crompton, *Adventuress*, p192.

207 'Independent Liberal Candidate: Mr Basil Murray Likely', p9.

208 Crompton, *Adventuress*, pp272-275.

209 'Fantastic New Turn in Ross-Shire: Mystery Man Arrives', *Aberdeen Press and Journal*, 9 January 1936, p7.

210 'Tory Opponent for Ex-Premier?' *Edinburgh Evening News*, 9 January 1936, p7.

211 Crompton, *Adventuress*, p273.

212 'Ross & Cromarty By-Election: Support for National Government Candidate Growing', *Inverness Courier*, 10 January 1936, p5.

213 'Fantastic New Turn in Ross-Shire', p7.

214 'Fantastic New Turn in Ross-Shire', p7.

215 'Sir Ian Macpherson's Letter', *Inverness Courier*, 10 January 1936.

216 'Inverness and Ross Link: Sir Ian Macpherson Chooses His Title', *Aberdeen Press and Journal*, 10 January 1936, p6.

217 'Ross and Cromarty: Mr Basil Murray Not To Stand', *Edinburgh Evening News*, 9 January 1936, p7.

218 MacDonald, Catriona M M *Whaur Extremes Meet: Scotland's Twentieth Century* (Edinburgh: John Donald, 2009), p228.

219 Hutchison, *Scottish Politics*, p23.

220 'Mr M. MacDonald's Opponent', *Daily Mail*, 10 January 1936, p11.

221 'Fresh Twist in Ross Election Tangle', *Aberdeen Press and Journal*, 10 January 1936, p7.

222 Martineau, Sir William. Letter, 8 January 1936. *Malcolm MacDonald Papers*, 3/4/34.

223 MacDonald, Malcolm. Letter, 9 January 1936. *Malcolm MacDonald Papers*, 3/4/12.

224 'Fresh Twist in Ross Election Tangle', p7.

225 'Fresh Twist in Ross Election Tangle', p7.

226 'Fresh Twist in Ross Election Tangle', p7.

227 Gardiner, *The Thirties*, pp241-242; Heffer. *Sing As We Go*, pp450, 490-491; Hutchison, *Scottish Politics*, pp12-14, 40-46; Harvie, *No Gods*, pp47-48, 51; Findlay, *Modern Scotland*, pp150-161; MacDonald, *Whaur Extremes Meet*, pp56-58, 92.

228 'Agriculture's Importance to Ross-shire', *Aberdeen Press and Journal*, 30 January 1936, p8.

229 'Ross and Cromarty: Mr Basil Murray Not To Stand', p7.

230 'Fresh Twist in Ross Election Tangle', p7.

231 'The Ross By-Election', *The Scotsman*, 10 January 1936, p8.

232 'Plea for Unity in Ross: "Victory for Government is Necessary"', *Aberdeen Press and Journal*, 10 January 1936, p7.

233 'Plea for Unity in Ross', p7.

234 'Plea for Unity in Ross', p7.

235 'The Ross By-Election', p8.

236 'Randolph Agrees to Fight', *Daily Mirror*, 11 January 1936, p4.

237 'Piquant Encounter with Mr MacDonald', *Daily Mail*, 11 January 1936, p9.

238 'Mr Churchill's Name Goes Forward', *Aberdeen Press and Journal*, 11 January 1936, p7.

239 Churchill, *His Father's Son*, p66.

240 'Mr Churchill's Name Goes Forward', p7.

241 'Mr Churchill's Name Goes Forward', p7.

242 'Mr Churchill's Name Goes Forward', p7.

243 'Liberal Puzzle in Ross and Cromarty', *The Scotsman*, 11 January 1936, p13.

244 'Liberal Puzzle in Ross and Cromarty', p13.

245 'Liberal Puzzle in Ross and Cromarty', p13.

246 'Mr Churchill's Name Goes Forward', p7.

247 'Mr Churchill's Name Goes Forward', p7.

248 'Liberal Puzzle in Ross and Cromarty', p13.

249 'Liberal Puzzle in Ross and Cromarty', p13.

250 'Liberal Puzzle in Ross and Cromarty', p13.

251 Description of the meeting has been collated from the following sources:
'Ross-shire By-Election Moves: Unionists Adopt Mr Randolph Churchill: Conditional Offer to Stand Down', *The Scotsman*, 13 January 1935, pp9-10;
'Critical Decisions in Ross Today', *Aberdeen Press and Journal*, 13 January 1935, p7;
'Tory Offer: Rejected by Ross Liberals', *Edinburgh Evening News*, 13 January 1936, p7;
'Unionist Meeting: Mr R Churchill's Bitter Attack on the MacDonalds', *Inverness Courier*, 13 January 1936, p6;
'Mr R Churchill Attacks The MacDonalds', *Evening Standard*, 11 January 1936, p5.

252 'Mr Churchill's Name Goes Forward', p7.

253 Churchill is using the word 'job' here in the sense of 'jobbery', the use of unfair means, particularly in politics, to secure a private end.

254 Harvie, *Travelling*, p128.

255 Cameron. 'Rival foundlings', p515.

256 'Magnanimity in Politics', *Manchester Guardian*, 13 January 1936, p8.

257 Churchill, *His Father's Son*, p130.

258 Churchill, *His Father's Son*, p72.

259 'The Election Issue: Socialist Candidate's Campaign', *The Scotsman*, 13 January 1935, p10.

260 'Dingwall Fire Brigade's Good Work', *Aberdeen Press and Journal*, 13 January 1936, p9.

261 'Keep It Dark', *Daily Mirror*, 13 January 1936, p12.

262 'The Ross By-Election: Nothing More Extraordinary', *The Scotsman*, 13th January 1936, p8.

263 'Premier Sends Message to Mr M. MacDonald', *The Scotsman*, 14 January 1936, p9.

264 'The Londoner's Diary: Timing a Telegram', *Evening Standard*, 14 January 1936, p6.

265 'Premier Sends Message to Mr M. MacDonald', p9.

266 'Premier Sends Message to Mr M. MacDonald', p9.

267 'Premier Sends Message to Mr M. MacDonald', p9.

268 'Premier Sends Message to Mr M. MacDonald', p9.

269 Birrell, Augustine, *Men, Women, And Books* (London: Elliot Stock, 1910).

270 MacDonald, Ramsay. Letter, 16 January 1936. *Malcolm MacDonald Papers*. 3/8/1.

271 'Ross and Cromarty: Dingwall Enthusiasm for Mr MacDonald', *The Scotsman*, 14 January 1936, p10.

272 'Eventful Day in Dingwall', *Inverness Courier*, 14 January 1936, p5.

273 'Ross and Cromarty: Dingwall Enthusiasm for Mr MacDonald', p10.

274 'Ross Score for MacDonalds', *Manchester Guardian*, 15 January 1936, p4.

275 'Ross and Cromarty: Dingwall Enthusiasm for Mr MacDonald', p10.

276 'Eventful Day in Dingwall', p5.

277 Sanger, *Malcolm MacDonald*, p108.

278 'Eventful Day in Dingwall', p5.

279 'An Infamous Campaign', *Inverness Courier*, 14 January 1936, p4.

280 'The Ross-shire Election', *Dundee Courier*, 14 January 1936, p6.

281 Gilbert, *Churchill: A Life*, p548.

282 Churchill, *His Father's Son*, pp125-126.

283 'Why Mr MacDonald Went to Ross-shire', *The Scotsman*, 15 January 1936, p11.

284 Churchill, *Twenty-One Years*, p12.

285 'The Issues In Ross: Absurd Situation Requires to be Clarified', *Aberdeen Press and Journal*, 14 January 1936, p6.

286 In his letter to Malcolm, Ramsay seems to suggest that the date of the leader article was 15 January, but he appears to be mistaken, as the article in question appeared in the 14 January edition.

287 MacDonald, Ramsay. Letter, 16 January 1936. *Malcolm MacDonald Papers*. 3/8/2, 3/8/3.

288 'Sir R Brooke Backs Mr Churchill: To Support Him at Dingwall Meeting', *Aberdeen Press and Journal*, 15 January 1936, p7.

289 'Sir R Brooke Backs Mr Churchill', p7.

290 'Sir R Brooke Backs Mr Churchill', p7.

291 'Malcolm MacDonald May Resign from Cabinet', *Evening Standard*, 14 January 1936, p11.

292 MacDonald, Ramsay. Letter, 16 January 1936. *Malcolm MacDonald Papers*, 3/8/2.

293 'How Liberals Approached Mr M MacDonald', *Daily Telegraph*, 15 January 1936, p14.

294 'Sir R Brooke Backs Mr Churchill', p7.

295 'Sir R Brooke Backs Mr Churchill', p7.

296 'Why Mr MacDonald Went to Ross-shire', p11.

297 'Sir R Brooke Backs Mr Churchill', p7.

298 'Why Mr MacDonald Went to Ross-shire', p11.

299 'Malcolm MacDonald May Resign from Cabinet', p11.

300 'Malcolm MacDonald May Resign from Cabinet', p11.

301 'Ross Liberals Still Want a Candidate', *Leicester Evening Mail*, 16 January 1936, p9.

302 'Malcolm MacDonald v. Randolph Churchill', https://youtu.be/NVr0HIPQZ1k?si=F2EtxXXbCFPy1kJd. Accessed 21 October 2024.

303 Information in this section has been collated from the following sources: 'Provost Smith Decides Not to Contest Ross', *Aberdeen Press and Journal*, 16 January 1936, p7; 'Provost Smith Declines to Stand', *The Scotsman*, 16 January 1936, p9; 'Ross and Cromarty Unionists: Loyalists Support Dominions Secretary', *Inverness Courier*, 17 January, p5.

304 Cameron, Ewan, 'The Political Histories of Modern Scotland'. *Scottish Affairs*, (85:1, 2013), pp1-28.

305 Hutchison, *Scottish Politics in the Twentieth Century*, p29.

306 Hutchison, *Scottish Politics in the Twentieth Century*, p29.

307 Brown, Alice, McCrone, David and Paterson, Lindsay, *Politics and Society in Scotland* (Basingstoke: Macmillan, 1996), p124.

308 'Mr MacDonald and Cabinet', *Daily Mail*, 16 January 1936, p11.

309 'Ross Conservatives Stage a "Rebellion"', *Daily Mail*, 17 January 1936, p11.

310 'Take It Easy', *Daily Mirror*, 16 January 1936, p11.

311 Information in this section has been collated from the following sources: 'Tumult at Churchill Meeting', *Aberdeen Press and Journal*, 17 January 1936, p7; 'Active Unionist Support for Mr Malcom MacDonald', *The Scotsman*, 17 January 1936, p13; 'Ross and Cromarty Unionists: Loyalists Support Dominions Secretary', p5; 'Samuelites Invite Another Candidate in Ross', *Evening Standard*, 17 January 1936, p13.

312 'Ross Conservatives Stage a "Rebellion"', p11.

313 'Ross Conservatives Stage a "Rebellion"', p11.

314 'Search For an Independent Liberal Candidate', *The Scotsman*, 18 January 1936, p17.

315 'A Text for Randolph Churchill', *Inverness Courier*, 17 January 1936, p6.

316 'Ross-Shire By-Election: To the Editor of the Inverness Courier', *Inverness Courier*, 17 January 1936, p6.

317 'Humbug in Ross and Cromarty', *Inverness Courier*, 17 January 1936, p4.

318 Churchill, *His Father's Son*, p129.

319 Cameron, 'Rival foundlings', p527.

320 'Shovels and Gumboots', *The Observer*, 19 January 1936, p18.

321 'Search For an Independent Liberal Candidate', p17.

322 'Another Liberal Withdraws', *Manchester Guardian*. 20 January 1936, p6.

323 'Search For an Independent Liberal Candidate, p17.

324 Cameron, 'Rival foundlings', p517.

325 'Search For an Independent Liberal Candidate, p17.

326 'Search For an Independent Liberal Candidate, p17.

327 Halton, MH. '"Turncoat? Nonsense" Says MacDonald', *Toronto Star*, 11 February 1936, p16.

328 'Ross Liberals May Yet Fight Seat', *Aberdeen Press and Journal*, 18 January 1936, p7.

329 'Search For an Independent Liberal Candidate', p17.

330 'Search For an Independent Liberal Candidate', p17.

331 Churchill, *His Father's Son*, p129.

332 Gilbert, Martin (ed), *Companion Volume 5. Part 2: The Wilderness Years 1929-1935* (London: Heinemann, 1981), p18.

333 Hutchison, *Scottish Politics in the Twentieth Century*, p39.

334 'Liberals' Secret Manoeuvres. *Dundee Courier*, 18 January 1936, p6.

335 'Ross Liberals May Yet Fight Seat', p7.

336 'Ross Liberals May Yet Fight Seat', p7.

337 'The King: Confined to His Room with a Cold', *Edinburgh Evening News*, 17 January 1936, p9.

338 'His Majesty Confined To His Room', *Aberdeen Press and Journal*, 18 January 1936, p7.

339 'The Snowstorm: Many Roads Blocked in the North', *The Scotsman*, 20 January 1936, p9.

340 'Another Liberal Fiasco in Ross and Cromarty', *The Scotsman*, 20 January 1936, p6.

341 'Scottish By-Elections', *The Scotsman*, 20 January, p8.

342 'Captain AR McDougal: Likely to Fight Ross-shire By-election', *Edinburgh Evening News*, 18 January 1936, p7.

343 'Another Liberal Fiasco in Ross and Cromarty', p6.

344 The Passing of a Great Campaigner. Land and Liberty', *Cooperative Individualism* (November-December 1955), p110.

345 'Another Liberal Fiasco in Ross and Cromarty', p6.

346 'Liberal Withdrawal', *Dundee Courier*, 20 January 1936, p6.

347 'Ross and Cromarty: "Yes," "No" Liberal', *Sunday Pictorial*, 19 January 1936, p4.

348 Another Liberal Fiasco in Ross and Cromarty', p6.

349 'Another Liberal Fiasco in Ross and Cromarty', p6.

350 'Another Liberal Fiasco in Ross and Cromarty', p6.

351 'Another Liberal Fiasco in Ross and Cromarty', p6.

352 'Another Liberal Withdraws', *Manchester Guardian*, 20 January 1936, p6.

353 Crompton, *Adventuress*, p274.

354 'Mr Churchill's Campaign: Attack on Sir Wm Martineau', *Inverness Courier*, 21 January, p7.

355 'Another Liberal Fiasco in Ross and Cromarty', p6.

356 'Letters to the Editor: Ross-shire By-Election', *Aberdeen Press and Journal*, 20 January 1936, p3.

357 'Ross and Cromarty By-Election', *The Scotsman*, 20 January 1936, p11.

358 Although he didn't originally coin the phrase, 'Three acres and a cow' is a political slogan most commonly associated with the radical politician Jesse Collings (1831–1920). 'Three acres and a cow', he said, were the minimum requirements for self-sufficiency. He used the phrase during political campaigning for land reform in the 1880s.

359 Devine, *The Scottish Nation*, pp430-438.

360 'Another Liberal Fiasco in Ross and Cromarty', p6.

361 'Experience More on the NC500', NC500: *The Ultimate Road Trip*, https://www.northcoast500.com/. Accessed 3 September 2024.

362 'Mr M MacDonald In Nursing Home', *The Scotsman*, 20 January 1936, p9.

363 'Liberal Withdrawal', *Dundee Courier*, 20 January 1936, p6.

364 Bartin, Andrew, *The Child Ballads, No 167.*

365 'The King's Illness', *The Scotsman*, 20 January 1936, p9.

366 'Grave News: Doctors' Statement After Consultation', *Edinburgh Evening News*, 18 January 1936, p7.

367 'Death of the King', *Daily Herald*, 21 January 1936, p1.

368 'Fireside Service in Millions of Homes', *Daily Herald*, 21 January 1936, p1.

369 'Announcer Asks All to Offer Prayer', *Daily Herald*, 21 January 1936, p2.

370 Watson, Francis, 'The Death of George V', *History Today*, 36:12, pp21-30.

371 'North Storm Fury Continues', *Aberdeen Press and Journal*, 21 January 1936, p4.

372 'Ross-shire By-Election: Independents Adopt a Candidate', *Inverness Courier*, 21 January 1936, p4.

373 'Ross and Cromarty Surprise', *The Scotsman*, 21 January 1936, p10.

374 MacDonald, Ramsay. Letter, 16 January 1936. *Malcolm MacDonald Papers*. 3/8/1.

375 'Surprise in Ross Bye-Election', *Dundee Courier*, 21 January 1936, p12.

376 'Ross and Cromarty Surprise', p10.

377 'Ross and Cromarty By-Election'. *The Scotsman*, 21 January 1936, p11. The quote, 'a foolish consistency is the hobgoblin of little minds' comes from Emerson, Ralph Waldo, *Essays* (New York: Charles E Merrill, 1907), p90.

378 'Ross and Cromarty Surprise', p10.

379 'Surprise in Ross Bye-Election', p12.

380 'Liberals Find a Candidate', *Daily Mail*, 21 January 1936, p4.

381 'Ross and Cromarty Surprise', p10.

382 'Independent Liberal to Contest Ross: Dr WS Russell-Thomas Adopted', *Aberdeen Press and Journal*, 20 January 1936, p6.

383 'Ross Liberals May Yet Fight Seat', p7.

384 'Liberals Find a Candidate', p4.

385 'Russell Thomas (politician)', https://en.wikipedia.org/wiki/Russell_Thomas_(politician). Accessed 3 September 2024.

386 'Independent Liberal to Contest Ross', p6.

387 'Independent Liberal to Contest Ross', p6.

388 'Ross and Cromarty Surprise', p10.

389 'Ross Liberals: Candidate Adopted Last Night', *Manchester Guardian*, 21 January 1936, p10.

390 'Independent Liberal to Contest Ross', p6.

391 'Death of the King', *The Scotsman*, 21 January 1936, p1.

392 'Independent Liberal to Contest Ross', p6.

393 'Storm Aftermath', *The Scotsman*, 22 January 1936, p4.

394 'Ross and Cromarty Truce', *The Scotsman*, 22 January 1936, p6.

395 Sanger, *Malcolm MacDonald*, p107.

396 'A Scandalous Report', *Inverness Courier*, 24 January 1936, p4.

397 'Truce Announced in Ross Election Contest', *Aberdeen Press and Journal*, 22 January 1936, p4.

398 'A Scandalous Report', p4.

399 'Truce Announced in Ross Election Contest', p4.

400 'Randolph Replies to "Courier"', *Inverness Courier*, 21 January 1936, p4.

401 'Mr Randolph Churchill and Ourselves', *Inverness Courier*, 21 January 1936, p4.

402 'Proclamation in Scotland.', *Aberdeen Press and Journal*, 23 January 1936, p7.

403 'Political Quiet In Ross', *Aberdeen Press and Journal*, 22 January 1936, p4.

404 'Miss Sheila as Housewife', *Dundee Courier*, 23 January 1936, p7.

405 'Political Quiet In Ross', *Aberdeen Press and Journal*, 23 January 1936, p4.

406 Muir, Willa, 'Women in Scotland' in Deane, Patrick (ed), *History in Our Hands: A Critical Anthology of Writings on Literature, Culture and Politics from the 1930s* (Leicester: Leicester University Press, 1998), p255.

407 Fraser, Roderick. Letter, 11 February 1936. *Malcolm MacDonald Papers*, 3/7/5.

408 MacEchern, John. Letter, 12 February 1936. *Malcolm MacDonald Papers*, 3/7/17.

409 Simpson, Barbara. Letter, 12 February 1936. *Malcolm MacDonald Papers*, 3/7/9.

410 'Miss Sheila as Housewife', p7.

411 Torrance, David. *The Wild Men: The Remarkable Story of Britain's First Labour Government* (London: Bloomsbury, 2024), pp219, 233.

412 'Sheila Lochhead', https://en.wikipedia.org/wiki/Sheila_Lochhead. Accessed 29 August 2024; 'MacDonald Family', *Amersham Museum*, https://amershammuseum.org/history/people/20th-century/mac-donald-family/. Accessed 29 August 2024; 'Ishbel Allan MacDonald Peterkin', *Find a Grave*, https://www.findagrave.com/memorial/100191685/ishbel_allan-peterkin. Accessed 29 August 2024; 'Hostess with the Mostest', *British Library*, https://blogs.bl.uk/untoldlives/2017/12/hostess-with-the-most-ess-and-so-much-more-introducing-the-ishbel-macdonald-archive.html. Accessed 29 August 2024; 'Shelia Ramsay Lochhead', *Find a Grave*, https://www.findagrave.com/memorial/100190176/sheila_ramsay-lochhead. Accessed 29 August 2024.

413 'Candidates at Dingwall', *Aberdeen Press and Journal*, 25 January 1936, p8.

414 'Ross and Cromarty: Some Impressions of the Contest', *Edinburgh Evening News*, 24 January 1936, p8.

415 This appears to be a misprint or misquote of Jeremiah 31:29, which should be 'The fathers have eaten sour grapes, And the children's teeth are set on edge'.

416 'Dornoch Dispute', *The Scotsman*, 21 May 1936, p11; 'Duty to Perform', *The Scotsman*, 22 May 1936, p12; 'Dornoch Church Dispute', *The Scotsman*, 18 May 1936, p12.

417 '"Turncoat? Nonsense" Says MacDonald.', *Toronto Star*, 11 February 1936, p16.

418 'Candidates and the Truce', *Inverness Courier*, 28 January 1936, p4.

419 'A Scandalous Report', *Inverness Courier*, 28 January p4.

420 'Another Reply from Mr Churchill', *Inverness Courier*, 28 January 1936, p4.

421 'Fight Resumed in Ross', *Aberdeen Press and Journal*, 30 January 1936, p8.

422 'Ross-shire By-Election', *The Scotsman*, 30 January 1936, p10.

423 'Ross-shire By-Election', p10.

424 'Ross-shire By-Election', p10.

425 'Personal Antagonisms in Ross', *Manchester Guardian*, 30 January 1936, p20.

426 The Ottawa Agreements stipulated quotas of meat, wheat, dairy goods and fruit from the Dominions which could enter Britain free duty-free. In return, tariff benefits would be granted by the Dominions to imported British manufactured goods. Farmers felt this seriously affected their business, allowing for cheap imports, while none of the benefits of the Agreement accrued to them.

427 'Ross and Cromarty Campaign Resumes', *The Scotsman*, 30 January 1936, p11.

428 Ross-shire By-Election', p10.

429 'Fight Resumed in Ross', p8.

430 'Hard Hitting in Ross Bye-Election', *Dundee Courier*, 30 January 1936, p11.

431 'Mr Churchill at Muir of Ord', *Inverness Courier*, 31 January 1936, p6.

432 'Fight Resumed in Ross', p8.

433 End of the Truce', *Edinburgh Evening News*, 29 January 1936, p11.

434 'Fight Resumed in Ross', p8.

435 'Lively Meeting at Muir of Ord and Dingwall', *Inverness Courier*, 31 January 1936, p5.

436 'Hard Hitting in Ross Bye-Election', p11.

437 Sanger, *Malcolm MacDonald*, p107.

438 'End of the Truce', p11.

439 This was when his father, Ramsay MacDonald, as Prime Minister established the National Government in response to the severe financial crisis engulfing the country.

440 'Lively Meeting at Muir of Ord and Dingwall', p5.

441 'Lively Meeting at Muir of Ord and Dingwall', p5.

442 'Ross-shire By-Election', p10.

443 'Politics on the Screen', *Inverness Courier*, 31 January 1936, p6.

444 'Gaelic Speaker's Tour', *Aberdeen Press and Journal*, 30 January 1936, p8. This Gaelic phrase does not mean what the paper suggests it did and is presumably a transliteration of something overheard. A more likely translation for 'Highlanders shoulder to shoulder' might be *Clann nan Gàidheal an Guaillibh a Chéile*. My thanks to Marcas Mac an Tuairneir for his advice on this matter.

445 Traditionally, fast days were held by the Church of Scotland on a weekday in preparation for the sacrament of communion on the following Sunday. Farm workers were given a day off, and local businesses would close.

446 'Sir John Simon's Advice to Ross-shire Liberals', *The Scotsman*, 31 January 1936, p10.

447 'Lively Meeting at Muir of Ord and Dingwall', p5.

448 Rather implausibly, his name appears to be Richard Adolph Plathen. 'Richard Adolph Plathen, "Officer in Charge of Fascists in Scotland"', *National Archives*, https://discovery.nationalarchives.gov.uk/details/r/C1257447. Accessed 27 September 2024.

449 'Fascists Spring a Surprise', *Dundee Courier*, 31 January 1936, p6.

450 'Blackshirt Organiser at Dingwall', *Aberdeen Press and Journal*, 21 January 1936, p9.

451 'Lively Meeting at Muir of Ord and Dingwall', p5.

452 Gardiner, *The Thirties*, pp441-444.

453 'Hitler's "Never Again"', *Dundee Courier*, 31 January 1936, p6.

454 'Hitler's "Never Again"', p6.

455 'Hitler's "Never Again"', p6.

456 Churchill, *His Father's Son*, pp90-91.

457 Churchill, *His Father's Son*, p98.

458 Levy, Mike. 'The "Red Duchess" – Katharine, Duchess of Atholl', *Basque Children*, https://www.basquechildren.org/-/docs/articles/atholl2019. Accessed 20 January2025.

459 'Sir John Simon's Advice to Ross-shire Liberals', *The Scotsman*, 31 January 1936, p10.

460 'Fortrose Meeting', *Inverness Courier*, 31 January 1936, p6.

461 'Sir John Simon's Advice to Ross-shire Liberals, p10.

462 'Dr Russell Thomas Charges Liberal Association With "Political Jobbery"', *Aberdeen Press and Journal*, 31 January 1936, p10.

463 'Sir John Simon's Advice to Ross-shire Liberals', p10.

464 'Sir John Simon's Advice to Ross-shire Liberals', p10.

465 Collins, Sir Godfrey. Letter, 29 January 1936. *Malcolm MacDonald Papers*, 3/4/55.

466 'Sir John Simon's Advice to Ross-shire Liberals', p10.

467 'Randolph Ramps Again', *Inverness Courier*, 31 January 1936, p5.

468 'An Odious Campaign', *Inverness Courier*, 31 January 1936, p4.

469 'The Issue in Ross and Cromarty', *Inverness Courier*, 31 January 1936, p4.

470 Churchill, *His Father's Son*, p97.

471 Churchill, *His Father's Son*, p80.

472 Churchill, *Twenty-One Years*, pp62-63.

473 'Situation Clarified in Ross Election', *Aberdeen Press and Journal*, 1 February 1936, p7.

474 Harvie, *No Gods*, p107.

475 Cullen, Stephen M. 'The Fasces and the Saltire: The Failure of the British Union of Fascists in Scotland 1932-1940', *Scottish Historical Review*, 88:2: 224, (October 2008), p310.

476 'Situation Clarified in Ross Election', p7.

477 'Nomination Day', *Edinburgh Evening News*, 31 January 1936, p3.

478 Compiled from: 'Rigours of Ross-shire Campaign', *The Scotsman*, 1 February 1936, p13; 'Situation Clarified in Ross Election', *Aberdeen Press and Journal*, 1 February 1936, p7; 'Two Car Mishaps: Mr McNeil Shaken', *Daily Telegraph*, 1 February 1936, p14.

479 'Rigours of Ross-shire Campaign', p13.

480 Mackenzie, Boyd. Private conversation with the author, 9 January 2025.

481 'Situation Clarified in Ross Election', p7.

482 Crompton, *Adventuress*, p73.

483 Churchill, *His Father's Son*, p480.

484 'Situation Clarified in Ross Election', p7.

485 Devine, *The Scottish Nation*, p319.

486 'Situation Clarified in Ross Election', p7.

487 'Quartet in Ross', *Aberdeen Press and Journal*, 1 February 1936, p6.

488 'The Scottish Elections', *Dundee Courier*, 1 February 1936, p6.

489 'Points of View: Ross and Cromarty By-Election', *The Scotsman*, 3 February 1936, p11.

490 'Football Has an Innings in Ross-shire', *The Scotsman*, 3 February 1936, p10.

491 'Double Attack on MacDonald', *Dundee Courier*, 3 February 1936, p5.

492 'Labour Campaign: Mr McNeil's Speech at Dingwall Last Night', *Inverness Courier*, 4 February 1936, p5.

493 Shaw-Mackenzie, Charles. Letter, 3 February 1936. *Malcolm MacDonald Papers*, 3/4/78.

494 'The Two "Bonnie Fighters of Ross"', *Daily Mail*, 3 February 1936, p19.

495 'Double Attack on MacDonald, p5.

496 'Football Has an Innings in Ross-shire', p10.

497 Harvie, *No Gods*, p48.

498 MacDonald, *Whaur Extremes Meet*, p94.

499 'Football Has an Innings in Ross-shire', p10.

500 Crompton, *Adventuress*, p195.

501 Linklater, Eric, *Magnus Merriman* (Edinburgh: Canongate Classics, 1990).

502 'Double Attack on MacDonald', p5.

503 'Still More Surprises In Ross Election', *Aberdeen Press and Journal*, 8 February 1936, p7.

504 'Liberal Candidate's Address: a New Deal', *Manchester Guardian*, 3 February 1936, p6.

505 'Still More Surprises In Ross Election', p7.

506 'Football Has an Innings in Ross-shire', p10.

507 'Scottish I.L.P.: Defeat of Proposal to Rejoin Labour Party', *The Scotsman*, 3 February 1936, p10.

508 'Ross By-Election Fight Warming Up', *Aberdeen Press and Journal*, 3 February 1936, p9.

509 'Ross Election Fight in Blizzard', *Aberdeen Press and Journal*, 4 February 1936, p5.

510 'Candidates Battle Through Blizzard', *Dundee Courier*, 4 February 1936, p7.

511 'Ross Election Fight in Blizzard', p5.

512 'Electioneering in Arctic Conditions', *The Scotsman*, 4 February 1936, p10.

513 'Politics in Blizzard at Ross', *Daily Mail*, 4 February 1936, p13.

514 'Ross-Shire By-Election: Campaign Enters Upon Its Final Week', *Inverness Courier*, 4 February 1936, p5.

515 'Electioneering in Arctic Conditions', p10.

516 Devine, *The Scottish Nation*, pp431-432.

517 'Candidates Battle Through Blizzard', p7.

518 'Sir William Martineau's Denial', *Inverness Courier*, 4 February 1936, p5.

519 'Electioneering in Arctic Conditions', p10.

520 'Socialists and the Mess of 1931', *Inverness Courier*, 4 February 1936, p5.

521 'Dominions Secretary: Home Producers Must Have First Place in Home Market', *The Scotsman*, 4 February 1936, p10.

522 'Labour Campaign: Mr McNeil's Speech at Dingwall Last Night', *Inverness Courier*, 4 February 1936, p5.

523 'Labour Campaign: Mr McNeil's Speech', p5.

524 'Labour Campaign: Mr McNeil's Speech', p5.

525 'Labour Campaign: Mr McNeil's Speech', p5.

526 Sanger, *Malcolm MacDonald*, pp107-108.

527 'Mr Churchill on Universities Result', *The Scotsman*, 4 February 1936, p10.

528 'The Scottish Elections', *Dundee Courier*, 4 February 1936, p6.

529 'A Good Omen', *Inverness Courier*, 4 February 1936, p4.

530 'Roosevelt's New Stroke: Wants Repeal of Own "AAA" Codes', *Dundee Courier*, 4 February 1936, p7.

531 'One New Squadron a Week For Air Force', *Daily Telegraph*, 11 January 1936, p11.

532 'Germany Nears Air Parity With Britain', *Dundee Courier*, 4 February 1936, p7.

533 'Candidate Goes to Meetings By Boat', *The Scotsman*, 5 February 1936, p15.

534 Mackenzie, Boyd. *Personal correspondence with the author*, 8 January 2025.

535 Sanger, *Malcolm MacDonald*, p108.

536 Rankin, HF. Letter, 28 December 1935. *Malcolm MacDonald Papers*, 3/4/4.

537 Rankin, 3/4/4.

538 Information collated from: 'Dr MacLean Watt Protests', *The Scotsman*, 5 February 1936, p11; 'By-Election Heat', *Edinburgh Evening News*, 5 February 1936, p7.

539 'Religious Issue at Ross', *Daily Telegraph*, 6 February 1936, p12.

540 'Candidate Goes to Meetings By Boat', p15.

541 Heffer, *Sing As We Go*, p508.

542 'Candidate Goes to Meetings By Boat', p15.

543 'Oats Policy: Mr M MacDonald Replies to Critics', *The Scotsman*, 6 February 1936, p8.

544 'Interim Interdict Granted to Mr McNeil', *The Scotsman*, 6 February 1936, p8.

545 'Sunday Golf Issue', *Dundee Courier*, 6 February 1936, p7.

546 'Oats Policy', p8.

547 Hutchison, *Scottish Politics in the Twentieth Century*, p50.

548 Parris, Matthew and Maguire, Kevin. *Great Parliamentary Scandals: Five Centuries of Calumny, Smear and Innuendo* (London: Robson Books, 2004), p116.

549 Boothby, Robert. *Boothby: Recollections of a Rebel* (London: Hutchinson, 1978), p110.

550 'Mr MacDonald in the Black Isle', *Inverness Courier*, 7 February 1939, p5.

551 'Untitled', *Inverness Courier*, 7 February 1936, p6.

552 'By-Election Heat', *Edinburgh Evening News*, 5 February 1936, p7.

553 'Points of View: Ross and Cromarty By-Election', *The Scotsman*, 6 February 1936, p13.

554 Dunbabin, J P D, 'British Rearmament in the 1930s: A Chronology and Review', *The Historical Journal*, (18:3,1975), pp587–609, p588.

555 MacDonald, Ramsay. Letter, 16 January 1936. *Malcolm MacDonald Papers*, 3/8/2.

556 Holman, Brett. 'The Air Panic of 1935: British Press Opinion between Disarmament and Rearmament', *Journal of Contemporary History*, 46:2, 2011, pp291-292.

557 Robertson, James C, 'The British General Election of 1935', *Journal of Contemporary History*, (9:1, 1974), pp151-155.

558 Holman, 'The Air Panic of 1935', p296.

559 Dunbabin, 'British Rearmament in the 1930s' p588.

560 Heffer, *Sing As We Go*, p553.

561 'Letters From Readers: Ross and Cromarty By-Election', *The Scotsman*, 7 February 1936, p13.

562 'A Telegram From the Twelve "Macs"', *Inverness Courier*, 7 February 1939, p5.

563 'Mr MacDonald in Black Isle', p5.

564 'Premier's Message to Ross-shire', *Aberdeen Press and Journal*, 7 February 1936, p7.

565 'Candidate in Nomination Day Crash', *Dundee Courier*, 1 February 1936, p7.

566 'Mr Boothby's Reply', *The Scotsman*, 7 February 1936, p11.

567 'Mr Baldwin's Tribute to Mr MacDonald', *The Scotsman*, 7 February 1936, p11.

568 'Mr MacDonald in Black Isle', p5.

569 'Mr Baldwin's Tribute to Mr MacDonald', p11.

570 'Fight for Ross Stiffens', *Daily Mail*, 7 February 1936, p13.

571 'Fight for Ross Stiffens', p13.

572 'Premier's Message to Ross-shire', p7.

573 'Mr MacDonald in Black Isle', p5.

574 'Mr Baldwin's Tribute to Mr MacDonald', p11.

575 'Liberals Chaffed', *Aberdeen Press and Journal*, 7 February 1936, p7.

576 'Mr McNeil's Views on Sabbath Question', *Inverness Courier*, 7 February 1936, p6.

577 'Mr MacDonald in Black Isle', p5

578 'Premier on the Issue', *Inverness Courier*, 7 February 1939, p5.

579 'National Interests in Ross and Cromarty', *Inverness Courier*, 7 February 1936, p4.

580 'Ross and Cromarty By-Election, 1936', *Inverness Courier*, 7 February 1936, p5.

581 'Candidates' Prospects in Ross-shire', *The Scotsman*, 7 February 1936, p13.

582 MacDonald, *Whaur Extremes Meet*, pp193-194.

583 Candidates' Prospects in Ross-shire', p13.

584 'Still More Surprises In Ross Election', *Aberdeen Press and Journal*, 8 February 1936, p7.

585 'Last Day of Ross Campaign', *Dundee Courier*, 8 February 1936, p7.

586 'Mr Churchill's Air Demands Cheered', *Daily Mail*, 8 February 1936, p11.

587 'Still More Surprises In Ross Election' p7.

588 'Candidates' Prospects in Ross-shire', p13.

589 'Candidates' Prospects in Ross-shire', p13.

590 'Last Day of Ross Campaign', p7.

591 'Still More Surprises In Ross Election', p7.

592 Churchill, Randolph. 'Ross and Cromarty: Men and Prospects', *Sunday Dispatch*, 9 February 1936, p14.

593 'Polling Today in Ross-shire By-Election', *Aberdeen Press and Journal*, 10 February 1936, p7.

594 'Ross-shire By-Election', *The Scotsman*, 8 February 1936, p12.

595 'Election Rigours: Arctic Conditions in Wester Ross', *Edinburgh Evening News*, 10 February 1936, p5.

596 'Ross-shire Polls Today', *The Scotsman*, 10 February 1936, p15.

597 MacDonald, Malcolm. Letter, 31 January 1936. *Malcolm MacDonald Papers*, 3/4/71.

598 'Mr Churchill's Meeting', *Aberdeen Press and Journal*, 10 February 1936, p7.

599 Churchill, *Twenty-One Years*, p119.

600 'Kingmaker by Sonia Purnell Review', *The Guardian*, 16 September 2024.

601 'Mr Churchill's Meeting', p7.

602 'Polling Today in Ross-shire By-Election', p7.

603 Mr Churchill's Meeting, p7.

604 'Polling Today in Ross-shire By-Election', p7.

605 'Ross-shire Polls Today', p15.

606 'Ross-shire Polls Today', p15.

607 'Mr Churchill's Meeting', p7.

608 'Ross-shire By-Election', *The Scotsman*, 8 February 1936, p12.

609 Description of the closing scenes collated from: 'Ross-shire Polls Today' p15; 'Polling Today in Ross-shire By-Election', p7.

610 Information in this section is collated from:
'Heavy Poll Recorded in Ross-shire', *Aberdeen Press and Journal*, 11 February 1936, p7;
'Polling Today in Ross-shire By-Election', *Aberdeen Press and Journal*, 10 February 1936, p7;
'Ross-shire Polls Today', *The Scotsman*, 10 February 1936, p15;
'A Heavy Poll: Crowd at a Booth at 7am', *The Scotsman*, 11 February 1936, p9;
'Polling Day Scenes in Constituency', *Inverness Courier*, 11 February 1936, p5;
'Big Constituency With Small Electorate', *Edinburgh Evening News*, 10 February 1936, p9;
'Election Rigours: Arctic Conditions in Wester Ross', *Edinburgh Evening News*, 10 February 1936, p5;
'Points of View: Ross and Cromarty By-Election', *The Scotsman*, 11 February 1936, p11;
'Tragedy of By-Election', *Aberdeen Press and Journal*, 12 February 1936, p7.

611 Harvie, *No Gods*, p49.

612 'Ross-shire Polls Today', p15.

613 'Declaration Scenes', *The Scotsman*, 12 February 1936, p11.

614 'Mr Malcolm MacDonald Wins', *The Scotsman*, 12 February 1936, p11.

615 'Ross Chooses Mr Malcolm MacDonald', *Aberdeen Press and Journal*, 1 2 February 1936, p7.

616 'Ross Chooses Mr Malcolm MacDonald', p7.

617 'Ross Chooses Mr Malcolm MacDonald', p7.

618 'Ross By-Election: Mr M MacDonald's Great Triumph', *Inverness Courier*, 14 February 1936, p6.

619 'Glasgow Skye Association', *Oban Times*, 22 February 1936, p2.

620 'Ross By-Election: Mr M MacDonald's Great Triumph', p6.

621 'A Notable Victory', *Inverness Courier*, 14 February 1936, p4.

622 'Mr Malcolm MacDonald Wins', p11.

623 'Mr Malcolm MacDonald Wins', p11.

624 'Ross Chooses Mr Malcolm MacDonald', p7.

625 Stewart, Alex J. Letter, 12 February 1936. *Malcolm MacDonald Papers*, 3/7/39.

626 'Ross By-Election: Mr M MacDonald's Great Triumph' p6.

627 '"Daddie's" Wire', *Edinburgh Evening News*, 12 February 1936, p9.

628 Sanger, *Malcolm MacDonald*, p108.

629 'Ross-shire By-Election', *The Scotsman*, 12 February 1936, p10.

630 'Ross Chooses Mr Malcolm MacDonald', p7.

631 'Malcolm MacDonald Wins Ross Seat', *Dundee Courier*, 12 February 1936, p7.

632 'The Ross-Shire Election', *Dundee Courier*, 12 February 1936, p6.

633 'A Notable Victory', p4.

634 'Ross-shire By-Election', p10.

635 'The Ross-Shire Election', p6.

636 'Thanks to Ross and Cromarty', *Inverness Courier*, 11 February 1936, p5.

637 'Thanks to Ross and Cromarty', p5.

638 'Ross By-Election: Mr M MacDonald's Great Triumph', p6.

639 '"Daddie's" Wire', p9.

640 Rothenstein, William. Letter, 12 February 1936. *Malcolm MacDonald Papers*, 3/7/10.

641 Donaldson, F Lewis. Letter, 13 February 1936. *Malcolm MacDonald Papers*, 3/7/86.

642 Marquand, *Ramsay MacDonald*, p782.

643 Crump, Norman. Letter, 12 February 1936. *Malcolm MacDonald Papers*, 3/7/38.

644 Eden, Anthony. Letter, 12 February 1936. *Malcolm MacDonald Papers*, 3/7/74.

645 Despencer Robertson, James. Letter, 13 February 1936. *Malcolm MacDonald Papers*, 3/7/90.

646 Cooper, Alfred Duff. Letter, 13 February 1936. *Malcolm MacDonald Papers*, 3/7/99.

647 Anonymous. Letter, N D *Malcolm MacDonald Papers*, 3/7/83.

648 'Obituary: Mr A L Bateman', *The Times*, 10 May 1957, p15.

649 Bateman, Arthur L, Letter, 13 February 1936. *Malcolm MacDonald Papers*, 3/7/95.

650 'No Comment', *Aberdeen Press and Journal*, 12 February 1936, p7.

651 Baldwin, Oliver, 'MacDonald to Right, MacDonald to Left, MacDonald in Centre While Europe Thunders', *Sunday Dispatch*, 16 February 1936, p16.

652 'Ross-shire By-Election', *The Scotsman*, 12 February 1936, p10.

653 'Election Expenses in Ross Contest', *Aberdeen Press and Journal*, 16 March 1936, p7.

654 'By-Election Expenses', *Aberdeen Press and Journal*, 18 March 1936, p7.

655 https://www.bankofengland.co.uk/monetary-policy/inflation/inflation-calculator. Accessed 12 September 2024.

656 Crompton, *Adventuress*, pp274-275.

657 'Votes at 18/8 Apiece', *Aberdeen Press and Journal*, 19 March 1936, p8.

658 'The MacDonalds Defined', *Edinburgh Evening News*, 20 February 1936, p6.

659 Findlay, *Modern Scotland 1914-2000*, p153.

660 MacDonald, *Whaur Extremes Meet*, p56.

661 MacDonald, *Whaur Extremes Meet*, p185.

662 Whatley, Patricia E, 'The Development of Medical Services in the Highlands and Islands of Scotland, 1843-1936', unpublished PhD Thesis, University of Dundee, 2013, p81.

663 'Highland "New Deal"', *Aberdeen Press and Journal*, 11 February 1936, p6.

664 Williams, Alan. *The Highlands and Islands Development Board 1965-70: Policy-making in an administrative setting*. MLitt: University of Glasgow, 1973, pp104-105.

665 Cameron, Ewan. *The History of Gaelic Scotland: The Highlands since 1880*. School of History, Classics and Archaeology Website, pp202-223.

666 UK Government. 'Scotland: Highlands and Islands Development', *Hansard*, 1 August 1939.

667 'Stories: Our Region', *Highlands and Islands Enterprise*, https://timeline.hie.co.uk/stories/our-region/. Accessed 25 September 2024.

668 'Our Region', *Highlands and Islands Enterprise*, https://www.hie.co.uk/our-region/. Accessed 30 September 2024.

669 UK Government. 'Debate on the Address', *Hansard*, 12 November 1936.

670 Heffer, *Sing As We Go*, p507.

671 Sanger, *Malcolm MacDonald*, p98.

672 'Malcolm MacDonald Papers', *Durham University*, https://reed.dur.ac.uk/xtf/view?docId=ark/32150_s13197xm06v.xml. Accessed 25 September 2024.

673 Malcolm MacDonald Papers', *Durham University*.

674 'Enoch Powell 1912–98', *Oxford Reference*. https://www.oxfordreference.com/display/10.1093/acref/9780191826719.001.0001/q-oro-ed4-00008596. Accessed 22 January 2025. Full quote is: 'All political lives, unless they are cut off in midstream at a happy juncture, end in failure'.

675 'Randolph Churchill', *Encyclopaedia Brittanica*, https://www.britannica.com/biography/Randolph-Churchill. Accessed 25 September 2024; 'Randolph Churchill', https://en.wikipedia.org/wiki/Randolph_Churchill. Accessed 25 September 2024.

676 'The Triumphs – and Tragedy – of Greenock MP Hector McNeil', *Inverclyde Now*, https://www.inverclydenow.com/hector-who/. Accessed 25 September 2024; 'Hector McNeil', https://en.wikipedia.org/wiki/Hector_McNeil. Accessed 24 September 2024.

677 'Dr Russell Thomas Joins Liberal National Party', *Edinburgh Evening News*, 10 June 1936, p9.

678 'Russell Thomas (politician)', https://en.wikipedia.org/wiki/Russell_Thomas_(politician). Accessed 25 September 2024.

679 'Election Rigours: Arctic Conditions in Wester Ross', *Edinburgh Evening News*, 10 February 1936, p5.

✡ ✡ ✡

INDEX

Page numbers in *Italics* indicate featured illustrations.

TIPPERMUIR BOOKS

Tippermuir Books Ltd is an independent publishing company based in Perth, Scotland.

PUBLISHING HISTORY

Spanish Thermopylae (2009)

Battleground Perthshire (2009)

Perth: Street by Street (2012)

Born in Perthshire (2012)

In Spain with Orwell (2013)

Trust (2014)

Perth: As Others Saw Us (2014)

Love All (2015)

A Chocolate Soldier (2016)

The Early Photographers of Perthshire (2016)

Taking Detective Novels Seriously: The Collected Crime Reviews of Dorothy L Sayers (2017)

Walking with Ghosts (2017)

No Fair City: Dark Tales from Perth's Past (2017)

The Tale o the Wee Mowdie that wantit tae ken wha keeched on his heid (2017)

Hunters: Wee Stories from the Crescent: A Reminiscence of Perth's Hunter Crescent (2017)

A Little Book of Carol's (2018)

Flipstones (2018)

Perth: Scott's Fair City: The Fair Maid of Perth & Sir Walter Scott – A Celebration & Guided Tour (2018)

God, Hitler, and Lord Peter Wimsey: Selected Essays, Speeches and Articles by Dorothy L Sayers (2019)

Perth & Kinross: A Pocket Miscellany: A Companion for Visitors and Residents (2019)

The Piper of Tobruk: Pipe Major Robert Roy, MBE, DCM (2019)

The 'Gig Docter o Athole': Dr William Irvine & The Irvine Memorial Hospital (2019)

Afore the Highlands: The Jacobites in Perth, 1715–16 (2019)

'Where Sky and Summit Meet': Flight Over Perthshire – A History: Tales of Pilots, Airfields, Aeronautical Feats, & War (2019)

Diverted Traffic (2020)

Authentic Democracy: An Ethical Justification of Anarchism (2020)

'If Rivers Could Sing': A Scottish River Wildlife Journey. A Year in the Life of the River Devon as it flows through the Counties of Perthshire, Kinross-shire & Clackmannanshire (2020)

A Squatter o Bairnrhymes (2020)

In a Sma Room Songbook: From the Poems by William Soutar (2020)

The Nicht Afore Christmas: the much-loved yuletide tale in Scots (2020)

Ice Cold Blood (2021)

The Perth Riverside Nursery & Beyond: A Spirit of Enterprise and Improvement (2021)

Fatal Duty: Police Killers and Killer Cops: the Scottish Police Force 1812–1952 (2021)

The Shanter Legacy: The Search for the Grey Mare's Tail (2021)

'Dying to Live': The Story of Grant McIntyre, Covid's Sickest Patient (2021)

The Black Watch and the Great War (2021)

Beyond the Swelkie: A Collection of Poems & Writings to Mark the Centenary of George Mackay Brown (2021)

Sweet F.A. (2022)

A War of Two Halves (2022)

A Scottish Wildlife Odyssey (2022)

In the Shadow of Piper Alpha (2022)

Mind the Links: Golf Memories (2022)

Perthshire 101: A Poetic Gazetteer of the Big County (2022)

The Banes o the Turas: An Owersettin in Scots o the Poems bi Pino Mereu scrievit in Tribute tae Hamish Henderson (2022)

Walking the Antonine Wall: A Journey from East to West Scotland (2022)

The Japan Lights: On the Trail of the Scot Who Lit Up Japan's Coast (2022)

Fat Girl Best Friend: 'Claiming Our Space' – Plus Size Women in Film & Television (2023)

Wild Quest Britain: A Nature Journey of Discovery through England, Scotland & Wales – from Lizard Point to Dunnet Head (2023)

Guid Mornin! Guid Nicht! (2023)

Madainn Mhath! Oidhche Mhath! (2023)

Who's Aldo? (2023)

A History of Irish Republicanism in Dundee (c1840 to 1985) (2024)

The Stone of Destiny & The Scots (2024)

The Mysterious Case of the Stone of Destiny: A Scottish Historical Detective Whodunnit! (2024)

Salvage (2024)

A Most Unsuitable Game: Celebrating Scottish Women's Football Fifty Years After the Ban (2024)

The Scottish Murder Book: Sensational Scottish Murder Trials. Book 1: Perth, Angus and Fife (2024)

William Soutar: Collected Works, Volume 1 Published Poetry (1923–1946) (2025)

William Soutar: Collected Works, Volume 2 Published Poetry (1948–2000) (2025)

The Road to Mons Graupius (2025)

'The Wheesht' The Best o Scots Hoose Yaldi (2025)

'The Perth Steamies': the Story of the Fair City's Public Washhouses, 1846–1976 (2025)

The Lass and the Quine (2025)

'The Old Divide': A History of Sectarianism in Scotland (2025)

Balkan Rhapsody (2025)

Shout. Collected Poems from the Corbenic Poets (2025)

An Odious Campaign: How the 1936 Ross & Cromarty By-election Shaped British Politics (2025)

A History of Perth Academy (Muriel Dunbar and Alan MacDonald, (2025)

A Wildlife Guide to Edinburgh (Keith Broomfield, 2025)

William Sandeman (1722–1790): Perthshire Entrepreneur and Cotton Pioneer (Anthony Cooke, 2025)

Barvick Falls (Rob McInroy, 2025)

FORTHCOMING

William Soutar: Collected Works, Volume 3 (Miscellaneous & Unpublished Poetry) (Paul S Philippou (Editor-in-Chief) & Kirsteen McCue and Philippa Osmond-Williams (editors), 2026+)

William Soutar: Collected Works, Volumes 4–6 (Prose Selections) (Paul S Philippou (Editor-in-Chief) & Kirsteen McCue and Philippa Osmond-Williams (editors), 2027+)

The Black Watch From the Crimean War to the Second Boer War
(Derek Patrick and Fraser Brown (eds), 2026)

Disasters, Accidents & Enquirers in Scotland (Gillian Mawdsley, 2025)

City Lives! A Dundee GP's Memoir of the NHS at its Height
(John Hulbert, 2025)

Ayont The Thistle (Jim Mackintosh, Alan Riach and James Robertson, 2026)

Scottish National Heritage: An Insider's View (Roger Crofts, 2026)

TIPPERMUIR
· BOOKS LIMITED ·

All Tippermuir Books titles are available from bookshops and online booksellers.
They can also bepurchased directly (with free postage & packing (UK only) – minimum charges for overseas delivery) from

tippermuirbooks.co.uk

Tippermuir Books Ltd can be contacted at

mail@tippermuirbooks.co.uk